Soviet Policy in Developing Countries

Soviet Policy in Developing Countries

EDITED BY **W. RAYMOND DUNCAN**

State University of New York at Brockport

ROBERT E. KRIEGER PUBLISHING COMPANY
HUNTINGTON, NEW YORK
1981

Original Edition 1970
Second Edition 1981

Printed and Published by
ROBERT E. KRIEGER PUBLISHING COMPANY, INC.
645 NEW YORK AVENUE
HUNTINGTON, NEW YORK 11743

Copyright © 1970 by
W. RAYMOND DUNCAN
Revised Edition © 1981 by
ROBERT E. KRIEGER PUBLISHING COMPANY, INC.

Printed in the United States of America

Library of Congress Cataloging in Publication Data

Duncan, Walter Raymond, 1936-
    Soviet policy in developing countries.

    Reprint of the edition published by Ginn-Blaisdell, Waltham, Mass.
    Includes bibliographical references and index.
1. Russia—Foreign relations—1953-1975.   2. Under-developed areas—Foreign relations.   I. Title.
[DK274.D8 1979]   327.47'172'4   78-20847
ISBN 0-88275-846-2

CONTENTS

THE CONTRIBUTORS

W. Raymond Duncan is a Distinguished Teaching Professor (Political Science) and Director of Global Studies, State University of New York, Brockport. His previous publications include *Soviet Policy in the Third World*, ed. (Pergamon, 1980); *Latin American Politics: A Developmental Approach* (Praeger, 1976): *Soviet Policy in Developing Countries* (Ginn-Blaisdell, 1970, edited with James Nelson Goodsell), plus numerous articles on Latin American politics and Soviet and Cuban policies in Latin America.

Orah Cooper and **Carol Fogarty** are economic analysts for the Central Intelligence Agency, U.S. Government. They have previously prepared parts of studies for the Joint Economic Committee, U.S. Congress.

Allan W. Cameron is a specialist in Soviet foreign relations, with emphasis on Southeast Asia. He edited *Viet-Nam Crisis: A Documentary History*, Volume I, 1941–56 (Cornell University Press, 1971) and *Indo China: Prospects after "The End"* (American Enterprise Institute, 1976).

Roger E. Kanet, Professor of Political Science, University of Illinois, Urbana-Chanpaign, Ill. His publications include articles on Soviet and East European policies in leading U.S. scholarly journals and *Soviet Economic and Political Relations with the Developing World* (Praeger, 1975), ed. with Donna Bahry; and *The Soviet Union and Developing Nations* (John Hopkins Press, 1974), edited.

Fred Warner Neal, Professor of International Relations and Government, Claremont Graduate School and University Center, Claremont, Calif.; and Executive Vice-President, American Committee on East-West Accord; his most recent work in *Detente or Debacle: Common Sense U.S.-Soviet Relations* (Norton, 1978).

Charles C. Petersen, professional staff member at the Center for Naval Analysis; wrote two chapters in *Soviet Naval Diplomacy*, ed. by Brad Desmukes and James McConnell (Pergamon Press, 1979); currently working on Soviet naval missions and air capabilities.

David Lynn Price, editor of Kuwait, Defense Correspondent for *Arab Times*, Kuwait; author of *Oil and Middle East Security* (Policy Papers Series: The Washington Papers, No. 41, 1977), Sage; and *The Western Sahara* (The Washington Papers, No. 63, 1979). Sage; author of articles in *Problems of Communism*.

Elizabeth Valkenier, research associate at the Russian Institute, Columbia University, author of several articles on Soviet policy in the Third World, including her essay The U.S.S.R., The Third World and the Global Economy, *Problems of Communism*, pp. 17-33; also author of *Russian Realist Art, The State and Society. The Peredvizhniki and Their Tradition* (Ardis Publishers, 1977).

PART ONE

EVOLUTION OF SOVIET POLICY

CHAPTER ONE

SOVIET POLICY IN THE DEVELOPING COUNTRIES

W. Raymond Duncan

Soviet policy in the Third World merits our attention as we enter the last two decades of the twentieth century. This is not simply due to Moscow's 1979 invasion of Afghanistan. Admittedly that event triggered the dramatic erosion in Soviet postwar Third-World relations, marked a return to Cold-War logic in America's policy planning, and escalated the Third World—in this case the Persian Gulf region—to a potential zone of great power confrontation. Other reasons compel us to examine the subject: the search for clues to the character of Soviet behavior, the quest for accurate assumptions by which to measure appropriate American policy responses, and some indication of the general impact of the Third World on U.S.-Soviet adversarial relations which so much condition contemporary international affairs.

Moscow's enlarged shadow in the Third World during the 1970s cannot be ignored. It first emerged in the mid-1950s under Nikita Khruschev's leadership and henceforth injected Marxist-Leninist precepts into the ex-colonial regions of the world, challenged U.S. conceptions of *détente* once the Richard Nixon-Leonid Brezhnev accords of 1972 introduced the idea, affected economic, military, and political outcomes in strategically important and raw-materials-producing countries, provided opportunities for a greatly expanding Soviet blue-water navy, and—given all that—consequently pulled the Third World into Soviet-U.S. confrontations.

As the years went by, the spreading Soviet presence in Africa, Asia, the Middle East, and Latin America increasingly consumed Washington's policy-making attention. Moscow's specter in the world's southern regions became the standard against which to measure U.S. power, frequently with the U.S. perceived at home to be slipping in the competition for influence and especially in its will to assert more vigorous military force after its Vietnam withdrawal. Moscow's invasion of Afghanistan in late 1979 became, in effect, the proverbial straw that broke the camel's back, the latest in a string of events—from Soviet involvement in Angola, Ethiopia, and Somalia, to Cuba and Vietnam—that resulted in the swelling wave of discontent over America's superpower status *vis à vis* the USSR. Russians in Kabul produced the seemingly inevitable return to Cold-War rhetoric and the "Carter Doctrine" of a renewed military build-up in light of a perceived Soviet "threat" in strategically critical Third-World areas. A study of Soviet Third-World relations, therefore, should help us determine to what extent this change in American foreign policy and the new climate of Cold-War politics is based upon accurate assessments of Soviet power in the lesser developed countries (LDCs).

The record of Soviet entry into and expansion within the Third-World during the 1970s is indeed impressive. By 1978, Moscow had extended economic credits and grants to over 85 countries, since its program began back in 1954, bringing its 24-year-total economic aid up to $17 billion.[1] And, by the end of the 1970s, Soviet trade with the developing countries represented an estimated 20 percent of the Soviet Gross National Product (GNP) compared with 11–12 percent at the beginning of the 1970s.[2] The USSR's military agreements with the LDCs totalled approximately $30 billion for the 1955–1978 period, with about 1,900 LDC nationals in the USSR for specialized military training by the end of 1978. Almost 10,800 Soviets were out in the LDCs training local personnel in the maintenance and use of military equipment.[3] As the year 1978 ended, the USSR and Eastern Europe together had an estimated 72,655 economic technicians in the

Third World, with the bulk in Africa and the Middle East.[4] All this must be estimated in light of Soviet interest in the Third World which began in 1954-55, compared to Moscow's earlier postwar record which demonstrated lack of enthusiasm for building Soviet-Third World ties.

Behind this impressive record of expanded Soviet power in the Third World lie discernible objectives, albeit inferred assumptions in that we do not know precisely what goes on inside the Politburo. It seems reasonable to assume that Soviet leaders envision the Third World excolonial countries as regions of opportunity to encourage national liberation movements away from Western control. To the extent these countries move into more independent foreign-policy practices, the Soviets appear to perceive the world "correlation of forces" between socialism and capitalism/imperialism moving toward the former.[5] The Third World also possesses important raw materials and markets for the USSR, can provide important strategic maritime functions for Moscow's blue-water navy, growing civilian merchant marine, and fishing fleet operations, and is a region of other opportunities for the USSR to play a superpower role through expansion of its global presence. These pragmatic national interests appear to outweigh the spread of communism, although ideological revolutionary goals of course have their lower echelon position in Moscow's foreign-policy strategy.

This set of objectives behind the great expansion of activities in Third-World countries lead to a central question not easily answered. Is the recent history of Soviet policy in the Third World, on balance, a story-book affair of unchallenged power applied at will, influencing Third-World leaders to act in ways they would not have acted in the absence of the Soviet presence? A positive "yes" can be argued if one carefully picks one's way through the record. As the 1970s unfolded, a number of pro-Soviet communist LDCs seemed to be within the Soviet orbit of power: Afghanistan, Angola, Cambodia, Cuba, Ethiopia, Laos, North Vietnam [which took control of the South in 1975], Mozambique, and South Yemen.[6] Other LDCs established strong ties with the USSR, such as India, Syria, Guinea-Bissau, Libya, and Grenada. In some cases, Soviet capacity to encourage LDCs toward pro-Soviet activities seemed rather spectacular, as in the case of Cuba, which, by 1979, sponsored approximately 19,000 troops in Angola and 15,000 in Ethiopia, where they fought on the side of pro-Soviet indigenous elements from 1975 (Angola) onwards.

Yet the negative dimension of Soviet capacity to influence Third-World countries is equally clear. Soviet power collapsed in Indonesia in 1966; fell from grace in the Sudan as that country demolished its communists in 1971; and ended in Egypt in 1972 when Moscow's advisers were thrown out. Somalia discharged the Soviets from their large missile and naval base at Berbera once the Kremlin determined to back Ethiopia in the Ogaden War, whereupon, ironically, the U.S. prepared to lease Berbera against Soviet moves in the Persian Gulf region in early 1980 after the Moscow invasion of Afghanistan. That invasion, moreover, appeared to mark the leading edge of a new era of strained relations between Moscow and the Third World. The LDCs voted in historic opposition to the Russians in Kabul under the auspices of the United Nations General Assembly in January 1980, followed by the sharp denunciation by Islamic countries of the Soviet Union shortly thereafter.[7] Beside massive Muslim reactions, with the exception of Syria and the People's Democratic Republic of Yemen (PDRY), all five members of the Association of Southeast Asian States (ASEAN; Singapore, Malaysia, Thailand, Indonesia, and the Philippines) were critical of the armed intervention, while Latin America and the Caribbean countries were also largely hostile. Cuba, in contrast, eventually reacted in favor of the invasion.

Behind these military and political events lie Moscow's economic relations with the LDCs, which are far from spectacular. The developing countries, in fact, account for a very small proportion of the USSR's total trade.[8] Much of the Soviet economic aid and credits to the LDCs go undrawn due to the more attractive Western capital goods,[9] and the Soviet Union does not participate in the Western-dominated international economic organizations of the world, e.g., the World Bank and the International Monetary Fund (IMF), which lend far more to the developing countries than the USSR.[10] Meanwhile, despite the Soviet Union's goal to exert great power on the decision-making influence in organizations devoted to global issues that affect the Third World, e.g., the World Food Council, the United Nations Law of the Sea negotiations, or the United Nations environmental deliberations, many

LDCs are increasingly critical of the Kremlin for its poor record in working toward global problems they deem imperative for their development goals. These issues include more available food, more capital and foreign aid as a higher percentage of the developed countries' GNP, and greater assistance in agricultural development. Looked upon in this perspective, Soviet power to influence events in the Third World may be far less than many observers have been willing to concede.

The troublesome issue in Soviet Third-World affairs is Moscow's growing tendency to accentuate military techniques of influence over economic leverage. This pattern seems relatively clear in Soviet policy toward Africa, South Asia, and Southeast Asia (support of Vietnam's military adventures). It is understandable, given the apparent recognition in Moscow that the world economic system continues under strong dominance by Western capitalism and that past Soviet foreign economic-aid programs have not produced as great change as anticipated earlier.[11] It is troublesome because first, even Soviet military policy in the Third World may be easily overestimated as to its real capability, and, second, because its high visibility became the dominant perception in Washington during the late 1970s, leading to escalated military spending and a new "Cold War" conceptualization of U.S.-Soviet relations after the Afghanistan affair. That Soviet military capacity can be overestimated centers upon the nature of the blue-water navy, the lack of capability for sustained large deployment of troops far from Soviet home bases, and its real difficulties in large-scale logistical support abroad.[12] The second issue—high visibility of its military power and the consequent reaction in Washington—is indicated by congressional and presidential reactions to Soviet troops in Cuba and to perceived Soviet-Cuban threat in Nicaragua under *Sandinista* leadership.[13] The American public consequently was well primed for the Soviet intervention in Afghanistan, especially so with American hostages in Iran raising levels of frustration within the United States.

In some ways Soviet behavior in the Third World appears to be at the brink of a new era, and in others the more traditional heavy-handed military responses in Soviet foreign policy seem to predominate. Moscow, for example, is more inclined to become involved in regional conflicts, with all the associated responsibilities

7

and commitments they imply. Its military-supply policies in Africa, the Persian Gulf, and Southeast Asia and its treaties of "friendship and cooperation" with several African and Middle East countries substantiate this trend. But, simultaneously, the Soviet Union is showing a new sense of world responsibility in stabilizing international institutions dealing with global issues that will serve the long-run interests of most states of the world. The Kremlin contributed significantly in a constructive manner to the negotiations on the new International Wheat Agreement (IWA) in 1977-79 and it at least is paying more lip-service to multi-lateral cooperation on grain issues on some bodies such as the International Wheat Council (IWC). Meanwhile, it is showing continued interest in the conclusion of a treaty to establish international laws and institutions to deal with a variety of issues associated with the territorial and open seas, as demonstrated at the Third United Nations Conference on the Law of the Seas. A number of authors now stress that the Soviet Union's increasing involvement in the international economic system and the nature of its global issues, e.g., food, energy, raw materials, ocean economics, etc., may be causing a reexamination of its future economic relations with the Third World—especially given underdeveloped country complaints about the weakness of Soviet responses to their problems.[14]

If we, indeed, are on the edge of a new era in Soviet-Third-World relations, an era nevertheless conditioned by Moscow's continuing military preoccupation, then the implications for U.S. policy are complex. To deal with a commonly perceived enemy pursuing a commonly agreed-upon policy is one thing, as was the case generally in the immediate postwar period that gave birth to the containment doctrine. But to develop a policy for conflicting foreign-policy trends is more difficult, especially when consensus is lacking on the rationale and operating principles in Soviet policy toward the Third World. How does Washington deal with its perceived Soviet military expansionism and power projections in lesser-developed arenas, when Moscow's behavior on other matters offers more cooperative avenues? While a posture of firm resistance and penalties for actions of the Afghanistan type are called for, the pursuit of U.S.-Soviet cooperation within international institutions seems required as well. Cooperation at the U.S.-Soviet level is imperative not simply to moderate international conflict in the nuclear age, but also because it is necessary to meet the major global problems faced by both countries and the Third World in the last two decades of the twentieth century.

The following essays examine the types of Soviet policy in Third-World settings, the range of behavior leading to Soviet–U.S. conflict, and a number of special issues in the study of Moscow's Third-World posture. They intend to contribute to a broadened understanding of Moscow's power projection which has become so vivid in recent years. While they do not pretend to have all the answers to questions about Soviet behavior in the southern regions of the globe, they do suggest the complex nature of Moscow's foreign policy and may help in the formulation of appropriate U.S. policy responses.

FOOTNOTES

1. *Handbook of Economic Statistics* (Washington, D.C.: National Foreign Assessment Center, Central Intelligence Agency, 1979), p. 116.
2. *Ibid.*, p. 99.
3. *Communist Aid Activities in Non-Communist Less-Developed Countries* (Washington, D.C.: National Foreign Assessment Center, Central Intelligence Agency, 1978), p. 2.
4. *Ibid.*, p. 14.
5. Donald S. Zagoria, "Into the Breach: New Soviet Alliances in the Third World, " *Foreign Affairs*, vol. 57(4) (Spring 1979): 733–754.
6. *Ibid.*
7. *New York Times*, January 6, 1980, p. E3.
8. *Communist Aid Activities in Non-Communist Less-Developed Countries* (Washington, D.C.: National Foreign Assessment Center, Central Intelligence Agency, 1977), pp. 8, 24, 25.
9. *Ibid.*
10. Robert Legvold, "The USSR and the World Economy: The Political Dimension," *The Soviet Union and the World Economy* (New York: Committee on Foreign Relations, 1979), pp. 1–16.
11. *Ibid.*
12. Charles C. Petersen, "Trends in Soviet Naval Operations," *Soviet Naval Diplomacy*, ed. Bradford Dismukes and James McConnell (New York: Pergamon Press, 1979), p. 75; Michael D. Davidchik and Robert B.

Mahoney, Jr., "Soviet Civil Fleets and the Third World," *Ibid.*, pp. 317-333.

13. *The New York Times*, July 18, 1979. Also *The New York Times, Washington Post*, and the *Christian Science Monitor* from August 30 onwards.

14. Elizabeth Kridl Valkenier, "The USSR, the Third World and the Global Economy," *Problems of Communism* (July-August 1979): 17-33.

CHAPTER TWO

SOVIET ECONOMIC AND MILITARY AID TO THE LESS DEVELOPED COUNTRIES, 1954-78

Orah Cooper and Carol Fogarty

INTRODUCTION

The USSR launched its aid program in the mid-1950s to promote Moscow's foreign-policy interests in the Third World. In the 24 years since then, the USSR has responded to aid opportunities in target areas throughout the world with nearly $47 billion of economic and military pledges to 73 countries. It has trained 50,000 students from 98 developing countries in academic disciplines and nearly 75,000 LDC nationals in military and technical skills. The record for Soviet personnel serving in LDCs in a single year (1978) was nearly 28,000 economic technicians and 11,000 military technical personnel (not including troops stationed in Egypt in the early 1970s).

Moscow's basic political objectives have remained constant—to erode Western influence and substitute its own; to counteract the Chinese challenge to its "leadership" of national liberation movements; and eventually to persuade Third-World countries that Soviet communism offers the only viable solution to their economic problems. To accomplish these objectives Moscow has

11

provided less-developed countries with alternative sources of arms, capital, and technical services on attractive terms. Initially, the Soviets gave preference to emerging states that followed a "non-capitalist path of development" and were on the road toward becoming "national democratic states." Ideology was overtaken by pragmatism in the mid-1960s when aid was offered with less concern for the political orientation of potential clients.

Anxious to assert a big power image in the Third World, the Soviets tried to fill the vacuum left by the withdrawal of colonial powers, while securing a foothold in areas of strategic importance. Moscow found arms its most direct and fastest route to influence in these countries which often were able to obtain economic assistance from non-Communist sources, but not military aid.[1] The Soviets also provided military personnel and advanced-weapons systems to states and nationalist groups ripe for conflict, most recently to the Arab belligerents in the Middle East, and for nationalist movements in southern Africa.

Nearly two-thirds of Moscow's $47 billion commitment and three-fourths of its $32 billion of deliveries since 1954 have been military related. In the first years of the program, when some developing countries were reluctant to accept large amounts of military assistance from Moscow, economic commitments roughly equalled the military. In the past 10 years military aid has outrun economic aid almost 2½ to 1, and, for most of those years, the Soviets have held second rank, after the United States, as an LDC arms-supplier.

Moscow has never been able to compete on a broad scale with the West, either in the size or kind of economic aid programs it has offered. Nonetheless, the heavy regional concentration and high visibility of its program often have given Soviet aid an impact beyond its size. Military aid has been competitive and has given Moscow prestige as a major international arms-supplier. While major Western powers would not or could not provide the modern weaponry developing countries craved, Moscow responded rapidly, often with favorable payment conditions. Because many new states felt that their political futures and even their survival hung on military stature and assured arms-suppliers, the Soviets were able to entangle many military clients in a web that deepened and prolonged their dependence on the USSR.

Moscow can respond quickly to crises with air and sea-lifts of large numbers of men and material to trouble-spots. Its most spectacular operation was in the 1973 Middle East War when the Soviets poured $4 billion worth of arms into Arab belligerents' inventories within 15 months. The 1975 venture into Angola was another bold display of Soviet supply capability. This was followed in 1977–78 by massive support to Ethiopia—on a scale unprecedented in the Soviet arms-supply record for a single country.

Economic assistance is viewed by Moscow as a low-cost expedient for forging links with the developing world. On few occasions has this aid—or the trade which has emanated from it—been cut off as a result of political changes in LDCs, strained relations between LDCs and the USSR, or changes in Soviet military supply policy toward a particular LDC. In Egypt, for example, Moscow's aid and trade programs continue in spite of Cairo's abrogation of major military and friendship treaties in 1976. While economic aid provides the materials, personnel, and ideas to encourage the growth of socialist institutions in aid-receiving countries, it also has established relationships which sometimes help assure the USSR certain strategic raw materials and goods and services from the LDC.

OPERATIONS OF THE PROGRAM

Moscow's first important use of aid was in Egypt. Using Czechoslovakia as a front, the Soviets answered Nasser's call for arms in 1955 with a $250-million military-aid package. The accord opened the door for a large Soviet military and economic presence in the Middle East. Egypt's acceptance of Soviet arms was followed by Western refusal to construct the Aswan Dam and a Soviet economic-aid commitment to Egypt that reached nearly a billion-and-a-half dollars. The $4-billion arms-supply relationship that evolved required some 17,000 Soviet military personnel (including troops) in 1971 to maintain it and created a relationship that crippled Egyptian military readiness after the cutoff of Soviet supplies.

Economic and military-assistance programs usually have worked in tandem. Generally, major military-aid recipients accepted arms-aid first, often during periods of perceived threats. These have frequently come with liberal terms, such as (a) discounts from list prices, which averaged 40 percent but were as high as 75 percent; (b) repayments stretched over 8–10 years, at 2-percent interest; and (c) payments in LDC commodities, rather than hard currency. Terms are no longer as concessional, and most sales, even to long-established recipients, are at higher prices than in the past and often for hard currency or oil. Discounts are no longer typical and in some cases prices may even be above those charged other customers.

Moscow's economic and military aid have been limited by historic ties and political affinities of LDCs. Thus, despite apparent Soviet willingness to sell to almost any less-developed country, arms-sales have been heavily concentrated in the same areas where Soviet economic aid has been extended. The largest share of the military and economic assistance has gone to nations on the Soviet borders, as well as to radical North African-Middle Eastern states. Together, these countries have received more than 55 percent of Soviet economic-aid commitments and nearly 50 percent of military-aid commitments.

Military

By 1974–78, Soviet military sales accounted for about 20 percent of the nearly $125-billion world sales to LDCs, while deliveries represented more than 25 percent.[2] Through these sales less-developed countries were able to obtain a wide array of modern military equipment, including their first jet fighters, supersonic jets, guided-missile systems, and missile-attack boats. Soviet sales in 1974–78 averaged $3.3 billion annually (in actual prices charged; $4 billion in U.S. production costs), and accounted for 55 percent of the nearly $30 billion of LDC arms orders placed with the Soviet Union in 1955–78.

Economic

The Soviet $17-billion economic-aid program has had a very different history. Deliveries have been slow, LDCs could get the aid elsewhere, and they could often obtain newer technology from non-Communist sources. Project-aid, the backbone of the program

TABLE 1
Soviet Economic Assistance to LDCs
(Million U.S. $)

	1956–78	1956–73	1974	1975	1976	1977	1978
*Agreements**	17,090	9,255	815	1,935	980	400	3,705
Africa	3,990	1,360	55	100	435	30	2,010
East Asia	260	160	100	—	—	—	—
Latin America	965	410	215	255	40	30	15
Middle East	6,920	3,770	200	1,050	500	—	1,400
South Asia	4,955	3,555	245	530	5	340	280
*Deliveries**	7,595	4,965	705	500	460	540	430
Africa	2,025	675	85	70	65	70	60
East Asia	145	145	Negl	Negl	—	—	—
Latin America	195	85	15	15	35	25	20
Middle East	3,340	2,105	245	320	225	280	165
South Asia	2,890	1,955	355	95	135	165	185

*Components may not add to totals shown because of rounding.

15

and always difficult to administer, has sometimes brought more grief than blessings. The program, initiated in 1954 by the flamboyant Khruschev, pledged large amounts of development-assistance which Moscow later found it could not always deliver as rapidly as expected by LDCs. After the first decade of aid and only 40 percent of the $3-billion commitment was delivered, commitments were made after more careful studies to assure project viability. Gradually, fewer lines of credit for development were offered. These were first replaced by commitments to specific projects and more recently by more general framework agreements. These newer agreements, in principle, which specify broad outlines for cooperation, are intended to allow flexibility in project-negotiations and implementation.

The basic operation of the economic-aid program has not changed much over the more than two decades of its history.

(a) Economic aid is still targeted at a few recipients that receive large credits often for highly visible, heavy industrial projects in the public sector.

(b) Almost all Soviet aid is tied to equipment purchases in the USSR. Rarely are commodities or hard currency extended.

(c) Moscow provides extensive technical assistance to help overcome the lack of local skills in implementing and operating aid projects. The USSR dispatched nearly 28,000 Soviet technicians to LDCs in 1977 and 1978 of which 65 percent acted as advisers and training officers on Soviet aid-assisted projects. These technicians have conducted geological surveys, drawn up plant designs, and supervised and performed technical tasks in the construction and operation of some 1,100 projects which the USSR has built or is building in LDCs. Large numbers of Third-World personnel are still going to the USSR for training, in addition to some 550,000 that have been trained locally.

(d) At least 95 percent of Soviet economic aid must be repaid—traditionally over 12 years at 2½-3-percent interest. Occasionally, the terms are more lenient, such as those usually given Afghanistan (which allow up to 50 years for repayment) and recent credits to India (20 years plus a three-year grace). Especially since the mid-1960s, however, credits have sometimes carried commercial-like terms that include downpayments, allow only 5-10 years for amortization, and carry high rates of interest. Most Soviet credits are repaid in commodities, often in the output of plants built with Russian aid. Soviet terms compare with average U.S. terms for official development assistance of more than 35 years and less than 3 percent; also grant-aid has comprised more than half of U.S. aid in recent years.

(e)   Increasingly, the USSR has extended economic assistance that will yield mutual benefits, such as border-dams in Iran, pipelines to carry natural gas from Iran and Afghanistan to the USSR, oil exploration in Iraq in return for oil, and geological surveys and exploration for minerals which the USSR has conducted in at least 30 countries of the developing world. The most recent example is the 1978-accord with Morocco to exploit phosphates with which Morocco will repay its debt to the USSR.

THE SHIFTING AID PICTURE

Military

Soviet arms-sales more than doubled in 1974-78, compared to 1969-73 (in a world market that had quadrupled) based largely on the massive resupply and buildup in the Middle East since the war in October 1973 and on the huge amounts of aid to Ethiopia in the past two years. In addition, the Russians moved more heavily into commercial sales, as opposed to concessional aid because of the availability of large OPEC funding for arms.

Before 1974, Moscow's military customers had included: Egypt, its only $4 billion customer; Syria, a $2.3 billion client; India and Iraq, each in the $1.5-$2-billion class; Indonesia, an $875-million client before 1965; Iran, Afghanistan, and Algeria whose orders ranged from $350-$600 million; and some two dozen LDCs that received small, often negligible, amounts of arms.

The larger sales following the 1973-War were accompanied by both accelerated training programs for LDC personnel in the Soviet Union and additional Soviet and Cuban support cadres in

TABLE 2

Soviet Economic Credits and Grants to Selected LDCs
(Million U.S. $)

	Total 1954–78	1977	1978
Total	17,090	400	3,705
Africa	*3,990*	*30*	*2,010*
North Africa	*2,920*	—	*2,000*
Algeria	715	—	—
Morocco	2,100	—	2,000
Other	105	—	—
Sub-Saharan Africa	*1,070*	*30*	*10*
Angola	15	5	1
Ethiopia	105	—	Negl
Chana	95	—	—
Guinea	210	—	—
Mozambique	60	5	—
Somalia	165	—	—
Sudan	65	—	—
Tanzania	40	18	—
Other	315	2	9
East Asia	*260*	—	—
Indonesia	215	—	—
Other	45	—	—
Latin America	*965*	*30*	*15*
Argentina	225	—	—
Brazil	90	—	—
Chile	240	—	—
Colombia	210	—	—
Jamaica	30	30	—
Other	170	—	15

TABLE 2 (Continued)

	Total 1954-78	1977	1978
Middle East	*6,920*	—	*1,400*
Egypt	1,440	—	—
Iran	1,165	—	—
Iraq	705	—	—
North Yemen	145	—	40
South Yemen	200	—	90
Syria	765	—	—
Turkey	2,380	—	1,200
Other	120	—	70
South Asia	*4,955*	*340*	*280*
Afghanistan	1,265	—	—
India	2,280	340	—
Pakistan	920	—	220
Other	490	—	60

less-developed countries that had purchased new modern equipment. The numbers of Soviet advisers and maintenance personnel in the LDCs rose to some 6,700 in 1974 and to 11,000 in 1978 with the largest numbers stationed in the Arab radical states and in Ethiopia (1978).

Kuwait and Iran bought military equipment in the USSR (a $50-million Kuwaiti order for missiles in 1977 and Iran's $800 million worth of ground equipment after 1973). Other oil producers (Algeria, Iraq, and Libya) placed over $7 billion of orders for Soviet equipment after 1973, which accounted for more than 40 percent of Moscow's $16.5 billion of arms-sales in 1974–78. At least another 15 percent of Soviet sales were placed by LDC customers whose purchases were financed by rich Arab states.

The loss of Moscow's most important customer, Egypt, was the most notable change in Soviet arms-client patterns after 1973. The loss was accompanied by (a) the emergence of Libya

TABLE 3
Soviet Economic Technicians in LDCs*
(Persons)

	1977	1978
Total	22,390	27,620
Africa	*7,520*	*11,575*
North Africa	*3,120*	*6,680*
Algeria	2,650	6,000
Libya	100	200
Morocco	150	250
Other	220	230
Sub-Saharan Africa	*4,400*	*4,895*
Angola	200	400
Ethiopia	150	600
Guinea	500	450
Mali	350	450
Other	3,200	2,995
East Asia	*65*	*35*
Latin America	*490*	*350*
Argentina	5	35
Bolivia	150	100
Brazil	25	25
Other	310	190
Middle East	*11,195*	*11,885*
Egypt	1,000	750
Iran	3,400	4,000
Iraq	3,800	3,950
Syria	1,200	1,100
Turkey	1,000	1,250
Other	795	835
South Asia	*3,120*	*3,775*
Afghanistan	1,300	2,000
India	1,100	1,000
Pakistan	500	575
Other	220	220

*Minimum estimates of number present for a period of one month of more. Numbers are rounded to the nearest five.

as Moscow's largest arms buyer (after 1973), (b) the marked expansion of Soviet sales to Iraq, Syria, Algeria, and India, and (c) the dramatic $2-billion supply-relationship established with Ethiopia in 1977-78—unprecedented in sub-Saharan arms-procurement history. Moscow has added half-a-billion dollars of orders in 1973 to its initial arms-sales to Peru—its only Latin-American customer (apparently a temporary one).

While these initiatives clearly reflect Soviet geopolitical interests, re-emphasizing Moscow's determination to maintain a presence in the Middle East and Indian Ocean areas, the Russians clearly have profited from these sales which now cover a large deficit in Soviet trade with LDCs and supplement Soviet hard currency earnings.

Economic

Fewer changes have occurred in Soviet economic assistance. The most notable has been a shift to the use of broad "framework" agreements and an increase in the number of large commercial accords. The framework accords are agreements, in principle, which explore possibilities for cooperation in designated areas without allocating definite amounts of aid until project-by-project-studies are completed. Accords are then drawn for each project either with supplier-type credits, commercial arrangements, concessionary-aid terms, or a combination of these arrangements for different parts of the package. At the same time that Moscow introduced framework agreements, it tried to synchronize its own requirements and production-plans with those of LDCs through joint Soviet–LDC committees. Moscow also has tried to expand its economic relationships through joint ventures (still limited to shipping and fishing) which Moscow is using in the case of fisheries to circumvent some of the limitations imposed on its own fishing fleet by the 200-mile territorial-waters limits.

Despite possibly harder terms overall, Moscow has continued to extend its largest credits to a select few. In general, the size of credits has increased. Partly because of higher project-costs and also because of the kinds of project-support provided, commitments in the past five years rose one-and-a-half times over those in the previous five years. Extensions in 1974–78 thus have accounted for almost half of the total amount of aid provided over the entire program period. Deliveries went up 25 percent

TABLE 4
Soviet Military Relations with LDCs
(Million U.S. $)

	Total 1956-78	1956-73	1974	1975	1976	1977	1978
*Agreements**	29,655	13,035	4,225	2,035	3,375	5,215	1,765
North Africa	4,965	485	1,825	535	—	1,800	315
Middle East	14,960	8,860	2,025	640	2,100	1,235	100
Other	9,730	3,690	375	860	1,275	2,180	1,350
*Deliveries**	25,310	11,240	2,310	1,845	2,575	3,515	3,825
North Africa	3,875	435	150	380	810	925	1,175
Middle East	13,800	7,755	1,780	975	1,065	1,125	1,095
Other	7,635	3,050	380	490	700	1,465	1,555

*Components may not add to totals shown because of rounding.

in 1974-78 but without marked improvement in the rate of drawdown.

The Program 1977-78

Despite a definite upward annual bias in Soviet military and economic commitments to LDCs in the latter part of the 1970s, annual pledges have fluctuated widely because of (a) changing political exigencies for the military, emergency and resupply operations; (b) long periods required for implementing economic aid and for absorbing military receipts into LDC inventories; (c) prolonged negotiations required for finalizing economic and military agreements and the lack of an annual rhythm in signing accords; (d) economic or political constraints within the USSR which affect aid determinations; and (e) the apparent lack of LDC interest, in some cases, in accepting Soviet offers or initiating requests.

The most dramatic swings in Soviet-aid history occurred for both the economic and military programs in 1977-78. Military pledges jumped to an all-time record ($5.2 billion) in 1977 and then plummeted in 1978 to their lowest level since 1973 ($1.8 billion). On the other hand, more than $3.7 billion of new economic assistance in 1978 followed the 1977 seven-year-program low and broke all former Soviet economic-aid extension records. These transactions demonstrated Moscow's continuing interest in expanding and reinforcing its Third-World connections. On the other hand, the kinds of agreements signed in 1977-78 made it apparent again that Russian aid had become as pragmatic as it is political. Moscow's military support to Ethiopia had a strong geopolitical basis, and the assistance for mining phosphates in Morocco was motivated by economic factors.

The increasingly commercial cast of Soviet assistance has been noted in (a) the harder repayment terms and higher prices for most military sales and (b) the $1.5 billion of hard-currency earnings Moscow has gleaned annually over the past several years from military sales (possibly as much as $2 billion in 1978). It also is reflected in an interest in exploiting aid-possibilities which eventually will provide goods to help support Soviet domestic industrial operations. The most noteworthy recent

23

TABLE 5
Soviet Military Technicians in LDCs*
(Persons)

	1977	1978
Total	10,200	10,800
Algeria	600	1,000
Egypt	—	—
Ethiopia	1,000	1,300
India	145	150
Iraq	1,050	1,100
Libya	990	1,300
Syria	2,170	2,400
Other	4,245	3,550

*Minimum estimates of number present for a period of one month of more. Numbers are rounded to the nearest five.

example of Soviet interest in LDCs material-supply-potential is the widely-publicized $2-billion Moroccan phosphate deal, signed in 1978. In this latest Soviet initiative to cultivate external long-term supply-sources for raw materials, the USSR is hedging against possible domestic shortages, either as a result of resource-depletion or prohibitive extraction or processing costs. Under the Soviet-Moroccan accord, the Russians have contracted for their first phosphate imports, with a 30-year supply line of 10-million tons a year.

Military Aid

Moscow has been pushing its more lucrative, more easily effective military-sales program. Sales for the two-year period (1977-78) were high despite the 1978 decline and despite Indian, Iraqi, and Syrian purchases of large amounts of Western equipment in their first important moves to diversify arms-supply sources. India broke a 17-year tradition by placing a $2-billion order for Anglo-French Jaguars which it selected in preference to the MIG-23 and SU-20 aircraft offered by the Russians. Iraq also bought $2 billion of arms (largely Mirage aircraft) from the West in the past 2 years, more than double its total previous purchases. The $240-million Syrian purchase of the Franco-German Hot and Milan antitank-missile system was Damascus's largest order ever placed in the West.

In addition to continuing a heavy supply program to its already important arms customers, Moscow's most decisive supply action was in the Horn of Africa. Following political decisions made late in 1976, the USSR shifted its alliance from Somalia to Ethiopia in an arms buildup unprecedented in size of character in the sub-Sahara. The $2 billion of modern weaponry to Ethiopia provided a class of sophistication new to the region and far beyond the capabilities of the Ethiopian military establishment to operate or maintain. Thus, in 1977, Addis Ababa sent a contingent of about 300 military trainees to the USSR, following this, in 1978, with almost a thousand. At the same time, about 1,300-1,500 Russian technicians in Ethiopia (in 1978) performed training and maintenance functions.

Arms for Ethiopia accounted for about 30 percent of total Soviet arms-sales in 1977–78. Four of Moscow's traditionally large arms customers—Libya, Algeria, Syria, and India—accounted for another 55 percent of total Soviet sales with their nearly $4 billion of orders for a wide range of weapons. Among the remaining 22 less-developed countries that purchased arms from the USSR in 1977–78, countries with Soviet-supplied arsenals such as Afghanistan, South Yemen, and Iraq bought more than $600 million of weaponry; Tanzania bought air and ground equipment, and Peru contracted for aircraft.

Deliveries under these accords scored new records in 1977 and 1978, rising to almost $4 billion in the latter year. These deliveries enabled military hardware to maintain its top rank as Moscow's most important export to the Third World. By the end of 1978, the Soviets had delivered about 85 percent of their total arms commitment to Third-World clients. The 1977–78 deliveries included an impressive array of first-time Soviet exports of advanced weaponry to the Third World, such as MIG-25 jet fighters to Algeria and Libya, IL-76 transports to Iraq, and SU-22 jet fighter-bombers to Peru. Among other important deliveries were: the first MIG-23 jet fighters to sub-Sahara (Ethiopia); and the late model MIG-21 Bis to Syria and Ethiopia. Syria also received continuing supplies of surface-to-air missiles, OSA-II guided-missile patrol boats, T-62 tanks, and a wide assortment of ground armaments.

The heavy flow of advanced weaponry which the USSR is pouring into LDC inventories has created an added burden on Soviet services for training local personnel in maintenance and use of the equipment. About 1,900 LDC nationals were in the Soviet Union at the end of 1978 for training. At the same time, almost 11,000 Soviets (double the number in 1973) were in less-developed countries in advisery-training roles to assemble and maintain equipment and instruct local units in combat techniques and the use and maintenance of new weapons.

Syria, which claimed the largest number of Russian technical personnel in 1973, continued as the top claimant in 1978, by which time it had received $2 billion of additional Soviet weapons. The next largest Soviet technical contingents were in Ethiopia, Libya, and Angola, each of these countries receiving large arms shipments after 1973. At the same time, the 1,500 Soviets stationed in Somalia early in 1977 all had departed by year-end.

Economic

Soviet economic aid, still a program of opportunity, depends not only on Moscow's assessment of cost-benefits but also on LDC response to aid-overtures and the kind of assistance offered. Soviet commitments rebounded to an all-time high in 1978 from their lowest level in 1977 since 1968. The $3.7 billion of credits extended in 1978 was more than double the previous record-year, 1975, and represents more than a fifth of all Soviet economic assistance committed to the Third World over the 24 years of the Soviet-aid program. The 1978-peak followed $400 million of extensions in 1977.

Even the 1978-data tend to understate the full extent of Russian economic-aid initiatives because many new accords carry no price tag. These general "framework" agreements depend on project-by-project consideration which draw actual allocations out over long periods. In 1977–78, framework-agreements were signed with Afghanistan, Costa Rica, Guyana, Morocco, Mozambique, Syria, and Ethiopia. Only in the case of Morocco and Syria have definite commitments already been made for specific projects. These amount to $2.3 billion.

Eighty-five percent of the aid extended in 1977 went to India—Moscow's first new aid to that country in more than a decade. Because a large part of the credit will be for an aluminum plant in which the Russians have a special interest, and because of Soviet eagerness to cement ties with this important Chinese neighbor, the terms of the credit were more concessionary than in earlier aid to India. The only other important agreement in 1977 was a $30-million credit to Jamaica—Moscow's first to that country—for geological prospecting, a cement plant, and training schools. During 1977, the Soviets also entered into large contracts, probably mostly on commercial terms, for (a) a second gas pipeline from Iran to the Soviet border, (b) a dam in Iraq to irrigate 1.6-million hectares of land and to provide 500 MW of power, and (c) a 240-MW power plant in Iraq.

The large pledges in 1978 stemmed almost entirely from the $2-billion Soviet–Moroccan accord—the USSR's largest commitment to a single project in the Third World—and $1.2 billion of industrial-development credits to Turkey. The aid to Turkey increases the amount of credits made available under a 1975-framework-agreement for financing (a) expansion of the Soviet-built steel and aluminum plants, (b) power plants, and (c) a new oil refinery. Looking to the future, Soviet and Turkish authorities also are viewing other possibilities for cooperation, which could involve billions of dollars of additional Soviet assistance.

Pakistan was the only other important aid recipient in 1978. A $220-million credit for financing increased costs at the Karachi steel mill brings Soviet aid to the project up to $650 million, three quarters of Moscow's total aid to Pakistan. Smaller amounts of aid also went to South and North Yemen, a token amount was extended to Latin America for power projects, and virtually nothing to sub-Saharan Africa despite big expectations in Angola and Ethiopia.

Soviet nonmilitary technical personnel in the Third World rose on the average by a third between 1975–76 and 1977–78. While large increases in the number present were noted in Africa, the Middle East, and South Asia, the African share of the more than

25,000 technicians present each year (in 1977–78) gained five percentage-points over 1975–76. A large percentage of the Soviets stationed in Africa continued to work outside the aid program; Soviet aid projects in Africa probably employed only half the Soviet technicians present on the continent. The rest of the Russians worked as administrators, teachers, and doctors on commercial construction jobs (as in Algeria, Libya, and Nigeria). Soviet technical personnel assigned to other areas of the Third World worked more often on aid projects, except in a few countries such as Iraq and Iran where the Soviets had captured large commercial contracts. Altogether the Soviets earned an estimated $50–75 million of hard currency a year from the non-project, nonaid technical services it provided in 1977–78.

EFFECTIVENESS OF THE PROGRAM

Reduced Western influence in Third-World countries has not necessarily led to a corresponding rise in Soviet influence. New governments often have translated anticolonialist positions into strong nationalist policies jealous of any foreign influence. Despite the commitment of some LDC governments to a "Socialist" system, they usually have wanted their own brand of socialism, and have not been attracted to Soviet Communist ideology, either by economic or military aid. Nonetheless, the Russians take a long-term view of the effectiveness of their program. While they continue to forge closer ties with a group of strategically situated LDCs, the Soviets enjoy economic returns from both military and economic aid.

Military assistance has been less problem-ridden than economic aid despite occasional setbacks—notably in Indonesia (in the mid 1960s) and more recently in Egypt and Somalia. For the most part they have had only a temporary effect on Moscow's expanding Third-World arms-sales. Thus, Soviet sales of military hardware more than doubled in the five years after the cutoff of supplies to Egypt, compared with the five years before.

Economic aid is often more able to endure strains created by new political alignments and changes in government. This holds true despite the disenchantment which often sets in during and after the economic aid implementation-period. Time-consuming surveys and feasibility studies required before construction work, as well as institutional, human, and economic obstacles in many of LDCs have hampered Soviet (as well as other) programs. The USSR has compounded the difficulties of administering its aid program by furnishing only materials, equipment, and technical guidance for projects.

Advantages to both donor and recipient have gone beyond the mere size of the exchanges as each party gains from the relationship. Many of Moscow's arms clients have had their aspirations for international power and prestige satisfied, while Moscow has built an LDC presence. In recent years, Moscow also has garnered a windfall in hard currency and has kept its trade with LDCs out of the red with arms-sales. The ranking position of the USSR as an LDC arms-supplier, the sophistication of the weapons it provides, and the dependent relationship it has created, all have contributed to a big-power image for Moscow. Soviet military technical assistance also has exposed LDCs to Soviet military institutions and techniques and undoubtedly has established important personal relationships with LDC military leaders. Moscow, through its aid program, has obtained base rights in several countries, the use of port facilities in Iraq and Syria (and previously in Egypt); during its venture into Angola, Mali, and Guinea made their airports available; Moscow has used facilities in India (and previously in Somalia) for naval and air intelligence operations.

The Soviets also must view economic assistance as productive and inexpensive. Foreign aid has imposed a negligible drain on Soviet domestic resources, despite burdens sometimes created by aid requirements levied against an already taut planning cycle. In return for aid, the USSR has received bauxite from Guyana, oil from Iraq, natural gas from Iran and Afghanistan, and aluminum from Turkey and India. The closer economic relations expanded Soviet–LDC trade to $12 billion in 1977 (20 times above 1955 level), representing 17 percent of total Soviet trade. Moscow's largest aid clients have become its major LDC trading partners. Egypt, India, Iran, and Iraq together accounted for nearly half of Soviet nonmilitary trade with the Third World between 1974 and 1977. Countries in the Middle East and South Asia were largely responsible for the almost 100-percent increase in Soviet–LDC trade between 1973 and 1977.

The USSR also must consider its recent Moroccan deal a coup. This latest effort to expand long-term procurement possibilities for strategic materials is part of Moscow's continuing effort to supplement its own supplies. Since the early 1960s, Russian geologists have inventoried the metals and minerals reserves of at least 12 countries in Africa, five in the Middle East, two in South Asia, and one in Latin America. Gas and petroleum exploration and exploitation assistance was provided fourteen less-developed countries. Until now the return flow has been limited to gas and oil, bauxite, and iron ore. By 1978, the USSR was receiving (a) 13-billion cubic meters of natural gas a year from Iran and Afghanistan through Soviet-built pipelines as repayment for economic and military aid; (b) 6-7-million tons of crude oil annually from Iraq and Syria from fields the Russians had helped to develop; and (c) 2.5-million tons of bauxite from Soviet-developed mines in Guinea.

Economic aid also made positive contributions to the development of some LDCs. For example, Soviet plants in India account for: 80 percent of India's output of metallurgical equipment, 60 percent of heavy electrical equipment, more than half of India's oil production, a third of its steel output, and a fifth of the electric energy generated.

In several instances when the USSR jumped in with aid offers for major installations turned down by other donors, Moscow gained extra prestige. The Bokaro steel mill in India and the Isfahan mill in Iran are classic examples. Moscow scored in some countries by its help for developing public-sector industrial complexes, though in some cases the administrative woes and under-utilized capacity have dampened the recipients' original fervor. In Egypt Soviet aid provided 70 percent of Egypt's power equipment, all of Egypt's aluminum production, three-fourths of the capacity at Egypt's only steel mill at Helwan, and refineries that fill half of Egypt's domestic needs.

PROSPECTS IN THE EARLY 1980s

While Moscow shifts its program tactics from time to time to accommodate new political or economic currents, no reduction in the scale or content of the aid program nor in Moscow's strategy for leadership in the Third World has become apparent.

Instead of backing off in the face of new massive OPEC funding for Moscow's most important aid clients, the USSR continued its small economic program even in oil-rich states, profiting from their wealth through larger arms-sales and big commercial deals.

Military Aid

On the military front, there are no signs of a letup in the Soviet sales effort. A slowdown might come from a market that is saturated momentarily and is winding down its orders. The heavy sales of the past few years will, in themselves, dampen chances for large new orders because of the time it takes for LDCs to absorb the large stocks of modern weaponry pouring into their inventories. The recent quest for alternative arms sources by some of Russia's largest customers (i.e., Iraq and India) could also lead to a gradual reduction in the scale of orders by some major Soviet buyers.

If the world arms-market settles into a more even annual procurement pattern, Soviet sales probably also will follow suit, with annual sales falling into the $2–$3-billion range. At a minimum, the USSR will supply complementary equipment and large quantities of spare parts and technical support to countries that have been large Soviet arms-buyers in the past. With the possibilities for increasing levels of instability in the Middle East, South Asia, and southern Africa, the USSR stands ready to offer rapid delivery of large quantities of equipment and services which would push Soviet sales even higher than before.

Economic

Economic assistance, while not expected to equal the 1978 record again in the next several years, should follow a more even pattern as definite commitments are negotiated under existing and new general framework agreements. Moscow is expected to maintain its aid tempo in traditional client areas—more often under framework agreements; at other times through specific accords for project assistance, as provided India in 1977. The Soviets also are expected to expand patterns of joint participation (in planning as well as in certain enterprises). They will continue to try to expand the commercial aspects of their program.

Commercially-oriented aid-overtures to Latin America especially should gain momentum, as Moscow exerts pressures on Argentina and Brazil for large sales of power equipment and on Mexico for sales of all types of machinery and equipment. Moscow will undoubtedly pursue negotiations with Jamaica and Guyana to exploit their bauxite deposits as part of its search for additional supplies to satisfy the USSR's own needs.

Note

The detailed information on Soviet foreign aid contained in this study is drawn from numerous official and nonofficial publications available to the public. A primary source for data concerning the Soviet program in the LDCs—aid extensions, drawings on credits, and technical assistance—is the annual reviews of the Communist aid-programs published by the Central Intelligence Agency. The most recent of the series, "Communist Aid Activities to Non-Communist Less-Developed Countries 1978" was published in September 1979.

Official publications, journals, and newspapers from LDCs and the USSR also have been invaluable sources, particularly the USSR Ministry of Foreign Trade's foreign trade yearbook series and monthly foreign trade magazines. Other useful sources include publications of the United Nations and the Organization for Economic Cooperation and Development.

CHAPTER THREE

EASTERN EUROPE AND THE DEVELOPING COUNTRIES

Roger E. Kanet

Prior to the Second World War, and even as late as the 1950s, the countries of Eastern Europe[1] maintained virtually no political, and only minimal economic contacts with those areas of the world now referred to as the Third World.[2] The establishment and consolidation of communist regimes in Eastern Europe in the late 1940s and the collapse of West European colonialism in the two decades following World War II were the two major sets of developments that prepared the stage for the recent growth of contracts between these two groups of states. However, in spite of the increasing significance of relations between Eastern Europe and the countries of the Third World, relatively few American scholars have devoted their attention to the subject. Although the evolution of Soviet relations with the noncommunist developing countries has elicited widespread scholarly interest in the West and the literature on virtually all aspects of this topic has continued to expand over the past twenty years, comparable concern for Eastern Europe has not been evident.[3]

The purpose of the present analysis is to provide an initial brief examination of the development of relations between the countries of Eastern Europe and the Third World. Of primary concern will be those factors that apparently motivate the CMEA member-states in establishing and expanding their relations with the developing countries and, in addition, the degree to which the policies of individual East European states coincide, both with the policies of other East European countries and with those of the Soviet Union.

EASTERN EUROPE AND THE
DEVELOPING COUNTRIES

To a very significant degree the policies of the East European countries—with the partial exception of Romania—have closely paralleled those of the Soviet Union throughout the Third World ever since the 1950s. The political leaders of the CMEA countries share a common view with the Soviets concerning the significance of the role of the developing world in the historic struggle with the capitalist West. Support for national liberation movements and for "progressive" regimes is an essential element of that struggle. This aspect of East European interest can probably best be seen in the upsurge of contacts with and support for revolutionary movements and regimes in Sub-Saharan Africa during the 1970s. Along with the Soviet Union and Cuba, several of the East European countries have played an important role in providing military and economic support to Angola, Mozambique, and Ethiopia, among others.[4] In the Middle East, the East European countries, with the visible and notable exception of Romania, have followed the lead of the Soviet Union in providing support of various types to the more "radical" of the Arab governments in their struggle with Israel.

In addition to the fact that East European political elites share a common world view with the Soviets, there is the added factor of Soviet efforts to insure that the members of the CMEA coordinate their foreign policies *vis-à-vis* the outside world, including the developing countries. The reports published at the conclusion of meetings between and among high-level Soviet and East European government and party officials in recent years virtually indicate that issues related to the Third World have been among the topics of common concern. In the words of a Soviet editorial on the significance of the series of summer meetings in the Crimea between General Secretary Brezhnev and the leaders of the East European communist parties, "Coordinated action heightens the effectiveness also of socialist foreign policy.[5]

In recent years, however, there has been evidence that factors other than ideologically-based interest or Soviet policy have increasingly stimulated East European concerns in the developing world. During the 1970s, in particular, Eastern Europe has turned to the Third World as both a market for industrial goods not easily sold on the world market and as a source of industrial raw materials, including energy.[6] Since the oil crisis of 1973-74 and the growing evidence that the Soviet Union is neither willing nor able to meet the expanding East European demands for petroleum imports, the East European states have been searching for new supplies of oil from countries throughout the Third World. While coordination has been an essential element in recent East European–Soviet political relations with developing countires, no comparable cooperation is yet visible in the economic sphere.[7]

Besides the general political interests of the CMEA countries in the developing world, there are more specific political concerns that have motivated at least two of the East European states. Both Romania and the German Democratic Republic have sought to bolster their international political position by expanding relations with Third World countries. Romania has been interested primarily in strengthening its autonomy *vis-à-vis* the Soviet Union by emphasizing its position as a developing country and by expanding its ties with other developing countries—much in the way Yugoslavia developed its international position as a non-aligned state in the 1950s and early 1960s.[8] The GDR, on the other hand, has been especially interested in establishing its position as a recognized sovereign state independent from the Federal Republic. While this motive clearly played a much more important role prior to GDR recognition by the West in the early 1970s, it apparently still influences GDR policies in the Third World.[9]

The following examines the development of both political-military and economic relations between the CMEA countries and the developing world. It deals with these relations at a relatively high level of generality, and attempts to point out those areas in which individual East European countries have tended to deviate from a common pattern in their policies.

POLITICAL AND MILITARY FACTORS
IN EAST EUROPEAN POLICY

Although the importance of economic factors in relations between Eastern Europe and the developing countries has grown significantly in the past decade, it would appear that political factors continue to play a very important role in most of those relations. Throughout the past thirty years, the countries of Eastern Europe, with the important exception of Romania, have adopted a position on virtually every major and minor development in the Third World that parallels almost exactly that of the USSR.[10] On issues such as the Arab-Israeli conflict, Indian-Pakistani relations, the national liberation struggle in southern Africa, and the need to eliminate the influence of the capitalist West from the developing world, the East Europeans have followed a political line virtually identical to that taken by the Soviets. The one important exception has been Romania, which has developed its own policies ever since the mid-1960s—policies which often are clearly distinguishable from those of the USSR. The most important issues relevant to the Third World on which the Romanians have refused to follow the Soviet lead have been the Arab-Israeli conflict, the role of China in the Third World, and the creation of a New International Economic Order. Not only has Romania been the only member of the CMEA that has continued to maintain diplomatic relations with Israel since the 1967 War, but it has been the only European communist state that has not condemned the Egyptian-Israeli peace agreement of 1979. In fact, Ceasecu reportedly played an important part in bringing Sadat and Begin together in the fall of 1977.[11] As has been already noted, this aspect of Romanian foreign policy is a part of Romanian effort to establish autonomy in relationship to the Soviet Union.

The area in which the coincidence of Soviet and East European policy has been most evident in recent years has been in relations with national liberation movements and revolutionary governments in Sub-Saharan Africa. As they did in the early 1960s in Ghana, Guinea, and Mali, East European governments have seemingly coordinated their military assistance programs in a number of countries with those of the Soviet Union. In Mozambique, for example, Hungary has been supplying military assistance and training officers of the Mozambique military, while Romania has reportedly agreed to assist in the training of Mozambique's military forces in the use of Soviet weapons.[12] This form of military cooperation between an East European country and the USSR is not new. As early as 1947-48, at the time of the creation of the state of Israel, Czechoslovakia, with the support and encouragement of the Soviet Union, provided military equipment and training in the use of that equipment to the Israelis, in order to support what the Soviets then viewed as the major challenge to Western influence in the Middle East.[13] Again in 1955, after Soviet policy on the Middle Eastern question had shifted, Czechslovakia again functioned as a Soviet surrogate when it acted as the intermediary for the initial major shipment of Soviet military equipment to a developing country—this time to Egypt.[14]

More recently, the most active of the East European states in the military field has been the GDR. In early 1979 it was estimated that between three-thousand and four-thousand-five-hundred East German instructors in police and security operations were working in various countries in Africa and the Middle East.[15] In all of the cases of East European military involvement in the developing world, there is a clear indication of cooperation with one another and with the Soviet Union. For the past recipients of military deliveries from Eastern Europe—in particular from Czechoslovakia, the GDR, and Poland—have been the very same countries that have received Soviet military exports.

However, while military assistance and sales have comprised an increasingly important part of Soviet relations with the developing countries, they have remained relatively less important for Eastern Europe. Soviet arms commitments to developing countries have increased from an average of slightly more than $390 million per year in the period 1955-68 to an annual average of more than $3,200 million since 1972. In the same period new commitments of economic assistance have risen from an average of $400 to $885 million per year for the two periods. The figures for Eastern Europe indicate that economic assistance continues to hold a much more important place, relative to military aid, in the policies of the East European countries as a group, than it does for the USSR. Commitments of new military aid have risen from $58 million per year in 1955-68 to $312 million annually for 1972-1978, while those of economic assistance have risen

TABLE 1

Arms Sales and Deliveries of USSR and Eastern Europe
to Noncommunist Developing Countries*
(In millions of current U.S. $)

	Agreements		Deliveries	
	USSR	Eastern Europe	USSR	Eastern Europe
Total	29,655	3,255	25,310	2,605
1955–68	5,495	810	4,585	745
1969	360	125	450	80
1970	1,150	50	995	80
1971	1,590	120	865	120
1972	1,635	150	1,215	70
1973	2,810	130	3,130	120
1974	4,225	530	2,310	165
1975	2,035	215	1,845	255
1976	3,375	215	2,575	315
1977	5,215	450	3,515	325
1978	1,765	465	3,825	325

*Central Intelligence Agency, National Foreign Assessment Center, *Communist Aid Activities in Non-Communist Less-Developed Countries, 1978: A Research Paper*, ER 79-10412U, September 1979, p. 2.

from about $150 million to more than $600 million per year (*see* Tables 1 and 3).[16] A small portion of that military assistance has been provided as training for the military forces of individual Third-World countries. During the period 1955 to 1978, for example, almost six-thousand military personnel from the developing countries received training in Eastern Europe—compared with almost 44,000 in the Soviet Union (*see* Table 2).

Soviet military assistance and arms-trade have been associated with attempts to gain a presence in various Third-World regions—

TABLE 2
Military Personnel from Noncommunist Developing Countries Trained in the USSR and Eastern Europe, 1955–1978*

	USSR	Eastern Europe
Total	43,790	5,965
Africa	13,420	1,400
North Africa	3,385	335
Algeria	2,045	200
Libya	1,265	65
Other	75	70
Sub-Saharan Africa	10,035	1,065
Angola	55	5
Benin	20	—
Burundi	75	—
Congo	355	85
Equatorial Guinea	200	—
Ethiopia	1,190	450
Ghana	180	—
Guinea	870	60
Guinea-Bissau	100	—
Mali	355	10
Nigeria	695	35
Somalia	2,395	160
Sudan	330	20
Tanzania	1,820	10
Zambia	85	—
Other	1,310	230
East Asia	7,590	1,710
Cambodia	30	—
Indonesia	7,560	1,710
Latin America	725	—
Peru	725	—

TABLE 2 (Continued)

	USSR	Eastern Europe
Middle East	15,630	2,485
Egypt	5,665	585
Iran	315	—
Iraq	3,650	680
North Yemen	1,180	—
South Yemen	1,075	20
Syria	3,745	1,200
South Asia	6,425	370
Afghanistan	3,725	285
Bangladesh	445	—
India	2,200	85
Pakistan	45	N/A
Sri Lanka	10	—

*Central Intelligence Agency, National Foreign Assessment Center, *Communist Aid Activities in Non-Communist Less-Developed Countries, 1978: A Research Paper*, ER 79-10412U, September 1979, pp. 5-6. Data refer to the estimated number of persons departing for training. Numbers are rounded to the nearest five.

in particular in such strategically important areas as the Eastern Mediterranean, the Horn of Africa, and southern Africa. While East European military assistance has been, in part at least, ancillary to that of the Soviet Union, it has also been motivated increasingly by financial considerations—as has that of the USSR itself—since military equipment supplied to some Third World countries is paid for in hard currency. In addition, countries such as the GDR have used the expansion of military ties of various sorts in the attempt to strengthen its international position.

Overall, the political and military relations of the East European countries with the Third World have grown immensely over the last two decades. East European states now maintain diplomatic

TABLE 3

Soviet and East European Economic Assistance to Noncommunist Developing Countries*
(In millions of current U.S. $)

	Agreements		Deliveries	
	USSR	Eastern Europe	USSR	Eastern Europe
Total	17,088	9,086	7,595	3,305
1954–68	6,081	2,385	2,870	800
1969	476	403	355	105
1970	200	196	390	145
1971	1,126	484	420	190
1972	654	915	430	170
1973	714	605	500	220
1974	816	914	705	230
1975	1,934	511	500	245
1976	979	773	460	370
1977	402	397	540	460
1978	3,707	1,502	430	365

*Central Intelligence Agency, National Foreign Assessment Center, *Communist Aid Activities in Non-Communist Less-Developed Countries, 1978: A Research Paper*, ER 79-10412U, September 1979, p. 11.

relations with the vast majority of the countries of the developing world. However, to a very substantial degree, these relations appear to be supportive of and ancillary to those of the Soviet Union. Only the Romanians have deviated in their policy from that of the Soviets and even they have coordinated certain of their activities with their Soviet allies—e.g., the military training in Mozambique.

THE ECONOMIC FACTOR IN
EAST EUROPEAN POLICY

The effort of the East European states to expand economic relations with the developing world has become an increasingly important element in their overall policy during the 1970s. It is in this area that policy coordination among the CMEA members has yet to be developed effectively. Trade between the European communist states and the developing countries has expanded by more than nine times during the course of the past two decades. Between 1960 and 1977 total trade turnover between the two groups of countries rose from $939 million to more than $8,500 million in current prices. However, as a percentage of the trade of the European Communist states, trade with the developing world has remained fairly stable. While trade with developing countries comprised 6.1 percent of total East European trade in 1960, by 1970 it had fallen to 5.9 percent. In recent years, it has risen to 7.1 and 7.7 percent in 1976 and 1977, respectively (*see* Table 4).

The growth of trade between the European communist states and the developing world is directly related to developments in the domestic economies of the European states and in trade relations with other major trading partners. The fact that virtually all of the East European countries are heavily dependent on imports of raw materials—in particular of energy—has meant that they have been interested in establishing stable, long-term agreements for the supply of petroleum and other raw materials from the developing countries. For example, prior to 1978, Poland's trade with Iraq consisted almost entirely of exports. In 1978, for the first time, Polish imports from Iraq, which consisted almost entirely of oil, exceeded imports. Prior to the overthrow of the Shah in Iran, most of the East European countries had signed agreements with Iran calling for expanded gas and oil imports. Kuwait, Libya, Mexico, and even Saudi Arabia have become the suppliers of increasing amounts of energy imports for the East European countries.[17] This search for new supplies of petroleum and natural gas is the result of a two-fold development during the past decade. First of all, the modernization drive in the domestic economies of all of the communist states has resulted in a rapidly expanding domestic demand for

for new supplies of energy, especially for their expanding petro-chemical industries. At the same time the Soviets have made clear that they cannot continue to meet these growing energy demands of their East European "partners," in particular if they are going to continue to export considerable amounts of oil and gas to Western Europe in order to cover the costs of imports of Western industrial goods and technology.

Given the chronic lack of convertible currency in the Communist states,[18] the primary method that has been employed to cover imports of petroleum and other industrial raw materials has been through barter agreements. Poland, for example, is presently building twenty major industrial projects in Iraq in which approximately 2,500 workers and specialists are engaged. In return, Iraq will make payment in oil exports in the coming years.[19] This represents a pattern that has become quite common in the trade between the European Communist states and many of the developing countries. Overall, economic and technical assistance programs of the East European countries have become increasingly related to the economic concerns of the donor country than has generally been true for Soviet economic assistance, even though the Soviets have, in recent years, begun to tie their project assistance to the needs of the Soviet economy.[20] Not only has East European assistance been motivated by the desire to ensure future oil supplies, it has also been closely coordinated with efforts to build up markets for East European industrial and agricultural equipment in the Third World. This aspect of East European economic assistance has been especially visible in Latin America where approximately seventeen percent of total East European credits have been committed (see Table 5). Virtually all of these credits have been supplied to cover exports of various types of East European industrial production to Latin America.

The distribution of East European economic assistance by region illustrates an important difference in this assistance from that provided by the Soviet Union. While the Soviets have concentrated their aid on a relatively small number of countries in the Middle East, North Africa, and South Asia (a total of almost eighty-seven percent of their assistance from 1954 to 1978), East European aid has been much more evenly distributed by both region and by country.

Table 4
Trade of East European States with the Noncommunist Developing Countries*
(In millions of current U.S. $)

	1960		1965		1970		1975		1976		1977	
	Exp.	Imp.	Exp.	Imp.	Exp.	Imp.	Exp.	Imp.	Exp.	Imp.	Exp.	Imp.
Bulgaria												
Total Trade	571	625	1,176	1,178	2,004	1,831	4,810	5,531	5,320	6,198	6,288	6,198
With DCs	18	13	52	37	125	81	463	209	430	238	650	340
Czechoslovakia												
Total Trade	1,929	1,816	2,688	2,673	3,792	3,695	8,158	8,874	8,745	9,410	10,495	10,888
With DCs	200	161	255	197	331	214	706	501	658	498	1,068	733
German Democratic Republic												
Total Trade	2,207	2,194	3,085	2,823	4,647	4,923	10,680	11,947	11,645	13,514	12,700	14,300
With DCs	89	90	131	120	183	182	431	483	473	605	597	715

Hungary

Total Trade	874	976	1,510	1,520	3,317	2,505	5,694	6,758	6,643	7,252	7,959	8,558
With DCs	58	58	107	113	137	177	364	498	392	524	473	640

Poland

Total Trade	1,326	1,495	2,228	2,340	3,548	3,608	10,510	12,752	10,969	13,823	12,405	14,767
With DCs	93	99	172	210	258	196	845	597	878	577	1,005	765

Romania

Total Trade	717	648	1,102	1,077	1,851	1,960	5,420	5,418	6,175	6,062	7,020	7,017
With DCs	40	20	68	55	153	117	985	732	1,089	1,087	1,173	1,031

Total Eastern Europe

Total Trade	7,624	7,754	11,789	11,618	18,159	18,522	45,272	51,280	49,497	55,626	56,867	61,728
With DCs	498	441	785	732	1,187	967	3,794	3,020	3,920	3,522	4,966	4,224
	6.5	5.7	6.7	6.3	6.5	5.2	8.4	5.9	7.9	6.3	8.7	6.8

*Central Intelligence Agency, National Foreign Assessment Center, *Handbook of Economic Statistics 1978: A Research Aid*, ER 78-10365, October 1978, pp. 67-68; 1977 data supplemented by Soviet Edonomicheskoi Vzaimopomoschchi Vzaimopomoschchi, *Statisticheskii Ezhegodnik Stran-Chenov Soveta Vzaimopomoshchi 1978*. (Moscow: Statistike, 1978, p. 325 for GDR and International Monetary Fund, *Directon of Trade Yearbook 1979*, p. 232 for Romania.)

TABLE 5

Soviet and East European Credits and Grants Extended to Noncommunist Developing Countries*
(In millions of current U.S. $)

	1954–1978				1977				1978			
	USSR	%	Eastern Europe	%	USSR	%	Eastern Europe	%	USSR	%	Eastern Europe	%
Total	17,088	—	9,086	—	402	—	397	—	3,707	—	1,502	—
Africa	3,989	23.3	2,350	25.9	31	7.7	154	38.8	2,010	54.2	627	41.7
North Africa	2,918	17.1	934	10.3	—	—	35	8.8	2,000	54.0	110	7.3
Algeria	716	—	524	—	—	—	—	—	—	—	—	—
Mauritania	8	—	10	—	—	—	—	—	—	—	—	—
Morocco	2,098	—	170	—	—	—	—	—	2,000	—	89	—
Tunisia	96	—	210	—	—	—	35	—	—	—	—	—
Other	—	—	20	—	—	—	—	—	—	—	20	—
Sub-Saharan Africa	1,071	6.3	1,416	15.6	31	7.7	119	30.0	11	0.3	517	34.4
Angola	17	—	88	—	6	—	N/A	—	1	—	76	—
Benin	5	—	N/A	—	—	—	—	—	—	—	—	—
Cameroon	8	—	—	—	—	—	—	—	—	—	—	—
Cape Verde	3	—	1	—	—	—	—	—	3	—	—	—

Country						
Central African Empire	3	—	—	—	—	—
Chad	5	—	—	—	—	—
Congo	28	60	—	3	—	—
Equatorial Guinea	1	—	—	—	—	—
Ethiopia	105	95	—	23	Negl	45
Gabon	–	2	—	—	—	2
Chana	94	105	1	—	—	—
Guinea	212	110	1	—	—	—
Guinea-Bissau	11	N/A	—	—	—	—
Kenya	48	—	—	—	—	—
Madagascar	20	Negl	—	—	6	Negl
Mali	90	23	—	—	1	—
Mauritius	5	—	—	—	—	—
Mozambique	5	17	5	12	—	2
Niger	2	—	—	—	—	N/A
Nigeria	7	80	—	—	—	—
Rwanda	1	—	—	—	—	—
Senegal	8	35	Negl	—	—	—
Sierra Leone	28	—	—	—	—	—
Somalia	164	6	—	Negl	—	—
Sudan	65	240	—	62	—	24
Tanzania	38	23	18	—	—	3
Uganda	16	—	—	—	—	—
Upper Volta	6	—	—	—	Negl	—

TABLE 5 (Continued)

	1954-1978				1977				1978			
	USSR	%	Eastern Europe	%	USSR	%	Eastern Europe	%	USSR	%	Eastern Europe	%
Sub-Saharan Africa (Continued)												
Zambia	9	—	62	—	—	—	—	—	—	—	12	—
Other	67	—	469	—	—	—	19	—	—	—	352	—
East Asia	261	1.5	552	6.1	—	—	—	—	—	—	170	11.3
Burma	16	—	173	—	—	—	—	—	—	—	140	—
Cambodia	25	—	17	—	—	—	—	—	—	—	—	—
Indonesia	214	—	292	—	—	—	—	—	—	—	—	—
Laos	6	—	4	—	—	—	—	—	—	—	—	—
Philippines	—	—	66	—	—	—	—	—	—	—	30	—
Latin America	964	5.6	1,500	16.5	30	7.5	90	22.7	15	0.4	244	16.2
Argentina	220	—	204	—	—	—	15	—	—	—	—	—
Bolivia	69	—	52	—	15	—	—	—	—	—	—	—
Brazil	88	—	621	—	—	—	—	—	—	—	200	—
Chile	238	—	145	—	—	—	—	—	—	—	—	—
Colombia	211	—	81	—	—	—	—	—	—	—	10	—

Country											
Costa Rica	15	—	12	—	—	—	10	—	—	—	—
Ecuador	Negl	—	19	—	N/A	—	—	—	—	—	—
Guyana	N/A	—	30	—	—	—	20	—	—	—	—
Jamaica	30	—	36	—	30	—	8	—	—	—	28
Mexico	N/A	—	35	—	—	—	35	—	—	—	—
Peru	25	—	216	—	—	—	1	—	—	—	—
Uruguay	52	—	31	—	—	—	—	—	—	—	—
Venezuela	N/A	—	10	—	—	—	—	—	—	—	—
Other	16	—	17	—	—	—	1	—	15	—	6
Middle East	6,918	40.5	3,712	40.9	—	—	148	37.3	1,399	37.7	441	29.4
Cyprus	—	—	5	—	—	—	95	—	—	—	—
Egypt	1,440	—	890	—	—	—	—	—	—	—	—
Greece	8	—	N/A	—	—	—	—	—	—	—	—
Iran	1,165	—	686	—	—	—	50	—	—	—	—
Iraq	705	—	493	—	—	—	—	—	—	—	—
Jordan	26	—	N/A	—	—	—	—	—	—	—	—
Lebanon	—	—	9	—	—	—	—	—	—	—	—
North Yemen	143	—	13	—	—	—	—	—	38	—	—
South Yemen	204	—	66	—	—	—	3	—	90	—	6
Syria	768	—	954	—	—	—	—	—	—	—	150
Turkey	2,380	—	396	—	—	—	—	—	1,200	—	85
Other	79	—	200	—	—	—	—	—	71	—	200

TABLE 5 (Continued)

	1954–1978				1977				1978			
	USSR	%	Eastern Europe	%	USSR	%	Eastern Europe	%	USSR	%	Eastern Europe	%
South Asia	4,956	29.0	872	9.6	341	84.8	6	1.5	283	7.6	20	1.3
Afghanistan	1,263	—	39	—	—	—	—	—	—	—	—	—
Bangladesh	304	—	159	—	—	—	—	—	—	—	—	—
India	2,282	—	455	—	340	—	—	—	—	—	—	—
Nepal	30	—	—	—	1	—	—	—	—	—	—	—
Pakistan	921	—	126	—	—	—	6	—	225	—	—	—
Sri Lanka	158	—	93	—	—	—	—	—	60	—	20	—

*Central Intelligence Agency, National Foreign Assessment Center, *Communist Aid Activities in Non-Communist Less-Developed Countries 1978: A Research Paper*, ER 79-10412U, September 1979, pp. 7–10. (N.B. components may not add to totals because of rounding.

Most of the East European countries initiated industrial-modernization drives in the early 1970s based on Western credits. It was assumed that, within a relatively short period of time, the new industries would be in operation and that the exports to the West of the products of these new factories would be used to repay the original loans. However, delays in completing the projects, the rising cost of imports resulting from worldwide inflation, recession in the West, and a variety of other factors have all proven this assumption false. The East Europeans have had to search for markets elsewhere—both within the CMEA community and in the developing world. Clearly the developing world represents a potential market for the surplus production of the East European states and, as the recent trade figures indicate, exports to the developing countries have been rising somewhat more rapidly than overall exports.

Another element of commercial relations between the developing countries and Eastern Europe that has been growing in importance has been the technical-services program (*see* Table 6). Initially, technical services were part of the economic-assistance program of the communist states. In recent years, however, an increasing percentage of East European technicians was being paid in hard currency for services unrelated to economic-assistance projects. Of approximately 44,000 East Europeans abroad in 1978, almost half were in Libya and an additional 10,000 were in Algeria, Syria, and other Middle Eastern countries.[21] At the same time that the number of East Europeans working abroad has risen, the number of technical personnel from the developing world receiving training in Eastern Europe has fallen. By 1978, only 3,300 technicians were resident in the Soviet Union and Eastern Europe—down from 4,390 four years earlier (*see* Table 7).

Another important aspect of long-term development-assistance provided by the Soviet Union and the East European countries has been the education of substantial numbers of academic students from the developing countries. The numbers of students have risen consistently and by 1978 more than 18,000 were studying in Eastern Europe—up from about 9,000 in 1970 (*see* Table 8). An interesting aspect of this program has been the focus on Sub-Saharan Africa. Since the inception of the academic training program in the late 1950s and early 1960s, close to forty percent of all students in Eastern Europe come from Black

TABLE 6
Soviet, East European, Cuban Economic Technicians Working in Noncommunist Developing Countries

	1970		1975		1977		1978	
	USSR	East Europe	USSR	East Europe	USSR and East Europe	Cuba	USSR and East Europe	Cuba
Total	10,600	5,530	17,785	13,915	58,755	6,575	72,655	12,525
Africa	4,010	3,150	5,930	10,290	34,390	5,900	43,805	11,420
North Africa	—	—	—	—	21,850	15	36,165	450
Sub-Saharan Africa	—	—	—	—	12,540	5,885	7,640	8,500
East Asia	100	60	25	30	125	0	85	0
Latin America	35	140	330	225	830	335	700	190
Middle East	—	—	—	—	20,010	330	23,890	915
South Asia	6,455	1,950	8,375	3,370	3,475	0	4,145	0

*Central Intelligence Agency, National Foreign Assessment Center, *Communist Aid to Less-Developed Countries of the Free World, 1975*, ER 76-10372U, July 1976, p. 8; *Idem*, for 1977, ER 78-10478U, November 1978, p. 9; *Idem*, *Communist Aid Activities in Non-Communist Less-Developed Countries, 1978*, ER 79-10412U, pp. 14-15.

TABLE 7

Technical Personnel from Developing Countries Receiving Training in the Soviet Union and Eastern Europe*

	USSR	USSR and East Europe combined	Eastern Europe
1965	—	2,000+	—
1970	1,020	—	530
1971	1,310	—	1,435
1972	1,355	—	975
1973	—	3,715	—
1974	—	4,380	—
1975	—	?	—
1976	4,250	—	?
1977	—	3,200	—
1978	—	3,300	—
Total 1954–1978	—	48,000+	—

*Through 1974, annual publications of Bureau of Intelligence and Research, U.S. Department of State, *Communist States and Developing Countries: Aid and Trade in* _____. For 1975 through 1978 *see* Table 6.

Africa, even though less than sixteen percent of total economic assistance has been committed to that region.

East European academic and technical training programs for students from the Third World have had two major purposes. First, they help to provide the skilled personnel needed to modernize the economies of countries receiving economic assistance and to staff the projects and programs established with East European aid. In this respect they represent an important component of the overall East European aid programs. In addition, however, the academic training program, in particular, is geared to prepare a future elite that, at a minimum, is favorably disposed toward the European Communist states.

TABLE 8

Academic Students from Developing Countries Being Trained in Communist Countries*

	All Communist Countries[1] 1970	All Communist Countries[2] 1975	All Communist Countries[3] 1977	USSR 1978	E. Europe 1978	China
Total	21,415	27,275	40,345	26,445	18,560	260
Africa	10,990	14,895	20,780	13,635	9,755	160
North Africa	2,115	2,370	2,965	2,035	1,520	20
Sub-Saharan Africa	8,875	12,525	17,815	11,600	8,235	140
East Asia	650	335	20	25	10	0
Latin America	2,425	2,940	4,445	2,760	1,890	0
Middle East	5,770	6,270	11,320	6,615	5,525	15
South Asia	1,580	2,825	3,780	3,400	1,375	80

[1] Approximately 12,500 of these students were in the Soviet Union, the remainder in Eastern Europe.
[2] Approximately two-thirds of the students were in the Soviet Union, most of the remainder in Eastern Europe.
[3] More than sixty percent of the students were in the Soviet Union, most of the remainder in Eastern Europe.
*For 1970 data, Bureau of Intelligence and Research, U.S. Department of State, *Communist States and Developing Countries: Aid and Trade in 1970*, p. 13. For 1975–1979 data *see* Table 6.

Even though there has been relatively little effort, to date, to coordinate the economic relations of the individual European CMEA members with the developing world—as has clearly occurred in the military and political spheres—there are recent indications that the European communist states plan to coordinate some of their economic activities in the developing countries in the future. Czechoslovak government officials announced in the spring of 1979 that the members of the CMEA envisage the joint supplying of complete industrial plants to Third World countries as a "new step" in economic cooperation. The primary purpose of this type of new cooperation will be to pay for increased imports of fuel, energy, and raw materials from the developing countries.[22] The success of such a cooperative program will depend not only on the ability of the communist states to compete effectively with Western suppliers of modern industrial equipment, but also on the continued willingness of developing countries to enter into what are still essentially barter arrangements. Unless the East Europeans are able to provide goods and materials competitive with those available from the West, it is likely that they will have to provide concessionary pricing of these goods and services and to continue to provide "commercial packages" that cover both exports and the provisions of technical assistance.

An additional question concerns the likelihood that East European investments in aid will pay off in future supplies of raw materials. The developing countries that are likely to be the most receptive to barter-type arrangements are the very ones that are the least developed and the least stable politically.[23] It is conceivable that the East Europeans will find it difficult to continue to negotiate such agreements with those countries in the Third World which command the resources that they are seeking.

Finally, the East Europeans, along with the Soviets, are learning that representatives of developing countries are unwilling to differentiate between capitalist and socialist-developed countries when making demands for the establishment of a new world economic order. Although the socialist countries have been willing to support, in principle, many of the demands of the developing countries, they have refused to commit themselves to guaranteed prices for raw materials or to specific amounts of economic assistance.[24] Only the Romanians, who have viewed themselves as part of the developing world, have been willing to support the specifics of the proposed new-world economic order.

SOME CONCLUDING REMARKS

What is clear from this very brief survey of East European relations with the developing world is that the East Europeans are more interested now in the potential role of the developing world in stabilizing and strengthening the economies of the CMEA members themselves than they are in most other matters relating to the Third World. The significant industrial growth that has occurred in most CMEA countries in the 1970s has resulted in a notable increase in both the need for raw materials and the availability of exportable industrial products. The developing countries—some of them at least—represent both potential suppliers of industrial raw materials and markets for a portion of the industrial exports.

However, in spite of Eastern Europe's growing economic interest in the Third World and the political stability that successful economic relations imply, the East Europeans are still involved in supporting revolutionary movements and regimes in consort with the Soviet Union. However, these two sets of relationships are not necessarily contradictory, for military–political support for a revolutionary movement may well be viewed as a means to ensure favorable future economic relations.

Overall, East European relations with the countries of the Third World have expanded markedly over the course of the past two decades. Political relations are now maintained with the majority of the independent states of Asia, Africa, and Latin America. In some isolated cases Eastern Europe, in conjunction with the USSR, has become the major supplier of economic and military assistance—e.g., in several of the more "radical" African countries. Insofar as individual East European countries have been able to have a political impact on the developing world, however, it has usually been in those areas where they have collaborated with their Soviet allies in providing support for "anti-Western" regimes or movements. Nevertheless, the available evidence seems to indicate that the East Europeans increasingly view the developing countries in relationship to their own economic needs and that policies toward the developing countries will be motivated even more than they have been in the past by economic, as opposed to political, factors.

Notes

1. Eastern Europe refers only to the European members of the Council for Mutual Economic Assistance and the Warsaw Treaty Organization, minus the USSR: Bulgaria, Czechoslovakia, the German Democratic Republic, Hungary, Poland and Romania.
2. Third World refers to the less-developed countries of Asia, Africa, and Latin America. The term will be used interchangeably with "less-developed countries" and with "developing countries."
3. In her excellent bibliography, *The International Relations of Eastern Europe: A Guide to Information Sources* (Detroit: Gale Research Co., 1978), Robin A. Remington lists only eight entries that deal with East European relations with the Third World. Three of these concern Yugoslavia, three treat the topic only peripherally in the context of Romanian foreign policy, and one touches on East Germany's relations with the developing world in the context of its larger foreign policy. Only one of the entries deals explicitly with East European relations separately from those of the USSR: Michael Kaser, "East European Development Aid: Comparative Record and Prospects," *The World Today*, 26 (1970): 467–478. An important recent contribution to the study of East European involvement in the Third World is the excellent series of articles on the relations of five East European countries (Bulgaria, Czechoslovakia, Hungary, Poland, and Romania) with the countries of Sub-Saharan Africa published by Radio Free Europe Research: R.N., "Bulgaria's Presence in Black Africa," *Radio Free Europe Research, RAD Background Report (RFER)*, (92), Bulgaria, 20 April 1979; Otto Pick, "Czechoslovakia's Presence in Black Africa," *RFER*, (77), Czechoslovakia, 19 March 1979; Aurel Bereznai, "Hungary's Presence in Black Africa," *RFER*, (50), Poland, 1 March 1979; Paul Gafton *et al.*, "Romania's Presence in Black Africa," *RFER*, (18), Romania, 23 May 1979; and William F. Robinson, "Eastern Europe's Presence in Black Africa," *RFER*, (142), Eastern Europe, 21 June. See also, Hans-Adolf Jacobsen, *et al.*, *Drei Jahrzehnte Aussenpolitik der DDR* (Munish: R. Oldenberg Verlag, 1979), Part V, pp. 641–738.
4. For example Hungary has developed interparty relations with a number of Marxist-Leninist parties in Africa and has promised military assistance to Mozambique. See Bereznai, "Hungary in Black Africa." Czechoslovakia has been providing military support to both Ethiopia and Angola. See Pick, "Czechoslovakia in Black Africa."

5. "Socialist Community Plans for the Future," *New Times*, 35 (1979): 1.

6. For example, Joachim Oesterheld, Ursula Padel, and Renate Wünsche, "DDR-Indien: Eine neue Etappe freundschaftlicher Beziehungen," *Deutsche Aussenpolitik*, 24 (3) (1979): 5-11.

7. At a recent conference of Africanists from the European communist states it was argued that economic relations of the Soviet Union and its European allies with Africa were developing erratically because of a lack of common principles, strategies and programs. See Bereznai, Hungary in Black Africa," p. 19.

8. For a recent analysis of Romanian foreign policy see Aurel Braun, *Romanian Foreign Policy Since 1965: The Political and Military Limits of Autonomy* (New York: Praeger Publishers, 1978). For a perceptive treatment of Yugoslav relations with the developing world and the importance of those relations for overall Yugoslav foreign policy, see Alvin Z. Rubinstein, *Yugoslavia and the Nonaligned World* (Princeton: Princeton University Press, 1970).

9. See, for example, Jacobsen, *et al.*, *Drei Jahrzehnte Aussenpolitik der DDR*, Part V.

10. In a study of East European voting at the United Nations Robert Weiner notes slight variations in voting on several issues related to the developing world. However, overall only Romania's position has deviated significantly from that of the Soviet Union or that of the other East European states as a group. Robert Weiner, "East Europe at the United Nations," in Ronald H. Linden, *Foreign Policies of East Europe: New Approaches* (New York: Praeger Publishers, forthcoming).

11. *RFER*, Romanian Situation Report, (36), 23 December 1977 and *Ibid.*, (7), 9 April 1979.

12. Bereznai, "Hungary in Black Africa," p. 20 and Gafton, "Romania in Black Africa," p. 11.

13. Arnold Kramer, *The Forgotten Friendship: Israel and the Soviet Bloc, 1947-1953* Urbana: University of Illinois Press, 1974), pp. 54ff.

14. For a recent discussion of the background of the Soviet-Czechoslovak arms shipment see Mohamed Heikal, *The Sphinx and the Commissar: The Rise and Fall of Soviet Influence in the Middle East* (New York: Harper and Row, 1979), pp. 57-60.

15. Elizabeth Pond, "E. Germany's Quiet African Role," *The Christian Science Monitor*, February 22, 1979, p. 6. In an earlier article Pond noted that East German military and security training was occurring in Guinea-Bissau, São Tomé, Angola, Mozambique, Ethiopia, and South Yemen, "East Germany's 'Afrika Korps'," *Ibid.*, June 26, 1979, p. 14. According to CIA estimates, only 1,300 East European military technicians were in developing countries in 1978, while 10,800 Soviets

were working abroad. See Central Intelligence Agency, National Foreign Assessment Center, *Communist Aid Activities in Non-Communist Less-Developed Countries 1978: A Research Paper*, ER 79-10412U, September 1979, pp. 3-4.

16. The data on Soviet and East European aid covers the years 1973-1977, for both Soviet and East European commitments of economic assistance rose almost exponentially in 1978. The Soviets signed agreements for $3,707 million in new aid—of which $2,000 million is for the development of phosphates in Morocco and an additional $1,200 million for industrial expansion in Turkey. Eastern European commitments for 1978 rose to $1,502 million—with about forty percent promised to Syria, Brazil, Burma, Angola, Turkey and the Philippines. See *Communist Aid Activities 1978*, pp. 11-12.

17. See *RFER*, Czechoslovakia Situation Report, (7), 21 February 1979; *RFER*, Poland Situation Report, (4), 27 February 1979; and *RFER*, Romania Situation Report, (2), 9 February 1979.

18. For a discussion of the hard currency debt of the East European states see Joan P. Zoeter, "Eastern Europe: The Growing Hard Currency Debt," and Kathryn Melson and Edwin M. Snell, "Estimating East European Indebtedness to the West," in U.S. Congress, Joint Economic Committee, *East European Economies Post-Helsinki* (Washington: U.S. Government Printing Office, 1977), pp. 1350-1368 and 1369-1395, respectively.

19. *RFER*, Poland Situation Report, (4), 27 February 1979.

20. For a discussion of Soviet assistance policy see Roger E. Kanet, "Soviet Policy Toward the Developing World: The Role of Economic Assistance and Trade," ed. Robert Donaldson, *The Soviet Union in the Third World* (Boulder: Westview Press, forthcoming).

21. *Communist Aid Activities 1978*, p. 13.

22. Czechoslovak Television, March 7, 1979; cited in H. G. Trend, "COMECON Joint Investments in Third World as Payment for Raw Materials?" *RFER*, Eastern Europe, (55), 9 March 1979.

23. A recent example of the negative impact of political instability on East European economic interests is visible in Iran. Soon after the overthrow of the Shah the new government cancelled a contract with the Soviet Union—and several other East and West European countries—which called for the construction of a second gas pipeline from Iran to the USSR. The Soviets were to receive additional Iranian natural gas and, in turn, were to expand their exports of gas to both Eastern and Western Europe.

24. Peter Knirsch, "The CMEA Attitude to a New Economic Order," *Intereconomics*, 13 (1978): 106-107; and Heinrich Machowski,

"Development Aid from the CMEA Countries and the People's Republic of China," *Intereconomics*, 14 (1979): 209. In an interesting article the Polish economist Stanislaw Polaczek has admitted that, although the socialist states are not responsible for the economic backwardness of the developing world, this does not mean that they should not commit themselves to increased assistance. He also discusses at some length the reasons that the proposals of the socialist countries concerning a new world economic system have not always received a positive response in the developing world. See Stanslaw Polaczek, "Nowy Miedzynarodowy lad ekonomiczny a kraje RWPG," *Sprawy Miedzynarodowe*, (12) (1978): 68-69; Marian Paszyński, "Kraje socjalistyczne w wielostronnej debacie o światowych stosunkach ekonomicynych," *Sprawy Miedzynarodowe*, (5) (1979): 85-96. For an excellent discussion of Soviet views of a new world economic order *see* Elizabeth K. Valkenier, "The USSR, the Third World, and the Global Economy," *Problems of Communism*, 28 (4) (1979): 17-33.

PART TWO

POWER PROJECTION IN THIRD-WORLD SETTINGS

CHAPTER FOUR

THE SOVIET UNION AND THE WARS
IN INDOCHINA

Allan W. Cameron

The fall of Saigon in April 1975 marked a resounding victory for the Communist regime in Hanoi: after thirty years of unremitting struggle it found within its grasp the goals of unification of Vietnam, expulsion of the Western "imperialists" and their influence, and domination over all Indochina. While the long-term balance of forces within Vietnam clearly favored Hanoi, in the last analysis the victory was made possible by the combination of United States withdrawal from the conflict and support from the Soviet Union.

The Soviet Union emerged as the major outside victor in the struggle, an outcome perhaps more fortuitous than planned. The North Vietnamese victory represented Moscow's first significant triumph in a proxy war, after defeats in Greece, Korea, and the Middle East, not to mention numerous other rebellions and insurgencies of lesser purport. Success in Vietnam was a major factor encouraging Soviet leaders to undertake similar ventures elsewhere, notably in Africa. Moreover, the failure of the United States to oppose the direct challenge presented by the 1975 Spring Offensive contributed to a Soviet evaluation of the "correlation of forces" which, discerning a weakening of the American position throughout the world, led, via Angola and the Horn of Africa, to the Afghanistan adventure of December 1979.

The course of the Indochina crisis for the first twenty years after World War II gave little indication that Soviet policy would be so successful. Indeed, for most of the period Moscow found its involvement in Vietnam to be difficult, frustrating, sometimes dangerous, and only occasionally rewarding. This analysis summarizes the course of that involvement, with concentration upon two crucial periods: the 1954 Geneva Conference, which ended the so-called "First Indochina War," and the years between 1963 and 1968, during which a major Soviet commitment to Hanoi's struggle was stimulated by the denouement of the Sino–Soviet Dispute and by massive American military intervention. In this complex picture, the relations of Moscow and Hanoi with the Chinese Communist regime figure almost as much as do their own bilateral interactions.

Throughout the thirty-year crisis, American policy was based in part upon a misconception, less of the nature of the struggle— a concerted effort to establish Vietnamese Communist rule over Vietnam and Indochina—than of the identity and character of the adversary. The Viet Minh movement, later the North Vietnamese regime, was never a controlled puppet of either of its major external allies, and neither China nor the Soviet Union had as much influence over Hanoi's policies as American decision-makers generally thought. Although many believed that China was the major adversary, it now appears that in fact Sino-Vietnamese relations were characterized more by tension than by cooperation for most of the period.

The Soviet objective was consistently the advancement of Moscow's own direct interests, first in Europe and then, as relations with Peking reached crisis, in Asia and in the world Communist movement. At no point did the leaders, from Stalin to Brezhnev, display more than nominal enthusiasm for the establishment of a Communist regime in Vietnam as a goal in its own right. Nor did Moscow place more than collateral emphasis upon the possibility of North Vietnam's victory in its struggle with the United States; an indeterminate conflict served the greater interests of weakening Washington's strength elsewhere and providing opportunity to win Hanoi away from the Chinese side in the Sino–Soviet Dispute. Moreover, the Soviet Union showed a consistent willingness to sacrifice the interests of its ostensible Vietnamese friends and allies to the pursuit of its own agenda, a phenomenon displayed most clearly in 1954 but also evident ten years later. Considerations of Communist internationalism and world revolution signified less than did the safeguarding of Soviet-Russian-interests; from this perspective Vietnam and Southeast Asia were consistently areas of, at best, secondary concern.

THE FIRST INDOCHINA WAR

The Soviet Union displayed little interest in Vietnam during most of the "First Indochina War" from 1945 to 1954. This situation changed, after the death of Josef Stalin in 1953, with the emergence of the fighting in Indochina as an issue of critical importance to the Western powers. Displaying considerable reluctance at every step, Moscow was forced during the fall and winter of 1953-1954 to give increased attention to the role of the struggle in the overall pattern of East-West relations, in large measure because the French attached so much importance to it. Even at the Berlin Conference in January and February 1954, a pivotal event because of the decision taken there to convene the 1954 Geneva Conference on Korea and Indochina, the Soviet Union agreed only grudgingly to consideration of the Indochina issue. Even at this stage Moscow's approach was influenced significantly by its relations with the Chinese Communist regime.

Until at least 1950, Soviet policy toward Vietnam and Indochina was largely derivative of concerns in Western Europe. The Indochinese Communist Party, later the Vietnam Workers' Party (VWP) and, after 1976, the Vietnam Communist Party, was formed and incorporated into the Communist International (Comintern) in the early 1930s through the efforts of Ho Chi Minh, then a responsible Comintern functionary in Asia. By the mid-1930s, however, the indigenous sections of the Party appeared to have become tied firmly to the French Communist Party (FCP), a relationship Moscow may have expected to continue after World War II.[1] Moscow's reaction to the Vietnamese "August Revolution" in 1945 was restrained, characterized by sparse and often inaccurate information; this situation continued for the first few years of fighting between the Viet Minh and the French. Soviet policy began to change toward active support of the Viet Minh after Andrei Zhdanov, in his speech inaugurating the Communist Information Bureau (Cominform) in September 1947, cited the Indochina War as an example of "a powerful movement for national liberation in the colonies and depend-encies," and indicated that Vietnam was "associated" with the anti-imperialist (Soviet) camp.[2] The crucial event, however, was the victory of the Chinese Communists in 1949, which pro-vided the Viet Minh with a supply source and rear area; it stimu-lated Soviet interest in Asian revolutionary movements, although Peking was to play a more obvious leading role in their support. In early 1950, Peking and Moscow granted diplomatic recog-nition to the Democratic Republic of Vietnam (DRV), thereby indicating their approval of the struggle and committing them-selves to its success. With the outbreak of the Korean War in June of that year, both the Communist and the Western powers came to view Indochina and Korea as complementary parts of the same Far Eastern problem. Moscow, for example, characterized the American role in Indochina as part of a "three-pronged in-vasion" of China, the other two being directed through Formosa and Korea,[3] while the United States responded with accelerated military assistance and political support to what it now, with French prompting, had come to perceive as a coordinated Com-munist campaign in Asia.

Soviet support for the Viet Minh struggle against the French had its roots in a revived desire to weaken the "imperialist" position, most immediately that of France, both in Europe and in the colonial world. France, the major continental anchor of NATO, was also its weakest link. Her position was crucial for the proposed European Defense Community (EDC), designed as the means to obtain a German contribution to European defense; the EDC treaties, signed in early 1952, had immediately become a primary target for Soviet propaganda and a source of consider-able controversy in Paris. For the Soviet Union these develop-ments, and the situation in Western Europe as a whole, were far more significant than Southeast Asia; the Indochina War was important primarily because it weakened France in Europe. The struggle in the French colony posed no direct threat to Moscow, but it bled France, forcing her to concentrate both attention and resources on an area that was, in global terms, peripheral. The war caused disruption and dissatisfaction in France, thus enhancing the position of the French Communist Party; it helped to keep the Socialists in opposition, and the support of the Socialists was essential if EDC were to be approved. Indochina also caused strains between France and her allies, particularly over the question of the amount of independence Paris should give to the non-Communist "Associated States of Indochina:" Vietnam, Laos, and Cambodia.

Together with the advent of the Eisenhower administration in the United States, the passing of Josef Stalin on March 5, 1953, marked the end of the post-World-War-II period during which the two major victors had contested the form and nature of the new world order. The new American leaders adopted a position marked by sharply belligerent rhetoric on both Korea and Indochina as well as on relations with the Soviet Union generally, in which Secretary of State John Foster Dulles' concept of "rollback" of Soviet influence and attention to the issue of "captive peoples" attracted the most attention. The "unleashing" of Chiang Kai-shek by withdrawal of the Seventh Fleet from the Formosa Strait, the characterization of the Korean and Indochinese Wars as interdependent parts of the same struggle in Asia, active support for EDC, and the threat to use nuclear weapons in Korea (made to Prime Minister Nehru of India by Dulles in May),[4] all reflected a policy marked by strong words but, it must be said, by cautious actions.

In this situation, the accession to power of a fractious and contending group of Soviet leaders produced virtually instantaneous crises in Soviet foreign policies on all fronts, although the extent of the difficulties was poorly recognized in the West. There are indications that Stalin's successors feared Western attempts, should Washington's actions match its rhetoric, to take advantage of the succession crisis, particularly by moving to change the situation in Central Europe. It can, indeed, be argued that in order to forestall any such move Moscow in essence offered to renegotiate European spheres of influence as defined by the 1945 Yalta and Potsdam Agreements. But President Eisenhower, rather than matching post-Stalin actions to the earlier rhetoric, adopted a conciliatory position in his speech of April 16, 1953, "A Chance for Peace," and Prime Minister

Churchill did the same when he, in the House of Commons on May 11, proposed negotiations with the Soviet Union "at the summit." When the Western powers failed to exploit the Berlin uprisings in June, the Soviet leaders apparently concluded that the crisis was past and that they could safely maintain positions which, despite the generally softer rhetoric in which they were presented, were essentially those of Stalin.[5] Out of Soviet pronouncements during the first post-Stalin weeks there now developed an accelerated "peace campaign" which emphasized "relaxation of international tensions" and the possibility of negotiations over specific issues and for which the major focuses were EDC and the internal situation in France.

This "peace campaign" was given credibility in the West by developments in the East, notably in Korea. There the Chinese at the end of March proposed resumption of the Panmunjom talks and suggested a compromise on the thorny problem of repatriation of prisoners of war over which the negotiations had broken down the preceding October. This initiative occurred in the midst of a crucial, and generally overlooked, episode of Sino–Soviet tension.

It appears that the Chinese had for some months been arguing for an end to the Korean War and for reorientation of Soviet aid (actually not provided *gratis* but through reimbursable credits) from military to economic purposes; in the face of Stalin's refusal to agree on either issue, Sino–Soviet relations had deteriorated badly. The transfer of power in Moscow appears to have produced additional disagreements with Peking, at least in part over the status to be accorded to Mao Tse-tung, Stalin's successors being unwilling to treat the Chinese leader as the world's senior Communist; Chou En-lai, not Mao, represented the Peking regime at Stalin's funeral. The tension was alleviated but not resolved by the conclusion of economic aid agreements at the end of March and by Soviet endorsement of the Chinese initiative in Korea.

While the move in Korea seems to have been primarily Chinese in origin, the Soviet Union immediately took credit for it, citing it as a concrete example of *Moscow's* willingness to contribute to a "relaxation of international tensions;" Western analysts at the time and later accepted this claim of a primary Soviet role. Consequently, the Western hope for talks with the new Soviet leaders on major issues, notably in Europe, was apparently reciprocated, with Korea attesting to Moscow's *bona fides*. From this flowed an extensive diplomatic exchange during the summer and fall, with both sides accepting the principle of talks at the foreign ministers' level but differing on the agenda. The three Western powers wanted four-power talks limited to specific European issues, but the Soviet Union demanded a five-power conference (including China) to consider the vague and catch-all "relaxation of international tensions." After the collapse of the Sino–American talks designed to prepare the political conference provided for in the armistice agreement, Moscow attempted to use the Western desire for discussion of Korea as an incentive for that five-power conference. When the Western powers rejected this proposal and refused to continue the diplomatic debate, the Soviet Union at the end of November abandoned its major position and agreed to the Berlin Conference of the four Foreign Ministers to be held in January 1954; the agenda consisted of Germany, Austria, disarmament, and "measures for the reduction of international tension," understood to include Korea.[6]

In this context, the worsening military situation in Indochina was of growing concern to the Western powers. Responding to increased and more effective Viet Minh actions supported and supplied by the Chinese, the United States was willing to grant substantially expanded assistance to the French, provided Paris would design and implement military plans acceptable to Washington; during 1953 these were incorporated in the so-called "Navarre Plan." French leaders were, however, increasingly driven by domestic political considerations toward finding some formula for multilateral discussion of Indochina as an analogue of the Korean talks. The French refused to talk bilaterally with the Viet Minh, a course commended by the Soviet press shortly after the conclusion of the Korean armistice; Paris sought an international gathering that would include at least China, identified as the major enemy, and perhaps the Soviet Union as well. The French Foreign Minister, Georges Bidault, hoped that such a meeting might produce a diminution of external support for the Viet Minh, but more pragmatically he recognized that such a satisfactory result was unlikely. Nonetheless, and of crucial importance, he and Laniel believed that the holding of a conference, even if unsuccessful, would demonstrate the French government's desire for a cessation of the fighting and would therefore mute the spreading internal opposition now shared by important segments of the center as well as the leftist parties. But the United States objected, urging the French to improve their military position through implementation of the Navarre Plan before risking multilateral conversations.

In advance of the Berlin Conference, neither the Soviet Union nor China demonstrated any clear interest in *multilateral* discussion of Indochina. Rather, the Soviet Union ever more actively, and the Chinese somewhat hesitatingly, advocated *bilateral* conversations between the French and the Viet Minh, a course for which neither prospective party had displayed enthusiasm. The Viet Minh finally stated a public position only in response to, and in support of, the Soviet "peace campaign;" as revealed first at the November 23, 1953, session of the World Peace Council meeting and then reiterated by Ho Chi Minh in his famous "interview" with the Swedish newspaper *Expressen* on November 29, it called for bilateral talks with Paris but on terms that amounted to French capitulation. Even so, the offer was perceived in many quarters as indicating Viet Minh willingness to negotiate an end to the fighting, and it thus had a tremendous impact in France where it increased the already considerable pressures on the government to find some means to end the war.

There was, however, little indication from the Western powers that Indochina would be an issue at Berlin, all the more so since, at the Bermuda Conference in December 1953, the Americans thought they had successfully disuaded the French from pursuing the matter. Yet, at Berlin, Bidault, frequently prodded from Paris, made a particular issue of the desirability of including Indochina on the agenda of any meeting that might consider Korea or Asian matters more generally. Foreign Minister Molotov of the Soviet Union did not raise this issue and showed little enthusiasm for discussion of it;[7] rather, he urged bilateral talks between France and the Viet Minh, even offering to act as an intermediary to arrange them.[8] Molotov devoted his formal efforts to the convening of a "five-power" conference to include China, using Korea as the issue to which the West would respond but holding out for consideration in that forum of the general "relaxation of international tensions;" he showed little receptivity to Bidault's argument that Indochina should also be a specific agenda item, which the French Foreign Minister reinforced by emphasizing the parallelism of Indochina and Korea and the need for the Great Powers to consider the only war then in process.

In this situation, Indochina was the subject of two sets of parallel and interactive negotiations. One was between the Western Foreign Ministers and Molotov and concentrated on the agenda of a conference to deal with Korea and, possibly, other Asian matters. The other was among the three Western ministers themselves, with Bidault assiduously attempting to obtain support for urging Indochina negotiations upon the Russian; in this he was supported by Anthony Eden, the British Foreign Secretary, but opposed by Dulles. The American opposition collapsed in the face of the conclusion that refusal to accommodate the French desire would not only have deleterious effects on the conduct of the war but might well cause the fall of the Laniel government, thereby also fatally damaging the prospects for French approval of EDC.[9] It was, therefore, Dulles, presenting the coordinated Western position on February 8, who proposed that a multilateral conference be held to consider Korea and, "after the Chinese Communist regime had shown a greater will for peace than in the past," perhaps Indochina as well.[10]

Molotov was cool to this suggestion, and much of the subsequent difficult negotiations were devoted to bringing him to accept multilateral consideration of the Indochina question as desirable in its own right rather than as just one of several Asian issues that might be considered at a five-power conference. In his counter proposal of February 11, the Soviet minister failed to mention Indochina at all,[11] although when Bidault challenged him he replied that "if it was important to mention Indochina, he thought it could be arranged." Bidault then inserted Indochina in a draft tabled later that day,[12] but Molotov, in a February 12 proposal for a general five-power conference, mentioned Indochina only in parentheses.[13] To this Bidault responded sharply that "to put Indochina in brackets was not appropriate for the one place in the world where war was still going on."[14]

Molotov's conduct casts doubt upon the assumption that the driving force in Soviet efforts at Berlin was to trade acquiescence to a multilateral conference on Indochina for Western agreement to include China and for French opposition to EDC.[15] While there is no question that a primary goal was to hinder if not prevent implementation of EDC, there is scant evidence of an attempt to do that at Berlin through a direct linkage of the Indochina and European issues. Rather, Molotov seemed to ignore the opportunity provided by Bidault's increasingly importunate efforts, showing a consistent reluctance to accommodate the French desire while advocating, outside the formal sessions of the Conference, bilateral Franco-Viet Minh efforts to find a solution. This Soviet position, although known to be unattractive to the French government, was compatible with that of the Viet Minh, who had been remarkably cool to the prospect of negotiations in any form unless they were a facade for French capitulation, and the Chinese, who had shown but limited enthusiasm for any negotiations at all.

The result, incorporated in the final communiqué issued by the Foreign Ministers on February 18,[16] was a compromise by which the Western powers agreed to what was in essence a "Big Five" conference, despite the disclaimers, while the Soviet Union accepted the Western agenda by agreeing to a large conference "for the purpose of reaching a peaceful settlement of the Korean question" and at which "the problem of restoring peace in Indo-China will also be discussed."[17]

One can only surmise about the reasons for the Soviet attitude on Indochina. One fundamental factor appears to have been that Sino–Soviet relations were less close than most analysts have believed; the "alliance" was apparently more an uneasy truce, begun with the events following the death of Stalin and lasting no longer than Khrushchev's "secret speech" in 1956 and the Moscow Conference of the ruling Communist parties later that year.[18] Throughout the restricted sessions at Berlin, Molotov repeatedly stated that he could not speak for the Chinese and that the Ministers must be sure that any proposal that envisaged Peking's participation would be acceptable to it;[19] although the Western Ministers tended to discount these protestations as mere posturing, there may have been more than a little substance to them.

Another factor was that Moscow had shown little interest in the Indochina War *per se*; rather, it appeared in Soviet statements primarily as a factor affecting French policies in Europe, and Soviet positions seem to have been motivated more by development of internal French opposition to the war than by concern for Indochina itself. This situation may have begun to change in the wake of the Korean armistice, as China began to increase substantially its support for the Viet Minh and the United States did the same for the French, but even in early 1954 Moscow clearly did not consider the Indochina war to be a dominant international problem. Molotov may even have been surprised by Bidault's insistence on an international conference on Indochina and by his ability to obtain the support of his colleagues for it.

The evolving situation presented two problems for Moscow. Should the Viet Minh, with Chinese support, win a major victory, China would reap the benefit; there is some reason to suppose this prospect may not have been entirely appealing to Moscow.[20] On the other hand, should the situation in Indochina stimulate a stronger American response, including perhaps intervention in Indochina and action against China itself,[21] the Soviet Union might become involved either because of its own commitments to the defense of China[22] or because of the outbreak of what Washington called "general war."[23]

While Moscow was increasingly concerned about the prospect of continued and expanded fighting, steps to avoid it could also be costly. Support for and participation in a multilateral conference could imply a Soviet commitment to see that a solution resulted, which would place Moscow in the position of having to impose conditions upon at least the Viet Minh if not the Chinese. Moreover, a solution reached in an international conference in which China was a participant could well redound primarily to the advantage of the Chinese, a prospect about which Moscow may well have been less than enthusiastic. Thus, at Berlin and during the subsequent weeks, Moscow stressed the advantages of a bilateral solution while downplaying the significance of Indochina talks at Geneva. The Chinese reaction to the forthcoming conference was initially somewhat hesitant, with Peking praising it in principle and for its Korean component, but treading delicately on the question of consideration of Indochina.

A major consequence of the Berlin decision, much though the prospective Geneva meeting may have been qualified and circumscribed in concept and in language, was to elevate the Indochina problem to a status directly concerning the "Great Powers" as a group, implying their right and responsibility, should they be able to agree, to specify and impose an appropriate settlement. In such a settlement, the rights and desires of the Indochinese states (the

DRV and the French-sponsored Associated States) would be sacrificed to whatever transcendental interests the Great Powers might define.

THE GENEVA CONFERENCE

The importance of the Geneva Conference was decisively increased during the spring as the Viet Minh attack on Dien Bien Phu developed into the crucial battle of the war and the threat of American military intervention made the problem the dominant one on the international scene. The effect in France was to transform expectations for Geneva from the possibility of progress toward an end to the war to the imperative to seek a solution under almost any terms short of outright capitulation; for Paris, the much desired conference had changed from a tactic to a combination of trap and salvation. For the Soviet Union the effect was the modification of an equivocal policy, in which attitudes toward Indochina were overwhelmingly conditioned by Moscow's interests in Western Europe, to one which accorded at least equal priority to a cessation of the war itself. Moscow appears to have been moved in that direction less by the successes of the Viet Minh[24] than by the prospect of an expanded conflict with direct American involvement.

As a result, Soviet policy came into a brief but decisive harmony with that of the British, whose Foreign Secretary, Anthony Eden, had reached the conclusion that the danger of escalation made a solution of the war essential and that only some form of partition could serve as an acceptable compromise. At Geneva, this proposition encountered obstacles from both East and West. The United States opposed any compromise, particularly one that would place "free" territory under Communist control, yet was ultimately driven to reluctant acquiescence by four factors. First was Washington's unwillingness, when it came to that, to intervene unilaterally. Second was the refusal of the British to participate in or acquiesce to a multilateral intervention generally on the Korean model. Third was the persistent unwillingness of the French to accept American participation in the war on terms which were, in essence, the renunciation of all colonial privilege. Fourth, and perhaps most important, was the prospect that categorical American opposition to a compromise solution would not only result in the fall of yet another French government, but would also fatally damage collective defense in Western Europe and perhaps even propel France toward an accommodation with the Soviet Union. Yet it was the perceived threat of American military involvement in Indochina that served as the motivating force for the progress of the negotiations as a whole and for the reluctant willingness of the Asian Communists to accept a compromise.[25]

On the other side, it was by no means clear that China came to Geneva favoring a compromise settlement; indeed, Peking's position during the first weeks of the Conference was certainly less than forthcoming, and was frequently in strident support of extreme Viet Minh positions. These derived from reluctance to accept any settlement in Indochina other than one that was effectively French capitulation, a stance that was understandable in view of the overall military situation and particularly the dramatic victory at Dien Bien Phu. Yet the Viet Minh were dependent on external military assistance, particularly from China,[26] and therefore were, like the non-Communist regimes in the Associated States, vulnerable to pressure from their supporters. For its part, the Soviet Union was a leading proponent of the need to end the fighting, but Molotov continued reluctant to have the "Great Powers" themselves define and impose a settlement.

During the first month of the Conference, those Communist attitudes were manifest in the discussion of two major issues. The first was the persistent Soviet effort to maximize the prospects of a bilateral solution through urging direct talks between the high commands of the two sides, French and Viet Minh, within a general framework of good offices to be provided by the Conference as a whole. Molotov seemed to believe that the Conference as a body could be concerned with matters such as supervision and control of an agreement, but that the specific modalities of an end to the fighting should be determined by the two parties. After much discussion, the Conference agreed at the end of May that the two high commands should undertake direct discussions in Geneva as well as in Indochina, and the French and Viet Minh conference delegations in June began contact on political as well as military matters through the so-called "underground military talks."

The second issue was that of the approach to the problems in

Cambodia and Laos. The Viet Minh, supported actively by the Chinese and somewhat less so by the Russians, insisted that all three Indochinese states be treated in the same fashion: if there were to be an end to fighting in Vietnam through a cease-fire and establishment of "regrouping zones" (that is, some form of partition), then there should be comparable arrangements in Cambodia and Laos, with the Viet Minh controlled "resistance governments" standing as the parties opposed to the French and, as such, participating in the Conference. The French and their allies argued that the situations in Cambodia and Laos were not analogous to that in Vietnam but were clearcut instances of invasion, and that the situation in both states could be returned to normal by nothing more than withdrawal of the Viet Minh forces. Although Molotov and Eden agreed on May 29 that the "resistance governments" need not be represented at the Conference, the impasse was not broken until June 16, after the fall of the Laniel government and the designation of Pierre Mendès-France as Premier, when Chou En-lai indicated in conversation with Eden that China would relax her support for the Viet Minh position.

By the end of May, the Viet Minh had accepted the principle of partition by endorsing two regrouping zones in Vietnam, but they insisted on control north of the thirteenth parallel (about halfway between Qui Nhon and Nhatrang) and on provisions for a "political" settlement (elections) that would virtually guarantee extension of that control over the French zone after a relatively short time. While the Soviet Union and China seem to have no problem with this in principle, it was clear that any such settlement would be unacceptable to the West. It was also clear that the "political" provisions had to be defined so as to avoid the implication that France had accepted defeat; the difficulty lay in finding a formula that would mask the fact that each side had to settle for something less than an optimum settlement, that would appear advantageous to both, and that would provide room for future maneuver. Even so, the Communist powers would have to exert considerable pressure to obtain Viet Minh acquiescence to anything to which Paris could agree and which its allies could accept.

The burden of obtaining the necessary Viet Minh concessions fell primarily to the Chinese. The key event was a meeting between Chou En-lai and Ho Chi Minh on the Vietnam-China border on July 5, 1954,[27] that may have dealt with specifics but probably concentrated more on convincing the Viet Minh leaders that they would have to acquiesce to and abide by the eventual agreement. The Vietnamese recently charged that it was Chinese pressure, particularly in early July, that brought them to accept a settlement on conditions less advantageous than they believed they deserved;[28] this pressure included the threat of terminating military aid.

Given the political situation in 1979, it is not surprising that the Vietnamese should blame the Chinese for all the ills of the Geneva Conference, or that they should avoid mentioning the role of the Soviet Union in making agreement possible. Yet it seems clear that the Soviet desire for a settlement was a crucial factor, even if Molotov himself did not directly undertake to coerce the Vietnamese. It is likely that the Soviet Union applied pressure to the Chinese, whose close relationship with the Viet Minh was obvious, perhaps on the question of whether and how much Moscow would support Peking in the event of American action in Indochina or against China herself; such pressure could have included threats to terminate further Soviet military and economic support.

In any case, Western sources make clear that it was Molotov's cooperative attitude that was instrumental in enabling the Conference to patch together an agreement—or, rather, a set of agreements of varying degrees of formality—to end the fighting. It was Molotov who suggested the compromise on the demarcation line (at the seventeenth parallel) and the two-year delay before the holding of elections (the Viet Minh wanted six months).[29] Molotov also hinted from time to time of his difficulties with his allies at Geneva. Still, Chou En-lai's forthcoming attitude during the later stages of the Conference won him grudging respect from the Western delegations, including the American, and the Geneva Conference saw the first tentative Sino-American contacts that led to the institutionalized conversations in Warsaw.[30]

The agreements concluded on July 20 and 21, while they did make possible an end to the Indochina fighting, were in fact far more equivocal than many later chose to interpret them. The French and the Viet Minh signed cease-fire agreements for Vietnam and Laos, the former of which provided for the provisional division that created North and South Vietnam, and the latter of which left two Laotian provinces under Pathet Lao control. The Cambodian high command signed its own agreement with the Viet Minh, under which all Vietnamese forces withdrew. The controversial Final Declaration of the Conference, signed by none of the participants and only equivocally supported by the United States, appears to have been primarily cosmetic. The fundamental goal was to end the fighting, partition was the means to do it, and the rest was window-dressing to enable the two sides to accept a situation each found less than wholly satisfactory.

For the Soviet Union, Geneva was a significant success. Moscow contributed to the end of the fighting in a way which allowed Molotov to appear as the peace maker and which resulted in the establishment of a Communist state in North Vietnam. There was some indication that Moscow now viewed Vietnam in much the same way as Korea: a divided country whose division served Soviet interests by temporarily eliminating open conflict while providing opportunity for further "revolutionary" progress in the future.

Chou En-lai's conduct, even if Chinese policy was constrained by Soviet pressure, contributed to a positive view of the Peking regime and of Chou himself and thus reinforced the overall peaceful image that China and the Soviet Union were now going to great lengths to project. It was, in fact, the Geneva period that saw the Chinese move into an active conciliatory policy, highlighted at the time by Chou En-lai's visit to India at the beginning of July and by his well-known agreement with Nehru on the "five principles of peaceful coexistence,"[31] a policy which reached its apex at the Bandung Conference in 1955.

If these Asian developments were successes for Molotov's policy, there were even more significant gains in Europe. There the main goals appear to have been to prevent the implementation of EDC and to create and exploit rifts among the Western allies. Developments immediately prior to and at the conference exacerbated the differences between the United States and Britain as well as between the United States and France. In Paris, the replacement of the Laniel government by that of Pierre Mendès-France in mid-June worked to the benefit of Soviet interests, for Mendès-France was known to be an opponent of EDC as well as of the Indochina war; the EDC treaty was effectively killed by the French National Assembly in August without the Premier making much obvious effort to save it. There is, however, no evidence to support the supposition that Molotov agreed to an end to the fighting in Indochina in return for a commitment from Mendès-France to oppose EDC; indeed, on at least one occasion in private conversation when Molotov raised European questions, Mendès-France refused to discuss them. Nonetheless, it is safe to assume that Molotov believed that the more he cultivated the French the less likely they were to accept EDC and the limitations on French sovereignty and status it entailed.

For these substantial gains the Soviet Union paid a small price. It was necessary to sacrifice many of the interests of the Viet Minh, who were constrained to accept compromise on nearly every issue from the location of the partition line to the delay in holding elections in Vietnam to the status of the revolutionary movements in Cambodia and Laos. There were numerous indications, then and later, that the Viet Minh were unhappy with the outcome.

Yet, for Ho Chi Minh and his colleagues, there was no viable alternative. Although not controlled by China and the Soviet Union, the Viet Minh depended on them for material and political support; nor were the Vietnamese Communists immune to the stated need to subordinate local interests in Vietnam to common objectives such as those of bringing peace to Asia and avoiding American intervention. Failure at Geneva might have led to an increased French effort with far greater American military support; since neither China nor the Soviet Union seemed willing to enter into a confrontation with the United States, Viet Minh military prospects would have been difficult. On the other hand, there were benefits to be obtained from accepting a cease-fire and temporary division of the country. Economic assistance was one, and the Soviet gift of a billion rubles to North Korea after the Korean armistice was a hopeful precedent.[32] More important, the Viet Minh obtained what was for them the most important part of Vietnam—the Tonkin delta, with Hanoi and Haiphong—and a recognition of their right to establish state power there.

Furthermore, the Geneva Agreements contained provisions which, if enforced by the Great Powers who theoretically subscribed to them, held out the probability of turning the half loaf into a whole one. Few challenge the contention that in the situation prevailing in July 1954 the Viet Minh could win any election

in Vietnam, and their control in the north allowed the establishment of a solid base should other actions become necessary. It
must have been difficult for them, as for others, to avoid the conclusion that no regime in the French zone would be viable, given
the depth of anti-French sentiment among the population, the
popularity of the Viet Minh nationalist appeal, and the political
and economic chaos in the State of Vietnam.

Moscow's policy toward Indochina during the First Indochina
War and at Geneva demonstrated that Soviet leaders were not
concerned primarily with the welfare of the Viet Minh or for their
success. Support for colonial revolution and the establishment of
a new Communist state, were less important than furthering
Russian interests. It should be stressed, however, that this self-
serving approach was not characteristic of just the Soviet Union;
Soviet policy at Geneva was successful because, on the matter of
ending the fighting in Indochina, Moscow's interests were similar
enough to those of Britain and France, and perhaps even of China,
to produce a concert that could elaborate and impose an acceptable if not appealing compromise.

BETWEEN THE WARS

During the years immediately following the Geneva Conference,
Soviet policy reflected satisfaction with the situation it had produced. Moscow extracted every iota of propaganda advantage
from its contribution to ending the Indochina fighting while showing little interest in the implementation of the political settlement.
Nor did Moscow demonstrate any great enthusiasm for the expansion of the "Socialist Camp" represented by the accession of the
Viet Minh to power in Hanoi. This situation would, however,
change as Soviet policy was increasingly conditioned by the
escalating disagreements and competition with China.

As the growing stability of the American-backed Diem regime
made unlikely a collapse in Saigon and the holding of the 1956
elections, Moscow showed little determination to provide active
support for the North Vietnamese case.[33] Even after the formal
inclusion of the Hanoi regime in the enumeration of the members
of the "Socialist Camp" at the beginning of 1955[34] the Soviet
Union's support for Vietnamese reunification was at best cool, as
indicated at the end of the year by failure to push the Chinese

suggestion that the Geneva Conference be reconvened. The merest hint of a change came in the October Revolution slogans, issued on October 25, in which Moscow for the first time endorsed the Vietnamese struggle "for the national unification of Vietnam on democratic foundations."[35]

Only in March 1956 did a senior Soviet official arrive in Hanoi, which had not been on the itinerary of Khrushchev and Bulganin during their much publicized tour of Burma, India, and Afghanistan the preceding fall. During his visit, Anastas Mikoyan emphasized in his public speeches the necessity for developing the economy of the peaceful north and avoiding war; his Vietnamese counterparts talked both of strengthening the north and of the necessity for friendly states to support the struggle for reunification and to insist upon the holding of elections. Mikoyan may bluntly have told the Vietnamese leaders that there would be no Soviet action to ensure fulfillment of the election provisions of the Geneva Agreements, that this was not an issue on which the Soviet Union intended to go to the mat with the Western powers, and that partition was a reality that must be accepted. Disagreement was signaled by the failure to issue the customary joint communiqué at the conclusion of the visit.[36]

The Mikoyan visit was nearly coincident with the series of diplomatic developments that confirmed the failure of the Geneva Agreements to produce a lasting resolution of the Indochina problem. The French decision in April to withdraw from Vietnam brought matters to an anticlimax as one of the two signatory parties of the cease-fire agreement in essence renounced all further responsibility. The reactions of all the powers were at best halfhearted; as they were disinclined either to enforce the election provision of the Final Declaration (which was of debatable legal standing in any case) or to take action to find a new formula for a political solution, the scheduled date for the Vietnamese elections was allowed to pass almost unnoticed. That Moscow viewed the existing situation as acceptable if not satisfactory was indicated, in January 1957, when the Soviet Union proposed that both Vietnams, as well as both Koreas, be admitted to the United Nations, a move that failed in the face of Western opposition to the admission of the two Communist states.[37]

Perhaps more important, the Mikoyan visit took place shortly after the 20th Congress of the Communist Party of the Soviet

Union (CPSU), held in February 1956, at which Khrushchev denounced Stalin in the famous "secret speech" and which saw the first formal manifestations of Sino–Soviet differences. As the Sino–Soviet Dispute developed into a matter involving not only Moscow and Peking but also the other Communist states and parties, North Vietnam and Ho Chi Minh began to acquire disproportionate importance. If success in the Dispute was dependent in part on the ability to marshal "votes" in the international Communist movement, then North Vietnam signified as much as any other Communist state, and perhaps more because of its historical avoidance of client status. If, for Moscow, the Asian Communism of Mao Tse-tung was the great threat to ideological rectitude and concrete progress, then it was important to muster support from other Asian parties. Here the Vietnamese occupied a special position because of Ho Chi Minh's impeccable credentials as an international Communist leader of considerable independent stature who might appear as a counterweight to Mao. Mikoyan's visit might therefore be explained as an effort to present the situation to Ho and to enlist his support on the side of the Kremlin's version of holy writ. If so, the results indicate that Hanoi was not willing to play that game.

Hanoi's position then, as later, was motivated by specific considerations of self-interest. The paramount goal was reunification of the country, an objective which, if it did not demand their active support, at least required that China and the Soviet Union not oppose it. But the thesis presented by Khrushchev at the 20th Party Congress, notably the need for peaceful coexistence, the possibility of avoiding wars between the Communist and Capitalist camps, and the possibility of "peaceful transition" to Socialism, could, to the Vietnamese, imply only that they should accept the current situation and endure the continued division of their country because that course was in the interest of the Communist movement as a whole as that interest was defined by the Soviet Union.

There is no indication that China was much more supportive, as its foreign policy was dominated by the "Spirit of Bandung" and the "five principles of peaceful coexistence." Indeed, the Vietnamese later alleged that China urged Hanoi to adopt the policy of "prolonged ambush," arguing that "the reunification of the country was a 'long struggle' and could not be achieved by using armed forces," that the Vietnamese should "defend the 17th parallel" and "lie low for a long time."[38]

If Hanoi was not to receive firm support and encouragement from either of the two Communist giants, there was little reason for commitment to either in their mutual ideological fratricide. On the contrary, there was much to be said for staying on the best possible terms with both and preventing the emerging differences from reaching such a serious level that a choice between them would be essential. From the beginning, therefore, the Vietnamese apparently attempted both to remain neutral and to mediate the Dispute.

Much of this activity was conducted personally by Ho Chi Minh, who was continually active in international affairs. In mid-1957 he toured Communist countries in both Asia and Europe, at least in part to obtain economic assistance. During this trip, he was in Moscow when Khrushchev expelled the "anti-party group" (Molotov, Malenkov, and Kaganovich) from the Soviet leadership, he was hailed during a visit to Yugoslavia, and in Peking Mao Tse-tung himself apparently urged Ho to show restraint with regard to the issue of reunification.[39] The Vietnamese leader was again in Moscow for the 40th anniversary of the Bolshevik Revolution in November 1957, when, like Mao Tse-tung, he participated in the meeting of the ruling Communist parties. The declaration that resulted was obviously a compromise between the Chinese and the Soviet positions, and Ho probably joined attempts to mediate between them. In January 1959 Ho attended the 21st Congress of the CPSU, at which Khrushchev asserted with even greater vigor the possibility of avoiding war between the Capitalist and Communist camps, and he was again in Moscow during July and August, prior to Khrushchev's visit to the United States. When the Soviet leader visited Peking later that year, on the occasion of the tenth anniversary of the Chinese Communist regime, Ho was also present.

During this period, Soviet policy showed indications of an effort to woo the Vietnamese. These included the publication of a Russian edition of Ho Chi Minh's selected works[40] and a significant expansion of Soviet-Vietnamese trade, which in 1959 more than doubled over that in 1958 and was to double again by 1962.[41] But the North Vietnamese continued to take a position of maximum impartiality, supporting both China and the Soviet

Union with words but with little action. It was, however, during this period that Hanoi apparently took the crucial decision to change its policy toward the south; in May, the Fifteenth Plenum of the Central Committee of the VWP for the first time called for armed struggle against the Saigon government,[42] and the new constitution, adopted in the fall, incorporated the goal of reunification as part of the fundamental law of the state. The Vietnamese now officially date "uprisings" in the south from late 1959.[43]

It seems probable that the sharp deterioration of Sino–Soviet relations removed one of the constraints on Hanoi's ability to conduct an independent policy and provided greater opportunities for maneuver; the North Vietnamese could now assume that in all probability one or the other of the Communist giants would support a more militant course if only to avoid abandoning the Hanoi regime to the other. This was not an unmixed blessing, for it also entailed increased pressure from both Peking and Moscow as the issues sharpened in 1960. According to Hanoi, the Chinese in May once again discouraged armed struggle to unify the country.[44] During the open Sino–Soviet disagreements at the Rumanian Party Congress in June, the Vietnamese delegation, headed by Le Duan, remained carefully neutral, but the VWP later issued a public statement stressing the need for unity. Later in the summer, Ho Chi Minh apparently made a secret visit to Moscow,[45] where he presumably discussed the Dispute, Soviet aid, and Hanoi's policy in South Vietnam.

The Third Congress of the Vietnam Workers' Party, the first since the end of the war against the French, was held in Hanoi in September. It was the occasion for mutual Sino–Soviet attacks so abrasive that the Vietnamese omitted speeches by foreign guests from their official English-language publications on the Congress. According to one authority, the Soviet delegate delivered a personal message to Ho from Khrushchev,[46] and the Congress was the occasion for an unusual private meeting between the Soviet and Chinese delegations.[47] From the internal point of view, the Congress was marked by adoption of a new five-year plan, for which new Soviet aid was a crucial ingredient, and by the decisions incorporated in the "Resolution of the Third National Congress of the Vietnam Workers' Party on the Tasks and Line of the Party in the New Stage." This important document noted the related goals of implementing "the socialist revolution in the north" and liberating "the south from the rule of the American imperialists and their henchmen, achieve national reunification and complete independence and freedom throughout the country."[48] This latter goal reflected a decision to expand efforts to overthrow Diem and led directly to the proclamation of the South Vietnam National Front for Liberation (NLF) on December 20.[49]

The meeting of the 81 Communist parties in Moscow at the beginning of December confirmed the depth of the Sino-Soviet Dispute and saw Ho Chi Minh again act as a mediator.[50] Among the major doctrinal differences considered was one of particular relevance to the situation in Vietnam. The Soviet Union argued that it was possible to avoid war, to achieve victory for Communist revolutionary forces through peaceful means, that "local wars" could too easily spread to global conflict, and that revolutionary gains should be attempted through other tactics. The Chinese, in contrast, contended that local wars waged by national liberation movements were both inevitable and desirable, and that they were unlikely to escalate into general conflict because of the overall strategic superiority of the Communist camp. If, as it appears, the North Vietnamese had embarked on a course of encouraging and supporting "national liberation" struggles in both Laos and South Vietnam, the Chinese position was, in principle, the more supportive; yet, according to the Vietnamese nearly twenty years later, the Chinese were at the time discouraging Hanoi from its efforts to expand the struggle in the south. In any case, the issue itself suggested that Vietnam might become a focal point for the competing arguments of the two Communist giants.

That competition was illustrated by developments in Laos in 1961 and 1962. There the Vietnamese-sponsored Pathet Lao forces were fighting the American-supported government in Vientiane, and the conflict was of particular concern to the Great Powers; indeed, outgoing President Eisenhower described Laos to his successor, John F. Kennedy, as a trouble spot of more immediate concern than Vietnam. By early 1961, the Soviet Union, then supplying the opponents of the Vientiane regime, was calling for an international conference, while China publicly urged continuation of the revolutionary struggle. After the King of Laos in February 1961 declared his country's neutrality, the argument mutated into one over whether a cease-fire should precede (the Soviet position) or follow (the Chinese position) the holding of an international conference. In due course, and as the result of a conference in Geneva, complicated and tenuous agreements were concluded to stabilize the situation, a result that appeared particularly advantageous to the Soviet Union because of the emphasis it placed on peaceful coexistence with the United States.

Although they had hegemonic ambitions, the Vietnamese interest in Laos at this time was more derivative of the developing struggle in South Vietnam. Hanoi's goal then and later was securing the supply route bypassing the demilitarized zone and ultimately known as the "Ho Chi Minh Trail." This produced further conflict with Peking, which urged caution in Laos lest the United States intervene with a consequent threat to both China and North Vietnam; the Chinese advocated a horizontal partition of Laos, with the Pathet Lao to control the north and the Vientiane administration the south. This the Vietnamese later denounced as "a wicked design aimed at securing Lao revolutionary forces' dependence on China and isolating the South Vietnamese revolution." [51]

The deteriorating economic situation in North Vietnam, in part a consequence of the devotion of effort and resources to the struggle in the south, reinforced Hanoi's need to remain on the best possible terms with both Moscow and Peking, the latter of which was the major external supplier of food throughout the war. Thus Ho Chi Minh preceded his presence at the 22nd CPSU Congress in October 1961 with a visit to Peking and a call upon Mao Tse-tung. At the Congress, Chou En-lai walked out in protest against Khrushchev's attacks on Albania; Ho Chi Minh did not mention Albania but did not walk out either, instead embarking on a tour of the Soviet Union. Shortly thereafter, on January 10, 1962, the Vietnamese made the first of a series of formal proposals "that a meeting be held between representatives of Communist and workers' parties to settle the discord together and that, pending such a meeting, the parties cease attacking one another in the press and over the radio." [52]

HANOI CAUGHT IN THE MIDDLE

As suggested by the formal North Vietnamese attempt to mediate, 1962 saw the beginning of the most difficult period of

Hanoi's relations with Moscow and Peking as both increased their pressure for the Vietnamese to select one side or the other. In its effort to maintain a neutral posture, Hanoi now discovered the disadvantages of its efforts to maintain a neutral position as it found itself, at the time of the overthrow of Ngo Dinh Diem in 1963, in imminent danger of irrevocably alienating at least the Soviet Union if not China as well. At this late date its almost desperate attempts to mend fences with Moscow were only marginally successful as Khrushchev in essence wrote off North Vietnam as a place where Soviet presence, influence, and assistance could have a productive effect.

In arguing that China and the Soviet Union should resolve their differences and fulfill their responsibility to consolidate the international Communist movement. Hanoi was also telling its two major allies that a continued struggle against imperialism was essential and, by implication, that they should support both Socialist construction in the DRV and the struggle in the south. Perhaps trapped by its own rhetoric, and certainly hoping to upstage the Soviet Union, China was now somewhat more forthcoming. When Ho Chi Minh and Nguyen Chi Thanh[53] visited Peking in the summer of 1962 to request military assistance for the south, "the Chinese government immediately provided 90,000 weapons for the people of South Vietnam."[54]

The contest for Hanoi's support was carried on by a series of Chinese, Soviet, and East European delegations to Hanoi in late 1962 and early 1963. As the pressure increased, the Politburo of the Vietnamese party brought matters into the open, on February 10, 1963, publicly calling on China and the USSR to resolve their differences.[55] This statement seemed to attribute the greater responsibility for healing the breach, and thus the greater responsibility for having caused it, to the Soviet leadership. Whether Khrushchev and his colleagues had already concluded that the North Vietnamese were beyond redemption is not clear, but Hanoi's statements now suggested a willingness to support the Chinese position as during the spring it joined Peking in blunt criticism of "Yugoslav revisionism."

The crucial event was a visit to Hanoi by Liu Shao-chi at the beginning of May, obviously to force the Vietnamese unequivocally to choose the Chinese side in the dispute. In public statements he strongly supported the armed struggle in South Vietnam, but Liu also told the Vietnamese that they could no longer remain neutral, that true Marxist–Leninists had to unite in smashing "modern revisionism," the Soviet leadership: "We cannot look on with folded arms or follow a middle course with regard to this important question of the struggle between conflicting principles."[56] As the Vietnamese later described the developments of the time, the Chinese attempted to obtain support for their "so-called 25-point program on the general line of the world communist movement," for their proposal "to convene a conference of eleven communist parties in an attempt to seize 'the leadership of world revolution' and to form a new communist international dominated by Beijing."[57]

> They were eager to get Vietnam's support to the idea, trying to use Vietnam's prestige and role in the world communist and national liberation movements. To this end, they even sought to buy over Vietnam by offering massive aid. Deng Ziaoping informed the Vietnamese leaders of the Chinese leaders' intention to give Vietnam one billion Chinese yuan in aid if Vietnam refused all aid from the Soviet Union.

Although the Vietnamese now claim that they rejected these proposals, Hanoi at the time appeared to move closer to the Chinese position, probably as a result both of Peking's pressure and of Moscow's disenchantment as well as of the inclinations of some factions in the leadership. During the summer, Hanoi attacked the Test Ban Treaty, which China had refused to sign, and produced fierce polemics against Yugoslavia and "modern revisionism," although stopping short of attacking Khrushchev by name. By all indications, the Soviet leader was thoroughly irritated both by Hanoi's position in the dispute and by its persistence in promoting armed struggle in Vietnam and in Laos, where it was generally known that Vietnamese forces had violated the 1962 agreement virtually from the outset. As a result, Soviet aid to Vietnam was substantially curtailed during the fall,[58] and there were other signs of broad estrangement between Moscow and Hanoi.

This situation produced a major crisis for the Hanoi regime, the curtailment of Moscow's aid leaving North Vietnam prospectively dependent on a China which, according to later Vietnamese reports, was providing considerably less than full encouragement and support for the struggle in the south, whose resources were limited, and whose long term intentions the Vietnamese suspected of being less than honorable. This crisis took place at perhaps the most inconvenient possible time for Hanoi, for the overthrow of Ngo Dinh Diem in November provided the most auspicious opportunity yet for triumph in the south, particularly when it was followed by the assassination of President Kennedy. In the ensuing confusion, the National Liberation Front did make significant gains, but there does not appear to have been the all-out effort to deliver the *coup de grâce* that could have been expected had the North Vietnamese leaders been able to devote their full attention to the struggle. Moreover, the situation may have highlighted reported factional differences within the Hanoi leadership over approaches to the war in the south as well as over the nature of relations with Moscow and Peking.

By the middle of December, Hanoi clearly had concluded that something had to be done lest all be lost. A cessation of anti-Soviet polemics was followed by a secret meeting of the VWP Central Committee that went on for some days. According to the communiqué published on January 20, 1964,[59] the session called for strengthening "the cohesion and unity of the socialist camp and the international communist movement," and managed to support the Chinese and the Soviet positions simultaneously while reinforcing the right of the Vietnamese to "creatively" apply Marxism–Leninism "to the specific conditions of our country." The Vietnamese return to approximate neutraliity was a remarkable feat of ideological legerdemain:

> Our party draws a clear political distinction between the Tito revisionist clique, lackey of imperialism, and people within the international communist movement [the Soviet leadership] who commit the error of revisionism or right-wing opportunism.

Through this formulation the Central Committee acquitted the Soviet leaders of the worst of the Chinese charges while at the same time acknowledging Peking's rectitude on the principle of the matter. The communiqé went on to state that "the VWP earnestly wishes that the Communist Party of the Soviet Union and the Communist Party of China continue talks to achieve solidarity and to create good conditions for the convening of the conference of representatives of communist and workers' parties," a reiteration of the mediation proposals of the past two years.

This virtuoso performance was followed, at the end of January, by a visit to Moscow of a party delegation headed by Le Duan. There it met not only with Khrushchev but also with a CPSU delegation headed by M. A. Suslov, the leading Soviet ideologue, thereby indicating that doctrinal questions were of great concern. In the communiqué issued on February 15, the two delegations pledged to "focus their attention on the common interests and goals that lead to the rapprochement of the two fraternal parties in their struggle against imperialism and to defend the cohesion of all anti-imperialist forces," while the CPSU delegation "declared its resolute support for the just struggle of the Vietnamese people against the aggressive imperialistic gendarme actions of the American imperialists in South Vietnam and expressed firm certainty of the final victory of the cause of the unification of Vietnam."[60] This was followed, on February 25, by a TASS statement condemning the United States for its actions in South Vietnam, officially endorsing "the struggle of the South Vietnamese people," and for the first time promising "the necessary assistance."[61]

The North Vietnamese ceased criticism even of those who failed to support the war in the south, and the press devoted itself to attacks on the United States and its "lackeys" and to the need for unity, particularly within the party. At the end of March, Ho Chi Minh convened a "Special Political Conference" as the occasion for a broad expression of support from all sectors of the society for the state, for the party, for the government, and for Ho Chi Minh himself. On April 21, the Central Committee of the VWP sent a letter to all Communist parties, once more calling for a resolution of the issues in dispute between the Russians and the Chinese and suggesting both a resumption of their bilateral talks and a later meeting of all Communist parties.[62]

Despite Hanoi's efforts to mend its fences, relations with Moscow remained strained as Khrushchev continued displeased by DRV activities in Laos and by the escalation of military operations in the south. According to one authority, the Soviet Union was so irritated by North Vietnamese actions that it was prepared to resign from its position as Cochairman, with Great Britain, of the semi-institutionalized 1954 Geneva Conference.[63]

Soviet coolness toward Hanoi was apparent at the time of the Tonkin Gulf crisis in August 1964. While Moscow routinely, if somewhat nervously, condemned the United States for its air attacks on the north,[64] the position it took in the United Nations Security Council was restrained. There the Soviet representative cautiously condemned the United States and introduced a resolution proposing an invitation to North Vietnam, not a member of the world body, to present its case.[65] The invitation was extended on August 7,[66] but on the following day Hanoi refused to accept the competence of the Security Council to consider the matter, arguing that only the signatory nations of the 1954 Geneva Agreements had the right to examine the United States actions.[67]

If the Soviet Union was less than fully supportive of the DRV, it appears that China was not much more so. The Vietnamese later alleged that the United States was able to act during the Tonkin Gulf crisis, and later as well, because "the U.S. imperialists were no longer worried about the Chinese rulers' reaction."[68] The Chinese rebuttal to this point notes a message, dated August 5, 1964, to Pham Van Dong and Van Tien Dung from Chou En-lai and Chief of the General Staff Lo Jui-ching "proposing 'to get to the bottom of the situation and introduce counter-measures in preparation for action,'" which was followed by official statements that China "will absolutely not sit idly by without lending a helping hand" and that "since the United States had bombed North Viet Nam, China had gained the 'right of action' to assist Viet Nam."[69] Yet even this Chinese defence suggests that Peking's action was composed primarily of rhetoric, not of concrete support.

During the fall, the North Vietnamese warned repeatedly that further American air attacks could be expected, and even claimed that some had taken place. Simultaneously Hanoi sought further aid, a process begun with a visit to Moscow by Le Duan in August. But the Soviet Union apparently responded by urging the Vietnamese to seek negotiations to deal with the conflict, a pressure Hanoi resisted; committed to a course which would accept nothing less than unification of the country under their control, the North Vietnamese leaders considered there was nothing to negotiate and, recalling the 1954 Geneva Conference, were suspicious that a Soviet negotiating agenda was not necessarily the same as their own.[70] For his part, Khrushchev had now "abandoned" Vietnam "as a place where the Soviet Union should not waste money and energy."[71]

EMERGENCE OF THE MOSCOW-HANOI ALLIANCE

The Soviet approach to Vietnam was changed fundamentally when Khrushchev was overthrown in October 1964 by a "collective leadership" in which Leonid Brezhnev and Aleksi Kosygin occupied the leading positions. It seems likely that one reason for their dissatisfaction was the course of the Sino-Soviet Dispute; whether policy toward Vietnam was also a factor is less clear, although the new leaders were to state that Khrushchev had "greatly neglected" both the Korean and the Vietnamese Communists.[72] When the new leaders discovered the degree to which Sino-Soviet differences were fundamental rather than situational, they returned to the earlier course of firm opposition, but, in contrast to Khrushchev, their tactic was less to force an open split in the international movement than it was to isolate China by wooing away her supporters; among these the DRV was one of the more important.

Rather than applying pressure, Moscow in essence determined to wean Vietnam from China through the provision of substantial military and economic aid. Although this was an area that maximized the Soviet advantage *vis à vis* the Chinese, the ultimate success of the tactic stemmed even more from other factors. Of these, the most important were the American decision to engage North Vietnam in a high-technology war, the decision of the Vietnamese leaders themselves to abandon prolonged guerrilla warfare for a more conventional approach, the growing Sino-Vietnamese hostility, the change in Peking's policy represented by its moves toward rapprochement with the United States after the election of President Nixon, and the qualitative change in the nature of the war resulting from the domestic effects in the United States of the 1968 Tet Offensive.

The new Soviet leaders seemed at first to think that it might be possible to stabilize if not resolve the dispute with the Chinese, but Chou En-lai's visit to Moscow for the October Revolution anniversary in November 1964 disclosed mutual intransigence, attributable as much to Chinese feelings that Khrushchev's overthrow justified their own position as to elements of constancy on the Soviet side. Even so, Moscow judged that the overall situation was not so firmly fixed as Khrushchev had imagined, that it might be possible to woo the North Vietnamese and others who had attempted to avoid commitment. And, in any case, the Vietnamese situation had a particular importance because of the threat of escalation and the impact of the war on Soviet relations with the United States. The decision to seek improved relations with Hanoi was signaled in January by the announcement that a high-level delegation, headed by Kosygin, would visit Hanoi. In advising the Hungarians of this development, Brezhnev and others said that Moscow desired to "reestablish close cooperation" with the Vietnamese, and outlined an approach to the Sino–Soviet Dispute that was based upon "an international consultative meeting of the Communist parties to reestablish unity in the international communist movement." [73]

The Kosygin delegation included senior military officials, suggesting that a decision had already been taken to provide Hanoi with military aid, primarily for air defense. It seems likely that exactly this kind of assistance had been requested by Hanoi after the Tonkin Gulf Crisis; the American air attacks on that occasion demonstrated the weakness of the North Vietnamese air defense system, while the increased tempo of the effort in the south, including the commitment of units of the North Vietnamese army beginning in the fall of 1964, strengthened the probability that the United States would strike the north. Kosygin's arrival at the beginning of February nearly coincided with Viet Cong attacks on American installations at Pleiku which stimulated—or at least provided the occasion for—retaliatory air attacks on the north on February 7 and 8. While this probably had no effect on the Soviet decision to support the Vietnamese, it certainly added some urgency to and increased the impact of that decision in Hanoi and elsewhere. The communiqué issued in Hanoi on February 10 stated:

The USSR government reaffirmed that, adhering to the principles of socialist internationalism, it will not remain indifferent to ensuring the security of a fraternal socialist country and will give the D.R.V. the necessary aid and support. The governments of the two countries reached an understanding on the steps that will be taken to strengthen the defense capacity of the D.R.V. and agreed to hold regular consultations on the above-mentioned questions.[74]

The communiqué also revealed some progress in working out a number of the other issues between Moscow and Hanoi, although there was no mention of the Soviet proposal for a consultative meeting of the Communist parties and Hanoi was subsequently to reject Kosygin's proposal of February 16 for a conference, without preconditions, on Indochina.

Despite its willingness to give military aid for the defense of the DRV, Moscow appeared somewhat more reticent about the provision of assistance for the struggle in the south. Immediately after the visit, Soviet leaders reported to the East European allies (who were expected to bear some of the aid burden) that the North Vietnamese believed that the Viet Cong would be successful with only North Vietnamese support but that Hanoi needed protection against American air attacks; the Soviet Union "had already agreed to send sophisticated material, including ground-to-air missiles, and to train Vietnamese personnel to man the missile batteries and to fly MIG fighters."[75] At this point, Soviet policy seemed to be based upon the provision of defensive military assistance to a "fraternal socialist country" under attack by the "imperialists," but to stop short of the kind of hardware that would enable Hanoi better to fight the war in the south. Yet the commitment of North Vietnamese units below the seventeenth parallel suggested that Hanoi had or would develop a need for that kind of assistance as well.

The Vietnamese did not limit their aid appeals to Moscow, apparently seeing the American air attacks as a compelling reason for a variety of sources to provide support. According to Peking, in April Pham Van Dong requested that the Chinese dispatch "support forces" including "some volunteer pilots, volunteer fighters . . . as well as other necessary personnel, including those personnel specializing in roads, bridges and other subjects."[76] Accordingly, say the Chinese, agreements were concluded.

But the course of relations with China was becoming increasingly difficult. In April, Le Duan and Vo Nguyen Giap in Moscow publicly thanked the Russians for their aid, and reportedly supported a Soviet proposal for "a Sino–Soviet–North Vietnamese summit conference to coordinate weapons shipments to Hanoi,"[77] a proposal stimulated by difficulties the Chinese had placed in the way of Soviet shipments.[78]

The catalog of North Vietnamese complaints was far broader than this example of Sino-Soviet pettiness. Hanoi later complained bitterly about Mao Tse-tung's interview with Edgar Snow in January 1965, in which the Chinese leader stated that the South Vietnamese could cope with their situation and that the Chinese would not go beyond their borders to fight; this, according to Hanoi, relieved Washington of any concern about a direct Chinese response to American actions.[79] They also claimed that Peking in February refused to support a joint statement condemning the United States, in March rejected "the Soviet proposal that the parties of the Soviet Union, China and Vietnam meet to discuss joint action in support of the Vietnamese people's stuggle against the U.S. aggressors," and "in April 1965, on two occasions, they rejected the Soviet proposal for joint action to ensure the security of the Democratic Republic of Vietnam. They explained why they rejected the Soviet proposal to set up an airlift via China and build airfields on Chinese territory to defend the Democratic Republic of Vietnam."[80] The Vietnamese interpreted these Chinese actions, notably the impeding of Soviet aid shipments, as an effort "to limit the Vietnamese people's ability to launch large-scale operations, particularly in the dry seasons"[81]

The beginning of sustained American air attacks on the north in the late spring of 1965, and the arrival of American ground combat units in the south, accentuated Hanoi's difficulties with the Chinese and accelerated the move toward the Soviet position. The Vietnamese claim that, despite the April agreement providing "in principle" for Peking to send pilots to Vietnam in June, the Chinese advised Hanoi "that the Chinese side could not send pilots to Vietnam because 'the time is not appropriate' and 'by doing so we could not prevent the enemy from intensifying their air raids.'"[82] To this the Chinese reply:

From October 1965 to March 1968, China dispatched to Vietnam support forces of over 320,000 men to undertake air defence, engineering, railway and logistics work. In a peak year, China's support forces totalled more than 170,000. Together with the Vietnamese people, the Chinese support forces defended the territorial air space of north Viet Nam with their lives. They ensured a smooth and unimpeded flow of traffic on the transportation lines in North Vietnam and enabled the Vietnamese People's Army to send large numbers of troops to South Vietnam for combat.[83]

Difficulties also arose over the situations in Laos and Cambodia, Hanoi later accusing Peking of trying to win over the Royal Government of Laos and of encouraging the "Pol Pot clique," over whom the Vietnamese allege the Chinese had secured control in 1965, to wage "an armed struggle against the Sihanouk administration, then allied with the resistance forces of Vietnam and Laos."[84]

Apparently, the well known Lin Piao article "Long Live the Victory of People's War," published on September 3, 1965,[85] was intended both as a contribution to a Chinese debate over the proper course to be followed in Vietnam and as a prescription for Hanoi.[86] It is not surprising that there should have been those in Peking, reputedly including Marshal Lo Jui-ching, then Chief of Staff of the Chinese People's Army, who favored both reconciliation with Moscow and a more militant line in Vietnam, but the views of the more powerful Maoist group prevailed. It was apparently these views that Lin Piao was presenting. With respect to Vietnam, he argued that massive American intervention had changed the character of the war, that the struggle in the south should take the form of protracted guerrilla warfare, that the Vietnamese should rely primarily on their own resources, and that assistance from Vietnam's allies would of necessity be limited. This last point meant not only that Vietnam should not rely on aid which China could not provide, but also that Hanoi should not accept aid from the Soviet Union.

The Lin Piao presentation was no doubt unwelcome in Hanoi, but the Vietnamese in the long run were to emphasize with pride the contention that their struggle was victorious because it relied primarily on Vietnamese resources (a claim that ignores the massive Soviet and East European assistance). Inherent in the Lin Piao position was Chinese willingness to, as the Vietnamese put it, "fight the Americans to the last Vietnamese,"[87] and Peking's later opposition to negotiations with the United States, for commitment to "protracted war" would obviate any benefit from that course. For Peking, the Vietnamese refusal in late 1963 and early 1964 to make an unequivocal commitment to the Chinese position suggested that Hanoi was not likely to become a firm and reliable supporter in the contest with Moscow but, rather, would exploit Chinese aid in its own direct interest. Peking therefore chose the course of providing sufficient assistance to fulfill international revolutionary obligations and to avoid driving Hanoi completely into the Soviet camp, but without straining Chinese resources or risking direct confrontation with the United States.

While difficulties with the Chinese were important in moving Hanoi toward Moscow, American policy may inadvertantly have been an even more significant factor. With their own resources and aid of the sort Peking was willing and able to supply, the North Vietnamese could have sustained a protracted "people's war" on the Chinese model in the south. But the attacks on the north, and the commitment of American and regular North Vietnamese units in the south, created a situation to which the Chinese could not respond; Peking did not have the resources to provide adequate air defense or to support a major conventional campaign without impairing China's own defense capability, and Chinese leaders feared that hostilities might spread to China herself if her involvement in Vietnam became too great.

The Vietnamese could have survived, as the Chinese argued they should, by simply digging in under the air attacks, dispersing their industry and population, minimizing the commitment of regular units in the south, and conducting a "protracted war." Hanoi was not, however, inclined to that course, and the willingness of the Soviet Union to provide high technology assistance of the sort the Chinese could not no doubt encouraged them to the contrary approach. The North Vietnamese decision to engage in conventional conflict against the South Vietnamese army, and later the United States, actually predated both the arrival of American combat units and the post-Khrushchev rapprochement with the Soviet Union. According to one authority, it was taken in early 1964 (probably about the time Hanoi decided to avoid full commitment to the Chinese position and to mend fences with Khrushchev) and was the source of some disagreement within the North Vietnamese leadership.[88] Once begun, however, this strategy acquired a dynamic of its own, with return to protracted guerrilla war ever more difficult both psychologically and practically.

North Vietnamese leaders did place importance on the preservation of industry and infrastructure in the north, particularly the logistic facilities to support the south; the new Soviet leaders were willing and able to assist in defending them. Sophisticated Soviet military equipment arrived as early as April 1965,[89] and by early 1966 Moscow had supplied ground-to-air missiles, radar controlled anti-aircraft guns, MIG-21 fighters, and probably some military personnel to assist with the operation of this complex technology.[90] Soviet aid fulfilled the obligation to defend a "fraternal socialist country" under attack by the "imperialists," and had a number of other benefits. It emphasized the area where the Soviet Union could best compete with the Chinese, in high technology items. It allowed Moscow to aid Hanoi without at the same time providing direct support to the struggle in the south. It gave Moscow leverage to force the Vietnamese closer to the Soviet position, illustrated perhaps by the fact that Hanoi sent a delegation to the 23rd CPSU Congress in March 1966, a meeting boycotted by the Chinese.[91]

Through its aid Moscow also acquired leverage to influence Hanoi to be somewhat more responsive in form if not in substance to the prospect of negotiations with the Americans. The Soviet Union was still concerned primarily with its relations with the United States; while constrained by a variety of factors to aid the Vietnamese, Soviet leaders were no doubt aware of the extent to which this could impair the prospects for detente. The problem was, therefore, that of appearing to occupy a moderate position while encouraging Hanoi to be more forthcoming in principle without necessarily making any substantive sacrifice. Such a Soviet approach may have been a factor in the formal statements of position represented by the "five points" put forward on March 22, 1965, by the NLF and the "four points" advanced by Pham Van Dong on April 8.[92]

It appears that the Soviet Union was not truly interested in bringing about meaningful negotiations, at least in part because Hanoi was hypersensitive to the possibility of being sold out; Moscow repeatedly refused to act as an intermediary. Moreover, it can be argued that the Soviet advocacy of steps such as bombing halts, ostensibly to facilitate negotiations, was designed to obtain breathing space both to build up the air defenses in the north and to allow Hanoi to concentrate its efforts in the south, with the goal being less a North Vietnamese victory than drawing the DRV toward the Soviet side in the continuing dispute with the

Chinese.[93] The Vietnamese, of course, had no interest in negotiating an end to the conflict on any terms other than those providing for ultimate victory, a position clear in their public statements and repeatedly demonstrated during the flurry of diplomatic activity in the 1965–1968 period.[94] For both Moscow and Hanoi, the maintenance of a public position of willingness to negotiate in principle helped to mobilize sympathy for the Vietnamese position and to complicate that of the Americans.

If the onset of the air war was a key factor influencing Soviet policy, giving Moscow the opportunity to maximize the prospect of obtaining a return for its aid investment, the Tet Offensive of February 1968, was the next turning point, for it changed both the course of the war and the participants' perceptions of it. For Hanoi, the crucial thing was less the sound military defeat suffered by its forces in the south than the almost complete lack of any uprising or expanded popular support. This may have convinced North Vietnamese leaders that "people's war" could not be a significant component of overall strategy, much less the major one as the Chinese suggested, but that a triumph could come only through military defeat of the enemy in a more conventional fashion, and without even reliance on large-scale popular sympathy, much less participation. If so, the rebuff at Khe Sanh suggested that existing capabilities for conventional warfare had to be upgraded significantly, something that could be done only with expanded Soviet aid, and that neutralization of the American combat capability might be essential. The consequences of Tet in the United States may have indicated to Hanoi that the course was feasible, for they prefigured the withdrawal of American forces.

For the Soviet Union, it was developments in the United States, not the battles on the ground, that were key. An American desire to reduce or eliminate its military commitment, to seek political and diplomatic extrication from the war, complemented the Soviet desire to exploit negotiations to minimize the deleterious effects of the war on detente. The American reaction to Tet may also have convinced Moscow that Hanoi could in fact win through a collapse of will in Washington comparable to that in Paris in 1953–1954. Thus Hanoi's desire for an increased conventional capability in the south was met by a Soviet willingness to extend its military assistance far beyond the defense of the north, thereby further solidifying North Vietnam as a member of the Soviet camp. Over the next several years, Hanoi was the beneficiary of massive Soviet military aid which, although not so large or so sophisticated as that provided in the Middle East, fundamentally changed the nature and capability of North Vietnam's forces.

China was less than pleased with these developments. According to the Vietnamese, Peking opposed the prospect of negotiations with the United States, declaring in April 1968, that "'the time has not come and a favourable position has not been secured for Vietnam's entering into negotiations with the United States. We have been making concessions too hastily.'"[95] Hanoi says the Chinese condemned the agreement to meet in Paris in return for a cessation of bombing north of the 20th parallel as, in effect, "a Vietnamese agreement with the United States and a big defeat and loss for the Vietnamese people, similar to the mistake in negotiating and signing the Geneva Convention in 1954," and

> ... the Chinese side brazenly accused Vietnam of negotiating with the United States on Soviet orders and requested the Vietnamese side to make a choice: Either Vietnam wants to defeat the United States, and thus must sever relations with the Soviet Union, or it wants to compromise with the United States, using Chinese aid in fighting the United States in order to fulfill its desire to hold negotiations with the United States, in which case Chinese aid would lose all its significance.[96]

The Vietnamese accuse the Chinese of reducing their aid, of threatening to sever party relations, and of inspiring disturbances and opposition inside Vietnam.

The Chinese deny the general allegations, although not the specifics, and maintain that their support for Vietnam was demonstrated by medical assistance given to Ho Chi Minh in China in 1967 and 1968 and by the provision of planes to carry North Vietnamese leaders back and forth between Hanoi and South Vietnam.[97] Yet the Chinese also state that "by July 1970 all the Chinese support forces had pulled back to China after fulfilling their internationalist mission."[98]

The Vietnamese allege that after the election of President Nixon the Chinese reversed their field and, instead of urging the Vietnamese to fight on, applied pressure to reach an agreement in furtherance of Peking's policy of "rapprochement with U.S.

imperialism."[99] Hanoi presents a litany of complaints about Chinese activities in Cambodia, along the Sino-Vietnamese border, in Laos, and elsewhere as evidence of Peking's inimical policy.

Between 1968 and 1972, while Hanoi engaged in "fighting while negotiating," the war on the ground reflected the copious Soviet support: Vietnamese guerrillas became high technology guerrillas. The 1972 Easter Offensive was a conventional attack very much on the Soviet pattern; while North Vietnamese forces were stopped by the South Vietnamese with substantial support from American airpower, and while the attacks disclosed deficencies in North Vietnamese organization and tactics, the offensive illustrated that Hanoi's forces were more than a match for their South Vietnamese counterparts. In this sense, the 1972 offensive was a harbinger of that in 1975.

The American reaction to the Easter Offensive, notably the resumption of bombing in the north and the mining of North Vietnamese harbors, produced a substantial protest reaction from the Soviet Union and Eastern Europe, demonstrating the extent to which Hanoi had moved toward alignment with Moscow; nonetheless, the Soviet leadership did not let the American actions interfere with the summit meeting with President Nixon scheduled for May. Hanoi now apparently concluded that its interests were best served by conclusion of an agreement with the Americans which would have the consequence of bringing about the removal of the remaining United States military forces; this course may have received Soviet encouragement. According to Hanoi, the Chinese, after the confusing failure to conclude an agreement in October 1972, brought pressure to bear on Hanoi to back down on several issues, notably withdrawal of its forces from the south and a North Vietnamese commitment to refrain from accepting military assistance.[100]

In this situation, the so-called "Christmas bombings"—"Linebacker II"—in December 1972 had a number of effects. The attacks demonstrated the American ability to penetrate Hanoi's sophisticated, Soviet-provided, air defense system almost at will and with very low losses, a factor that appears to have impressed both North Vietnam and the Soviet Union. But the substantial scale of the attacks led to a broad international outcry, spearheaded by Soviet propaganda organizations, about "carpet bombing" of populated centers, an allegation hardly supported by

Hanoi's claim of 1,318 dead.[101] More important, the attacks seem to have convinced Hanoi that the United States had the ability and will to impose heavy punishment on the north; this helped with the conclusion of the 1973 Paris Agreements and demonstrated that Washington had a sanction adequate to enforce adherence to their terms.

The 1973 agreements were a substantial victory for Hanoi, for they brought about the withdrawal of American combat forces from Vietnam and incorporated a number of concessions staunchly opposed by the Saigon government. Based on the results of the 1972 offensive, Hanoi appeared confident that it could win a conventional campaign in the south at some time in the forseeable future provided it corrected some obvious failings—notably in logistics and tactical air defense—and provided that American power were not applied. Between 1973 and 1975, as Hanoi and Saigon jockeyed for position and advantage in fierce struggles little reported in the American press, the North Vietnamese devoted considerable effort to building a logistic base in the south, including the construction of all-weather roads and pipelines, and to upgrading its military organization, equipment, and training.

Hanoi originally believed it would have to refrain from attempts to seek final victory until after 1976, when Nixon would no longer be President, not so much because of an understanding reached with Washington as because of the demonstrated willingness of that administration to conduct "Linebacker II" type operations to enforce it.[102] The willingness of Washington to apply that sanction in event of violation of the apparent agreement that there should be a "decent interval" before resumption of the full-scale North Vietnamese effort to conquer the south was fatally undermined not so much by the War Powers Act as by Watergate, the diminution of executive power that accompanied it, and the resignation of President Nixon. When the United States failed to respond to the initial stages of the offensive—which had not been planned to achieve final victory—the North Vietnamese concluded that they could proceed, although the speed and extent of their success stunned them nearly as much as it did everyone else.

MOSCOW'S QUALIFIED VICTORY

Hanoi's military triumph was not one of "people's war" on the Chinese pattern but of conventional conflict based on Soviet operational doctrine and conducted with Soviet equipment. For both Moscow and Peking, therefore, the fact that the North Vietnamese finally won was less important than the way they did it, and the Vietnam War was a defeat for the Chinese in their contest with the Soviet Union. For the Vietnamese, success derived from the abandonment of Chinese doctrine for that of the Russians, a shift based less on ideology and conviction than on a pragmatic, if internally controversial, decision about the best way to conduct the struggle with the Americans.

The postwar situation has confirmed Hanoi's fundamental estrangement from the Chinese and its commitment to the Russians. It would, however, be a mistake to conclude that Hanoi is firmly under the Soviet thumb, however much the Vietnamese regime—and its satellites in Vientiane and Phnom Penh—now identify themselves closely with the Soviet camp. On both sides, the considerations that underlie the current alignments are primarily those of self-interest, not those of ideology; to expect them to remain indefinitely in congruence would be to ignore the fact that perceptions and positions of self-interest change rapidly in a tumultuous world.

Moscow's position on the winning side was to some extent fortuitous. Vietnam was geographically and culturally distant, under independent and obstreperous leadership, in a part of the world of relatively low priority in the spectrum of Russian national interests. After 1965 Soviet policy in Vietnam was driven as much by considerations external to the struggle itself as it had been during the First Indochina War; the willingness to supply the North Vietnamese military machine derived less from a conviction that this was the way to win the war or to promote revolution than from a desire to woo Hanoi away from Peking. Moscow simply has never been that concerned about developments in Indochina in their own right; the possibility of establishing Communist regimes there has not been a conditioning factor in Soviet policy, has not been sufficiently important to warrant the sacrifice of other interests.

The unexpected North Vietnamese triumph may have demonstrated to Soviet leaders the wisdom of a flexible policy, the foreign policy equivalent of situational ethics, which enabled the maintenance of distance when the situation was unfavorable, involvement when it appeared Soviet interests could benefit immediately and directly, all irrespective of interstate obligation or

103

ideological mandate. Similarly it illustrated that benefits could flow from the simple if expensive technique of providing copious assistance, just as success in 1954 flowed from a willingness to use pressure and to sacrifice Vietnamese interests.

The Soviet share of the victory, while impressive, is not total. Moscow has not established a strong position in Southeast Asia; its influence is dependent on the sufferance, or the indebtedness, of the Vietnamese. Peking may have been rebuffed, and all the more so given the equivocal results of its attempt to "punish" Hanoi in 1979, but China, not the Soviet Union, is still the power whose presence most conditions the region, and the United States remains at least a potential factor. Moreover, Hanoi's policies since 1975 may not have been those that Moscow, in the best of all possible worlds, would have preferred from its one protegé in Southeast Asia.

But, overall, the North Vietnamese victory itself signifies less for Moscow than what the circumstances of that victory say about the broader situation. Certainly it illustrated the unwillingness or inability of Washington to prevent it, a situation in which developments in the United States were far more important than those in Southeast Asia. While Peking has been shown to have more bark than bite, perhaps Moscow has now concluded that Mao Tse-tung was in part right, that the United States is a "paper tiger" vulnerable to tactics that exact a high cost in money, blood, and will. If the Americans are reluctant to face the prospect of "another Vietnam," then the Soviet Union may find advantage in the creation or support of "other Vietnams," in Africa or the Middle East or Asia. To this challenge the United States has yet to find an appropriate and effective response.

FOOTNOTES

1. See, for example, the report of relations between the French party and the Vietnamese Communists in September 1945, Harold R. Isaacs, *No Peace for Asia* (Cambridge, Massachusetts: The M.I.T. Press, 1967), pp. 173-174.
2. Andrei Zhdanov, "The International Situation," *For a Lasting Peace, For a People's Democracy!*, November 10, 1947, p. 2.
3. *Pravda*, December 21, 1950, p. 3.

4. "... Secretary of State Dulles' explicit statement to Nehru on 22 May—viz., if a truce could not be arranged [in Korea], the U.S. could not be expected to refrain from using atomic weapons .. : ." United States, Central Intelligence Agency, "Asian Communist Employment of Negotiations as a Political Tactic" (RSS No. 0177/66, November 1966, "Sanitized Copy" declassified and released to the author, February 22, 1979), p. 28.

5. This process was capped by the downfall of Beria who was alleged, among other things, to have urged concessions to the West in Germany.

6. Even so, Moscow continued to condition its approach on French politics, refusing to hold the Conference in early January in anticipation of a possible governmental crisis in Paris in the middle of the month upon the inauguration of the new President; the Constitution required the existing government, under Premier Joseph Laniel, to resign, but Laniel was asked to continue by the outgoing President, Vincent Auriol, and his successor, René Coty, and the National Assembly on January 6 accorded its confidence.

7. In reporting on the prospective Geneva Conference to the Senate Foreign Relations Committee in executive session on February 24, Dulles observed: "I may say that this idea of a possible negotiation with reference to Indochina was put forward primarily by the French, not by the Russians." United States, Congress, Senate, Committee on Foreign Relations, *Executive Sessions of the Senate Foreign Relations Committee (Historical Series)*, Volume VI: *Eighty-Third Congress, Second Session, 1954* (Washington: Government Printing Office, 1977), p. 160.

8. News article by Clifton Daniel, *The New York Times*, February 12, 1954, p. 3.

9. See Dulles' candid comments to the Senate Foreign Relations Committee on February 24, in *Executive Sessions of the Senate Foreign Relations Committee, 1954*, pp. 153-184. See also Dwight D. Eisenhower, *The White House Years: Mandate for Change*, Garden City, N.Y.: Doubleday & Company, 1963), pp. 342-344.*

10. "Minutes of Restricted Meetings of the Four Foreign Ministers at Berlin, February 8-18, 1954" (declassified and released to the author by the Department of State, March 1980), Monday, February 8, 1954, 3 P.M., pp. 2-3.

11. *Ibid.*, Thursday, February 11, 1954, 3:00-5:10 p.m., pp. 2-3.

12. *Ibid.*, pp. 10-11.

13. "Mr. Molotov then reverted to the Soviet proposal which, he said, named two items. If the French preferred, he said, it would be possible to be more precise. We could stipulate both Korea and Indochina. In fact, Mr. Molotov said we could then have the following agenda for the conference:

---

*See supplement on page 114.

'1. The Korean Political Conference
2. Statements on subjects mentioned above (which would include or specify Indochina) and the exchange of views on these subjects.'

This would then provide a definite framework for the conference and for the statements which would be made at it."

Ibid., Third Restricted Session, Friday, February 12, 1954, 11:30 a.m., p. 5.

14. *Ibid.*, Fourth Restricted Session, February 15, 1954, 11:00 A.M., p. 6.

15. Compare with Allan W. Cameron, "The Soviet Union and Vietnam: The Origins of Involvement," in W. Raymond Duncan, ed., *Soviet Policy in Developing Countries* (Waltham, Massachusetts: Ginn-Blaisdell, 1970), pp. 187-188; Donald Lancaster, *The Emancipation of French Indochina* (London: Oxford University Press, 1961), pp. 290-291; Philippe Devillers and Jean Lacouture, *End of a War: Indochina 1954*, Alexander Lieven and Adam Roberts, trans. (New York: Frederick A. Praeger, 1969), p. 55; Robert F. Randle, *Geneva 1954: The Settlement of the Indochinese War* (Princeton, New Jersey: Princeton University Press, 1969), p. 21; and János Radványi, *Delusion and Reality: Gambits, Hoaxes, & Diplomatic One-Upmanship in Vietnam* (South Bend, Indiana: Gateway Editions, Limited, 1978), p. 6.

16. "Final Communiqué Issued by the Foreign Ministers of the United States, France, the United Kingdom, and the Soviet Union at the Berlin Conference," extract, in Allan W. Cameron, ed., *Viet-Nam Crisis: A Documentary History, Volume I: 1940-1956* (Ithaca, New York: Cornell University Press, 1971), Document 99, pp. 229-230.

17. Dulles' understanding of the result was stated to the Senate Foreign Relations Committee on February 24: "The resolution is so drawn that there can very well be the fact that the holding of a conference on Indochina would be deferred pending the outcome of the Korean negotiations. . . . It implied that [Korea] should come first. I would not want to say that I am sure that the order of events will be closely followed, but I do feel confident that there will be first a Korean political conference, and then that out of the position, military position, in Indochina, and the attitude of the Russians and the Chinese Communists, will come the final decision as to when to go into Indochina, the Indochina phase of this matter, and just who should be there. Those matters were not finally settled." *Executive Sessions of the Senate Foreign Relations Committee, 1954*, pp. 160-161.

18. Compare with my own earlier characterization: "The last half of 1953 saw the beginning of the honeymoon between Moscow and Peking which lasted until sometime in 1955:" Cameron, "The Soviet Union and Vietnam," p. 185. Compare also Harold C. Hinton, *Communist China in World Politics* (Boston: Houghton Mifflin Company, 1966), p. 245.

19. For example, at the February 15 session: "Mr. Molotov said he wished to draw the attention of his colleagues to a difficulty which the Soviet Government faced and which should not be forgotten. If they were considering the matter of participation of the Chinese People's Republic, they must be sure that their invitation would be acceptable to it. The Soviet Union is not in a position to speak for the Chinese Communists today and China should be asked if the proposal was acceptable to her." "Minutes of Restricted Meetings of the Four Foreign Ministers at Berlin, February 8-18, 1954," Fourth Restricted Session, February 15, 1954, 11:00 A.M., p. 3.

20. See Dulles' testimony to the Senate Foreign Relations Committee on February 24: "I am not at all sure that the Russians want the Chinese to win a great victory in Southeast Asia." *Executive Sessions of the Senate Foreign Relations Committee, 1954*, p. 171.

21. In a speech to the American Legion in St. Louis on September 2, 1953, Dulles had warned of direct action against China should Peking send its own army into Indochina; see Cameron, *Viet-Nam Crisis*, Document 88, pp. 204-205. This threat seemed to be reinforced by Dulles' famous "massive retaliation" speech on January 12, 1954: United States, Department of State, *Bulletin*, Vol. XXX (January 25, 1954): pp. 107-110.

22. Those commitments included direct participation in air defense: "The Chinese working people knew that the Soviet Air Force divisions that were urgently sent to China at the request of its government stopped the piratical raids by Kuomintang airplanes against CPR territory. During the tense time of the 1950-1953 Korean War, Soviet air units closed China's skys to American aircraft." I. Aleksandrov, "Contrary to the Interest of Peace and Socialism," *Pravda*, April 7, 1979, p. 4, condensed translation in *The Current Digest of the Soviet Press*, Vol. XXXI, No. 14 (May 2, 1979), pp. 2-4. See also "Soviet Government Statement," *Pravda* and *Izvestia*, April 5, 1979, p. 2; translated in *ibid.*, pp. 1-2.

23. In his February 24 presentation to the Senate Foreign Relations Committee, Dulles said: "I did have [at Berlin] a feeling of some apprehension on the part of the Russians that, for reasons of their own, they were not particularly anxious to have the Chinese Communists get out of hand to any extent which would cause risk, at least, of a general war. I do not think the Russians want to have a general war, I do not. I think there was a chance, at least, that they do not want the Chinese Communists to take steps which might precipitate a general war, despite the views of Soviet Russia." *Executive Sessions of the Senate Foreign Relations Committee, 1954*, pp. 171-172.

24. It is difficult to accord much credence to the contention in *Khrushchev Remembers* that "the situation was very grave. The resistance movement

in Vietnam was on the brink of collapse." *Khrushchev Remembers* (Boston: Little, Brown and Company, 1970), p. 482. The contention is, however, supported by János Radványi, a former Hungarian diplomat from time to time involved in relations with North Vietnam; see *Delusion and Reality*, pp. 6-10.

25. For example, a later Vietnamese account claimed: "Besides, acting in concert with the French, the Chinese delegation raised at every turn the spectre of an American intervention in Indochina which could prolong and widen the conflict. It used the warlike declarations of American public figures and the hard-line attitude of Dulles and other American representatives to exert pressure on Vietnam." Hoang Nguyen, "Twenty Five Years Ago: At the 1954 Geneva Conference," *Vietnam Courier*, No. 8 (August 1979), p. 5.

26. The Chinese now state that a "Military Advisers' Mission" was present with the Viet Minh forces from 1950 to 1954, and that "all the arms and ammunition, communication equipment, food, and medicines used and expended in this [Dien Bien Phu] campaign were supplied by China:" "More on Hanoi's White Book," *Beijing Review*, Vol. 22, No. 48 (November 30, 1979), p. 11, citing an article by *Renmin Ribao* and Xinhua commentators published in *Renmin Ribao* on November 21, 1979, under the title "Sino-Vietnamese Relations During Viet Nam's Anti-French, Anti-American Struggle."

27. See the text of the brief communiqué, in Cammeron, *Viet-Nam Crisis*, Document 127, p. 283.

28. See Hoang Nguyen, "Twenty Five Years Ago: At the 1954 Geneva Conference," pp. 4-5; see also "The Truth About Vietnam–China Relations over the Last 30 Years," "White Book" released by the Foreign Ministry of the Socialist Republic of Vietnam (SRV) on October 4, 1979, broadcast by Hanoi Domestic Service in Vietnamese, 1100 GMT, October 4, 1979, in United States, Foreign Broadcast Information Service, *Daily Report: Asia & Pacific*, Vol. IV, No. 204, Supplement 031 (October 19, 1979), Part Two, "China and the Termination of the Indochina War in 1954." In these retrospective, and clearly somewhat self-serving, accounts, the Vietnamese make no mention of the Ho-Chou meeting. They also claim that the Viet Minh leadership maintained its uncompromising position until July 10, on which date the Central Committee of the VWP received a message from Chou En-lai that argued "we should avoid complicating matters and engaging in time-consuming discussions and prolonged negotiations, so as not to allow the U.S. to sabotage the conference." "The Truth About Vietnam–China Relations over the Last 30 Years," p. 10.

29. Devillers and Lacouture, *End of a War*, pp. 292-293. This account is apparently based on still generally unavailable French materials.

30. The Geneva Conference was the occasion for conversations between Wang Ping-nan, then Secretary General of the Chinese Foreign Office, and Ambassador U. Alexis Johnson over the status of American prisoners in China and Chinese nationals in the United States.

31. The principles were first stated in the Sino-Indian agreement on the status of Tibet, concluded on April 29, 1954.

32. In 1955 the Soviet Union granted 400 million rubles "without recompense" to North Vietnam; see the Joint Comminiqué issued in Moscow on July 18, 1955, in Cameron, *Viet-Nam Crisis*, Document 164, p. 387.

33. Indeed, even the extent to which the North Vietnamese believed that the elections would be held is called into question by Hanoi's public calls, as early as September 1954, for the overthrow of Diem. One could argue that, despite later attempts to justify a militant course by pointing to the failure to hold elections, the North Vietnamese from the outset believed that victory would come only through collapse or overthrow of the Saigon government.

34. In Molotov's foreign policy report to the Supreme Soviet on February 8, 1955; see *Pravda*, February 9, 1955, pp. 2-3.

35. *Pravda*, October 25, 1955, p. 1.

36. For Soviet coverage, see *Pravda*, April 2-6, 1956. North Vietnamese reports were broadcast by Vietnam News Agency International Broadcast Service in English, April 4-6, 1956.

37. United Nations Document A/SPC/1.9 LIMITED, "USSR Draft Resolution of January 24, 1957;" see the consideration of the matter in United Nations Documents A/SPC/SR17 through A/SPC/SR22, records of the Special Political Committee, January 23-30, 1957.

38. "The Truth About Vietnam–China Relations," pp. 13-14.

39. *Ibid.*, p. 13.

40. Ho Chi Minh, *Izbrannye Statii i Rechii* (Moscow: Izd-vo Polit-ry, 1959).

41. See "Soviet Trade with South-East Asian Countries," *Yuva Newsletter*, No. 1 (April 1962), p. 36; and No. 2 (January 1963), p. 1.

42. Radványi, *Delusion and Reality*, p. 26; see the account of his April visit to Hanoi on pp. 16-27.

43. "The Truth About Vietnam–China Relations," p. 14.

44. *Ibid.*, pp. 14-15.

45. See P. J. Honey, *Communism in North Vietnam: Its Role in the Sino-Soviet Dispute* (Cambridge, Massachusetts: The M.I.T. Press, 1963), pp. 76-77.

46. *Ibid.*, p. 78.

47. Donald S. Zagoria, *The Sino-Soviet Conflict 1956-1961* (Princeton, New Jersey: Princeton University Press, 1962), p. 337.

48. *Third National Congress of the Viet Nam Workers' Party, Volume I* (Hanoi: Foreign Languages Publishing House, 1960?), p. 221.

49. It now seems clear, with the abandonment of pretense that followed the North Vietnamese victory in 1975, that the National Liberation Front was from the beginning a creation and creature of Hanoi, however much some Western analysts may have argued for its status as an independent entity and however much it may from time to time have appeared to follow policies divergent from those of Hanoi.

50. See the account of part of Ho's efforts in *Khrushchev Remembers*, pp. 483-484.

51. "The Truth About Vietnam-China Relations," p. 16.

52. Cited in "Text of Statement of the Politburo of the Lao Dong Party Central Committee, February 10, 1963," in Honey, *Communism in North Vietnam*, Appendix A, p. 182.

53. A member of the Politburo and Director of the Political Department of the Vietnam Peoples' Army (VPA), Nguyen Chi Thanh was apparently in direct charge of the struggle in the south. He died in 1967, probably killed in a B-52 raid.

54. "More on Hanoi's White Paper," p. 13. Chinese weapons began to appear in quantity in the south in 1965 and 1966.

55. Text in Honey, *Communism in North Vietnam*, Appendix A, pp. 181-185.

56. "Comrade Liu Shao-chi's Speech at a Meeting in His Honour at the Nguyen Ai Quoc Party School, Hanoi," May 15, 1963, in *Joint Statement of Chairman Liu Shao-chi and President Ho Chi Minh* (Peking: Foreign Languages Press, 1963), p. 33.

57. "The Truth About Vietnam-China Relations," p. 15.

58. See the news story by Seymour Topping, "North Vietnamese Economy Reported Failing," *The New York Times*, December 20, 1963, p. 20. See also King Chen, "North Vietnam in the Sino-Soviet Dispute, 1962-1964," *Asian Survey*, Vol. 4, No. 9 (September 1964), Note 53, p. 1034; P. J. Honey, "North Vietnam Quarterly Survey, No. 11," *China News Analysis*, No. 508 (March 13, 1964), p. 5; and J. P. Honey, "North Vietnam, Quarterly Survey, No. 12," *ibid.*, No. 520 (June 12, 1964), p. 1.

59. Broadcast by Hanoi, VNA International Service in English, 1210 GMT, January 20, 1964, in United States, Foreign Broadcast Information Service, *Daily Report: Far East* (hereafter cited as FBIS Far East), No. 15-1964 (January 22, 1964), pp. JJJ1-JJJ6.

60. "Communiqué on Meeting in Moscow of Representatives of the Communist Party of Soviet Union and of Vietnam Workers' Party," *Pravda*

and *Izvestia,* February 15, 1954, p. 1, translated in *The Current Digest of the Soviet Press,* Vol. XIV, No. 7 (March 11, 1964), p. 32.

61. Broadcast by TASS in English, 1338 GMT, February 25, 1954, in United States, Foreign Broadcast Information Service, *Daily Report: USSR & East Europe,* No. 39-1964 (February 26, 1964), pp. BB1-BB3.

62. Broadcast by Hanoi, VNA International Service in English, 1413 GMT, April 29, 1964, in FBIS Far East, No. 85-1964 (April 30, 1964), pp. JJJ1-JJJ2.

63. Donald S. Zagoria, *Vietnam Triangle: Moscow, Peking, Hanoi* (New York: Pegasus, 1967), p. 11. The precipitant issue was Laos: see Great Britain, Parliament, Papers by Command, *Documents Relating to British Involvement in the Indo-China Conflict 1945-1965* (London: Her Majesty's Stationery Office, Cmnd. 2832, 1965), Documents 149 and 150, pp. 239-240.

64. Moscow was concerned about the dangers of an expanded war; see *Pravda,* August 8, 1964, p. 1.

65. News article by Thomas J. Hamilton, *The New York Times,* August 6, 1964, pp. 1, 8.

66. News article by Sam Pope Brewer, *The New York Times,* August 8, 1964, pp. 1-2.

67. Text in Polski Instytut Spraw Miedzynarodowych, *Zbiór Dokumentów,* Vol. XX, No. 7-8, 1964, pp. 1255-1260.

68. "The Truth About Vietnam-China Relations," p. 16.

69. "More on Hanoi's White Paper," p. 14.

70. See Allan E. Goodman, *The Lost Peace: America's Search for a Negotiated Settlement of the Vietnam War* (Stanford, California: Hoover Institution Press, 1978), pp. 6, 12. The fact that Hanoi had apparently been willing to talk with Ngo Dinh Nhu in 1963 suggested that it was not opposed to talks provided they were clearly in its own interest; see Dennis J. Duncanson, *Government and Revolution in Vietnam* (New York: Oxford University Press, 1968), p. 339 and p. 411, note 114.

71. Radványi, *Delusion and Reality,* p. 37.

72. *Ibid.,* p. 38.

73. *Ibid.*

74. "Joint Statement of Delegations of Union of Soviet Socialist Republics and Democratic Republic of Vietnam," *Pravda,* February 11, 1965, pp. 1, 3; *Izvestia,* February 12, 1965, pp. 1-2; translated in *The Current Digest of the Soviet Press,* Vol. XVII, No. 6 (March 3, 1965), pp. 9-11. Ho Chi Minh headed the Vietnamese delegation, but the joint statement was signed by Pham Van Dong.

75. Radványi, *Delusion and Reality,* pp. 39-40.

76. "More on Hanoi's White Paper," p. 14; ellipsis in the original.

77. Zagoria, *Vietnam Triangle*, p. 50.

78. William E. Griffith, *Sino-Soviet Relations, 1964-1965* (Cambridge, Massachusetts: The M.I.T. Press, 1967), p. 76.

79. "The Truth About Vietnam-China Relations," p. 16; the Mao Tse-tung interview is described at length in Edgar Snow, *The Long Revolution* (New York: Random House, 1972), pp. 192-223.

80. "The Truth About Vietnam-China Relations," pp. 17-18. See also Griffith, *Sino-Soviet Relations, 1964-1965*, pp. 72-73; Zagoria, *Vietnam Triangle*, pp. 49-50.

81. "The Truth About Vietnam-China Relations," p. 18.

82. *Ibid.*, p. 17.

83. "More on Hanoi's White Book," p. 14.

84. "The Truth About Vietnam-China Relations," pp. 18-19.

85. *Peking Review*, No. 32 (August 4, 1967), pp. 14-35.

86. For analysis of the context and substance of the Lin Piao article, see D. P. Mozingo and T. W. Robinson, *Lin Piao on "People's War:" China Takes a Second Look at Vietnam* (Santa Monica, California: The RAND Corporation, Memorandum RM-4814-PR, November 1965); Zagoria, *Vietnam Triangle*, pp. 67-83; and Uri Ra'anan, "Peking's Foreign Policy 'Debate,' 1965-1966," in Tang Tsou, ed., *China in Crisis, Volume 2: China's Policies in Asia and America's Alternatives* (Chicago: The University of Chicago Press, 1968), pp. 23-71. Hanoi does not mention the Lin Piao article or the Chinese debate in "The Truth About Vietnam-China Relations."

87. "The Truth About Vietnam-China Relations," p. 20; Hanoi attributed this description to General Maxwell Taylor.

88. See Douglas Pike, *History of Vietnamese Communism, 1925-1967* (Stanford, California: Hoover Institution Press, 1978), pp. 117-119, and Note 5, p. 164.

89. Radványi, *Delusion and Reality*, p. 41.

90. Zagoria, *Vietnam Triangle*, p. 51.

91. *Ibid.*, pp. 51-52.

92. Texts in Great Britain, Parliament, Papers by Command, *Recent Exchanges Concerning Attempts to Promote a Negotiated Settlement of the Conflict in Vietnam* (London: Her Majesty's Stationery Office, Cmnd. 2756, 1965), pp. 33 and 51.

93. This argument is developed at length in Radványi, *Delusion and Reality*.

94. For a useful summary and analysis, see Goodman, *The Lost Peace*, chapter 2.

95. Quoted in "The Truth About Vietnam-China Relations," p. 19.

96. *Ibid.*, pp. 19-20.

97. "More on Hanoi's White Book," p. 15.

98. *Ibid.*, p. 14.

99. "The Truth About Vietnam-China Relations," p. 21.

100. *Ibid.*, p. 23.

101. For example, World Peace Council, *The World Accuses* (Helsinki: Information Centre of the World Peace Council, 1972). This pamphlet, and many others of the time, were printed in East Germany, whose staunch support of North Vietnam, like that from Cuba, illustrated the degree to which Hanoi had moved to the Soviet position.

102. The clearest statement of this belief appears in an article by Generals Vo Nguyen Giap and Van Tien Dung, published on June 30, 1975:

> The enemy's biggest surprise was the timing of the general offensive. This was one of the key factors that rendered him completely and strategically passive. The U.S. imperialists and their henchmen miscalculated; they thought they still had 2 more years [from 1975] to implement their scheme to sabotage the Paris agreement. They thought that our armed forces and people would be forced to sit and watch them repress the southern compatriots and gradually destroy the revolution's gains. Therefore, they were caught completely unaware when our general offensive erupted.

"Great Victory of the Spring 1975 General Offensive and Uprising," published on June 30, 1975, in *Nhan Dan* and *Quan Doi Nhan Dan* and in the July 1975 issues of *Hoc Tap* and *Tap Chi Quan Doi Nhan Dan*, broadcast by Hanoi in Vietnamese to Vietnam, 1100 GMT, June 30, 1975, in Foreign Broadcast Information Serivce, *Daily Report: Asia & Pacific*, Vol. IV, No. 134, Supplement 9 (July 11, 1975), p. 35. In many respects this article is more frank and forthcoming than the better-known analysis published a year later by Van Tien Dung: *Great Spring Victory, ibid.*, Vol. IV, No. 110, Supplement 38 (June 7, 1976); also published in the United States as Van Tien Dung, John Spragens, Jr., trans. *Our Great Spring Victory: An Account of the Liberation of South Vietnam by General Van Tien Dung, Chief of Staff, Vietnam People's Army* (New York: Monthly Review Press, 1977).

*Supplementary addition to footnote 9 on p. 105.

An official source states that, as a condition for United States accession to discussion of Indochina at Geneva, the French undertook not to agree "to any arrangement which would directly or indirectly result in the turnover of Indochina to the Communists." United States, Department of State, Historical Division, *United States Policy on Indochina 1945—May 8, 1954 With Emphasis on Events Preliminary to the Geneva Conference*, Research Project No. 370, July 1955 (declassified and released to the author by the Department of State, October 26, 1979), p. 16.

CHAPTER FIVE

MOSCOW AND HAVANA IN THE THIRD WORLD

W. Raymond Duncan

Had the Cuban Revolution occurred in 1953, when Fidel Castro first attempted to overthrow the U.S.-dominated Fulgencio Batista regime, it might not have succeeded. For, at that time, the Soviet Union, under Joseph Stalin's waning days, was not especially interested in the Third World, let alone Latin America.[1] But, happening as it did in 1959, followed in 1961 by Fidel Castro's turn to Marxism–Leninism, the revolutionary movement in Cuba created a remarkable opportunity for projection of Soviet policy into Washington's backyard. By then, the adventuresome Nikita Khrushchev controlled the tiller in Soviet foreign policy, had launched the first Sputnik, and was building Moscow's military might into superpower status. With the Kremlin also embarked upon a major economic and military aid offensive in the world's underdeveloped areas, Cuba's unexpected break with the United States under Castro's Marxist leadership was simply too good a chance to pass up.

Once established as a revolutionary state, Cuba's relations with the USSR blossomed into one of the most significant ties in Moscow's greatly expanded Third-World posture. Havana's enormous importance was demonstrated by its twenty-year collaboration with Moscow [1959–1979], especially through a rough period in the 1960s when Fidel Castro's insistence upon armed struggle clashed with Moscow's peaceful approach to the Third World. Cuba's evolving significance in the Third World domain, at least from Soviet perspectives, is underscored by the high visibility it enjoys in Soviet news media and scholarly publications, the attention commanded by leading Cuban political figures visiting Moscow, and the diplomatic, cultural, trade, and military links between the two countries.[2] Cuba had become a star among Third-World regimes by the end of the 1970s, a point dramatically illustrated by Cuba's geographic location in a region— Latin America—that otherwise was of far less priority compared to more geographically proximate areas of sensitive strategic concern to the USSR, along its borders, e.g., Iran or Afghanistan.

The importance Moscow attaches to Cuba is demonstrated by several types of aid and trade statistics. Consider that Moscow extended a total of $94 million in economic credits and grants to all of Latin America between 1954 and 1978.[3] This compares to the approximately $7 billion extended to the Middle East, $5 billion to South Asia, $3 billion to North Africa and $1 billion to Sub-Saharan Africa during the same period.[4] These figures suggest the generally lower priority of the Caribbean and Latin America in Soviet economic aid and trade perspectives compared to other Third-World regions. But here Cuba is the big exception to Latin America and the Caribbean as a whole. Moscow extended many types of economic help to Cuba after 1960, to include direct subsidies for Havana's trade deficits with Moscow, payment for Cuban sugar above the prevailing world market price, lowered prices for Soviet petroleum products, supplies of military equipment, and direct credits for economic development.[5] Subsidies directed to bilateral trade deficits amounted to about $3.8 billion between 1960 and 1974. Moscow paid three-to-five-times more for Cuban sugar during the 1970s than the prevailing world market prices, and provided several hundred million dollars in credits for economic development in this period.[6] At the same time, it is estimated that the Kremlin extended about $1.5 billion in arms-transfers during the 1960s, which rose to several billion dollars in the following decade.[7] By the late 1970s, Soviet aid to Cuba had risen from an estimated $3 million per day during the 1960s to approximately $9 million per day.

Much has been written about this fascinating affair, through its stormy period in the 1960s into the era of foreign policy convergence between Moscow and Havana objectives in the 1970s.[8] And as might be expected, considerable debate centers over the issues of just how much influence Moscow exerts over Havana in its external posture—in Africa, the Caribbean, Central America— and to what extent a Soviet-backed Cuba represents an expanding Communist threat to the Americas and the United States. Some observers perceive sharp Soviet control over a Cuban "proxy" in Communist international politics, while others accentuate the independent threads of Cuban self-interests in its overseas activities.[9] However, one concludes, a number of implications ensue for United States foreign policy toward Cuba and the USSR in its special Cuban context.

The purpose here is to examine Soviet and Cuban foreign policies in terms of those elements which will help to understand not only the nature of the relationship, but as well the implications for Washington as we move into the future. It is the overall benefits and costs derived for Moscow, as well as for Havana, that we are after. This requires a probe of the extent to which Cuban foreign policy reflects an independent dimension which constantly underlies changing foreign policy directions, and the overall limits to Soviet–Cuban influence in the Third World. Toward this end, four levels of analysis are explored: (1) Cuba and Latin America in Moscow's Third-World posture, (2) policy convergence between Moscow and Havana in the 1970s; (3) independent aspects of Cuban foreign policy; and (4) limits to Soviet and Cuban influence in Third-World settings.

CUBA AND LATIN AMERICA IN MOSCOW'S
THIRD WORLD POSTURE

Soviet objectives in Cuba, as in the Latin American and other developing regions, are tied to central driving forces in Moscow's overall Third-World posture. One key goal is to project influence where opportunities exist, certainly as a means to enhance Soviet security, but also to raise Moscow's status as a global power. The means to do so include a variety of policy instruments: extended aid and economic credits, technical assistance, training of client state personnel, and, perhaps most important of all, military arms transfers. Projecting Soviet power abroad also means an extended Soviet *presence* in Third-World countries through diplomatic contacts, cultural exchanges, and trade missions, as well as the presence of Soviet military advisers and equipment. The result is a growing importance of Moscow's blue-water navy and merchant marine, both of which perform a variety of functions in Soviet security and great power politics, but which of course require ports of call and naval facilities in the Third World—which make a distance location like the Caribbean and Latin America important in this respect.[10]

Beyond security, other state interests—inspired by both pragmatic realism and ideology—appear to operate in Soviet international politics. Moscow shows increasing concern about access to markets and raw materials, as do all countries in the last quarter of the twentieth century where demand for natural resources is increasing while supply appears less certain. At the same time, the Kremlin is in need of strengthened trade ties to augment their hard currency, access to international fishing waters to help in food supply and to food markets abroad when grain and food crops fail within the USSR. These security and state interests appear to outweigh any drive to expand worldwide communism, since they are actively pursued throughout the Third World despite the fate of local communist parties.[11]

Yet ideological perceptions nevertheless continue to shape Soviet policy in the Third World. This is demonstrated by the emphasis in Soviet analyses on reducing western influence where possible by strengthening what Moscow calls the world "correlation of forces" between socialism and capitalism/imperialism in favor of the former.[12] And in much of Soviet writing there is brave talk about the decline of Western capitalism, although increasingly this prognosis was tempered in the 1970s with discussion of the continued durability of the West's capitalist economy.[13] Notably, Soviet writers began to describe Latin America in the late 1970s as a special case within the Third World where Western capital exercised an especially strong hold, defined as "dependent capitalism" of a scale much greater than in Africa and Asia.[14] Cuba's own Marxist–Leninist break away from this situation during the 1960s naturally gives it unique prominence in such a setting and an additional reason for Soviet attention.

SOVIET POLICY IN LATIN AMERICA
AND CUBA COMPARED

This foreign policy backdrop helps to explain Soviet objectives toward Cuba and the benefits derived from the relationship. They parallel those goals sought elsewhere in Latin America, although, as we shall see, Cuba is a unique actor that provides special opportunities for the Soviet Union to expand its power far beyond the Caribbean, Central, or even South America. But the comparison of Cuba with Latin America in Soviet policy objectives is as good a place as any to begin the analysis.

First, both Cuba and Latin America provide a range of opportunities for expanded Soviet activities in one part of the Third World—the part geographically closest to the United States, leader of the "imperialist" camp in Soviet perspectives. They include establishment of resident diplomatic missions, trade and consular offices, providing economic and military technicians, cultural exchanges and inviting academic students into the Soviet Union for training. Consider that 700 Soviet economic technicians were in Latin America and the Caribbean by 1978, about 100 Soviet military trainers were in Peru by 1977, 2,760 students were being trained in the USSR—all of this compared to a dismal record before 1955—and you have a distinct record of increased Soviet participation in Latin American affairs from the 1960s into the 1970s.[15]

Second, both Cuba and Latin America are regions of raw materials and markets. Cuba's sugar and nickel are matched by grain and meat from Argentina, tin from Bolivia, and bauxite from Guyana to mention only some of the available raw materials in the region. But equally important here is the Soviet emphasis on raw materials being placed under Latin American rather than foreign ownership through multinational corporations.[16] Hence Cuba and other Latin American and Caribbean states are encouraged by the Soviet Union to nationalize natural resources operations where possible. Cuba is the established leader in this trend, but Moscow perceives other encouraging efforts by Guyana and Jamaica in bauxite.

It should be stressed here that any movement toward nationalized raw materials industries is perceived by a number of, but not all, Soviet analysts as part of a larger economic trend. It is one of

Latin America trying to gain increased leverage in its economic life *vis à vis* the United States. Thus Soviet commentators in the mid-1970s hopefully discussed the "anticapitalist" and "anti-imperialist" movement in Latin America. Characterized by raw-materials diplomacy, formation of the new Latin American Economic System (SELA) which did not include the United States, the development of the Caribbean Free Trade Association (CARIFTA), and the birth of the joint Caribbean Shipping Company of eight countries (NAMUCAR), it was seen by some Soviet writers as further evidence of a successful trend leading to weakening of "imperialism's position."[17]

Third, Cuba and Latin America are outlets for the flexing of Soviet maritime strength. While Cuba is the more visible partner in this respect, Moscow's merchant marine made visits to other Latin American countries, e.g., Brazil, Chile, and Peru. The Soviet Union has offered fishing aid to a number of Latin American countries, e.g., Argentina, Chile, and Peru; by the late 1970s joint fishing ventures were underway with Argentina, Ecuador, Guyana, and Peru.[18] To be a great power requires naval strength, and judging from Soviet maritime activities in Cuba and Latin America, these western hemispheric regions play an important role in that pursuit, helping to guarantee Moscow's access to the oceans as major transportation routes and as sources of food and other resources.

Fourth, both areas provide opportunities for Moscow to weaken its "capitalist" opponents in another way: by encouraging Caribbean and Latin American *political* as well as economic inde-pendence. Any change toward increased political autonomy *vis à vis* the United States south of the Rio Grande is looked upon favorably by Moscow, given its broad Third-World approach, and especially since they can help to modify a capitalist-dominated economic system in the region. Just as the Kremlin jumped upon Cuba's radical nationalist bandwagon early in the 1960s, it also supports verbally Panama's Canal policy, the Puerto Rican inde-pendence movement, and the *Sandinista* victory over Nicaragua's 34-year dictatorship headed by Anastasio Somoza, and other politically leftist movements in Grenada, Guyana, and Jamaica. Moscow distinctly is in favor of "national liberation" movements in this part of the world, as it is in Africa and Asia, although it does not back its verbal commitments with direct military force.

CUBA'S SPECIAL POSITION IN SOVIET
POLICY OBJECTIVES

Cuba's unique position and advantages for Moscow within this Latin American setting is identifiable in terms of several constant forces at work in Cuba's own foreign policy pronouncements and activities. Of major significance is that previous to the Cuban Revolution of 1959 Latin America had not been a notably fruitful arena for Soviet-induced expansion of communism, nor for special political and economic advantages. The emergence of a communist state with a governing Communist Party, albeit under strong nationalist pressures, made possible Soviet economic, military and political ties with a Latin American antiimperialist critic of the United States, one lying, moreover, just ninety miles off the Florida coast. With Washington's encirclement of the Soviet Union through its military alliances in Western Europe, the Middle East, and Southeast Asia since the late 1940s and early 1950s, the Cuban connection must have produced considerable satisfaction to a country in quest of great power status, increased physical security, and countervailing pressures on the United States.

From the onset of the relationship, Castro's Cuba attracted the Soviet Union for a number of reasons. These have remained generally constant since then. Castro, for example, began to reduce United States power in Cuba through expropriation of its foreign investments and minimizing its military influence. This effort coincided with growing attention in other Latin American countries to the primacy of state control over economic life and certainly over raw materials—a trend that grew remarkably in Latin America and the Caribbean during the 1960s and 1970s. It is not strange, then, that many Soviet analysts perceive Cuba to be historically at the leading edge of change in United States-Latin American relations, where U.S. power became gradually eroded through the region's state efforts to control natural resources and internal processes of economic development.[19] While a growing Soviet debate is now at work over just how much control U.S. economic power exerts within the hemisphere, the leading role of Cuba in undermining Washington's once clear dominance is clearly acknowledged.[20]

Castroite diplomacy soon began to cause multiple problems for the United States which sought to conduct a strong diplomatic posture in the region's multilateral decision-making machinery. Washington's frequent overreaction to perceived Cuban influence in the Caribbean and Central America through the years since Castro's victory undermined its larger goal considerably. First in the Bay of Pigs event of 1961, then the Dominican Republic crisis of 1965, and years later in congressional overreactions to the Soviet troops in Cuba and to *Sandinista* guerrilla challenges to Nicaragua's Anastasio Somoza, Washington conducted an ill-fitting diplomacy that heightened Latin American disaffection with the United States. The Soviets could naturally look upon this trend as a generally favorable situation to augment their own aid, trade, and technical projects or, barring that, to lower at minimum U.S. status in the region.

Castro also became, and continued to be over the years, the principal Latin American antiimperialist critic of the United States. While this posture evolved through several twists and turns, Cuba has remained a country of high visibility in attacking U.S. "imperialism" in Latin America and elsewhere in the Third World. Castro has used antiimperialist denunciations of North American policy very effectively since 1961 to encourage a nationalist-oriented dedication to work, struggle, self-sacrifice, austerity, commitment to national progress, and superpatriotism from most Cubans on the domestic scene. At the same time, his antiimperialism is consistent with international Communism and Marxism-Leninism, which view the United States as the leader of the imperialist camp. This combination of nationalism and Marxism-Leninism makes Castro's Cuba a vital piece on Moscow's international chessboard. For unlike the pre-1959 period, revolutionary Cuba produced a Latin American government led by a ruling Communist Party (although dominated by Castro) playing the chief antiimperialist role in the Western Hemisphere rather than a less powerful local communist party following the Soviet line as in pre-Castro days.

Cuba's communism and nationalism also set forth a new model of development strategy in the Caribbean and Latin America. It emphasized not only state control over the economy and national unity of people within the state, but also the common economic and international political problems of other states within the Caribbean, Central and South America. Cuba's version of development, then, began to propel the island increasingly into the ranks of progressive Third-World countries—eventually into the top leadership position by 1979—and set the island up as an alternate development model to be emulated if desired by other hemispheric countries. As Cuba's own impact on Jamaica, Guyana, Grenada, and Nicaragua began to be felt during the late 1970s, this socialist development model and leadership role in the non-aligned movement, as demonstrated at the Sixth Conference of Nonaligned Countries, in Havana, August 1979, was not lost to Soviet observers.[21]

To sum up these constant features of Cuban domestic and foreign policies that condition Moscow's attraction, we can look to Soviet observers. They stress that the Cuban Revolution marked a major event in expanding their version of the "world socialist system" in its evolving struggle with capitalism and imperialism.[22] It provided Moscow with key opportunities to weaken United States imperialism in its "strategic rear" within the Caribbean area and to help shape what the Soviets refer to as the world "correlation of forces" between socialism and capitalism/imperialism increasingly toward the former.[23] And the Cuban Revolution became instrumental in restructuring inter-American relations in ways that reduced United States political power in the Western Hemisphere. As one Soviet commentator put it in 1978, revolutionary Cuba had become "a shining example of what might be achieved by a people who have rejected the capitalist path of development and embraced the road to building socialism."[24] Given the twenty-year ties with Cuba [1959-1979], Moscow's premier example of Soviet-supported Marxism–Leninism in the developing world and thereby of Soviet world-power significance for the Third World, the Kremlin must interpret its Cuban link as largely successful. This perception is sharpened all the more by Moscow's policy defeats elsewhere, e.g., in Egypt and Somalia in 1972 and 1977, by Chile's ill-fated communist experiment under Salvadore Allende between 1970-1973, and by the general lack-luster performance of Latin American communist parties.

POLICY CONVERGENCE IN THE 1970s

The changing features of Cuban foreign policy can best be described as convergence toward those pursued by the USSR, beginning in the late 1960s and continuing into the 1970s. To place this convergence into proper perspective requires a brief background note on the nature of Soviet–Cuban relations during the 1960s, especially between 1966 and 1968, one of exceptional divergence between the two countries. Havana insisted upon armed struggle during this period as the major road to change, confronted the pro-Soviet Latin American communist parties as weak and ineffectual in their "united broad fronts" dedicated to peaceful change, purged the Cuban political regime of pro-Soviet Communists in 1968, and gave low key treatment to Soviet visitors and anniversary celebrations

This independent approach resulted in considerable limits on Moscow's Latin American profile. For it led to splits within the Latin American communist movement, weakened communist party flexibility, and contributed toward Latin American unity among governments opposing Havana. By implication, Castro's armed struggle thesis contributed also toward growing Latin American suspicion of the Soviet Union in support of this radical "trouble-maker" in the Caribbean, while raising somewhat the U.S. position in hemispheric affairs—one previously undermined by Washington's Bay of Pigs fiasco in 1961. Certainly the whole affair was not amenable to Moscow's projection of its own relations through peaceful government-to-government links and stress upon peaceful broad fronts for the Latin American communist parties. Something had to give in Havana's posture, as it did by late 1968 when Castro revised his foreign policy to bring it into closer adjustment with the USSR.

From the 1970s onwards, Havana's foreign policy shows convergence with the USSR in many ways. In so doing it began to help promote Soviet–Third-World objectives, not only in the Caribbean, Central, and Latin America, but also in Africa, the Middle East, and within the nonalignment movement itself.

The adjustments in Cuban foreign policy from the late 1960s onwards, especially after 1970 when Cuba suffered a major economic setback in its sugar harvest which made the island even more intrinsically dependent on Soviet economic assistance, are clear in different geographic settings. In Latin America, Castro's move away from the violent road to change led to improved diplomatic relations with a number of governments in the region. Where Cuba had embassies only in Chile (until September 1973) and Mexico (which continued its diplomatic relations with Havana after the 1959 revolution), its embassy ties extended to Argentina, Colombia, Peru, and Venezuela by 1970. Havana became exceptionally active in the Caribbean during the 1970s, where the Soviet Union also began to emphasize progressive forces of change in its media. By 1979, Cuban embassies or embassies with nonresident ambassadors could be found in the Bahamas, Barbados, Grenada, Guyana, Jamaica, and Trinidad and Tobago. Meanwhile, Cuban school-construction teams, doctors, and technical assistants were at work in Guyana and Jamaica. In nearby Central America, Havana established a consulate with Costa Rica and embassies with Panama and Nicaragua (after Somoza's overthrow by the *Sandinistas* in 1979). And, as in the Caribbean, Cuba began to send teams of school teachers into Nicaragua during late 1979 and early 1980, personnel which reached 1,200 people by January 1980.[25]

As a Caribbean country with Caribbean cultural understanding, Cuba does in this region with its school-construction teams, educators, technical assistants and doctors what the Soviet Union cannot do—achieve ready acceptance and quick communication links through common cultural and historic ties. In doing so, Cuba's interests converge with those of the Soviets: both seek to ride the tide of national liberation movements, to strengthen indigenous national and leftist economic groups, and overall to share up the correlation of forces in favor of socialism as opposed to capitalism/imperialism. But within these Third World Caribbean and Central American settings, where Cubans work much easier than Soviets, one envisions Moscow riding the Cuban shirttails, an extra benefit for supporting Havana whose Caribbean version of proletarian internationalism fits the region's cultural complexities.

Cuba also began talks with the United States and pursued a number of policies designed to smooth the road toward renewed diplomatic and economic relations.[26] It also initiated diversified trade ties with West European countries and Japan. Each of these steps must have been perceived as potentially useful to the USSR, to the extent they might strengthen, on the one hand, *detente* between Moscow and Washington and, on the other, Cuba's own internal economic development. The latter would help to take some economic strain off the USSR which, given Cuba's increasingly heavy debt, would be of potentially great benefit.

Consider also Soviet and Cuban convergence in North Africa, South Africa and the Middle East. In contrast to Latin America, these regions provided enlarged opportunities for Moscow to apply military power in support of "national liberation" movements. And while Cuba had dropped its armed struggle thesis for Latin America, it found in Africa and the Middle East a substitute outlet for its militant revolutionary tendencies—in a region less likely to run the risk of direct confrontation with the United States and where its own forces could be combined with the logistical support, military arms, and military leadership of the USSR. Africa and the Middle East, then, became geographical focal points of both Soviet and Cuban support for compatible revolutionary movements.

A brief statistical overview indicates the convergence of Soviet and Cuban policies in these arenas. By 1978, the Soviet Union and East Europe had sent 12,070 military technicians into Africa, matched by 38,650 from Cuba. The bulk of Cuban military forces were in Angola (19,000) and Ethiopia (16,500), followed by 800 in Mozambique, 200 in Libya and Guinea, 150 in Equatorial Guinea, 140 in Guinea–Bissau and 15 in Algeria.[27] Elsewhere in the Middle East were 4,495 Soviet and East European military technicians, compared to 1,150 Cubans, the majority being in South Yemen (1,000) and Iraq (150). Cuban military advisers arrived in Angola in 1975 to train Angolans, and later that year additional Cuban troops went into action, while the Soviets provided weapons, economic assistance and logistical support—all of which required close policy coordination between the two countries.[28] Subsequent joint Cuban and Soviet military operations in Ethiopia during 1977–78 required continued close joint coordination, especially since Soviets and Cubans both were directly involved in the fighting against Somalia in the Ogaden area of eastern Ethiopia.[29] Certainly it can be argued that neither the Angolan or Ethiopian military operations could have been executed by the Cubans or Soviets alone.[30]

Both the Soviets and the Cubans, along with East European countries, also provide economic technicians to African and Middle Eastern countries. By 1978, the Soviet Union and East German technicians amounted to about 7,500 in Sub-Saharan Africa, compared to Cuba's approximately 11,000; these forces were located principally in the same countries where military personnel were active.[31] The Soviets and East Europeans stationed about 36,000 economic technicians in North Africa, most of them in Algeria and Libya, matched against Cuba's 450 in that region, most of them in Libya. And in the Middle East the Soviets and East Europeans had approximately 24,000, Cuba about 1,000. It should be noted here that the manpower in a number of these regions, especially in Sub-Saharan Africa, e.g., Angola, Ethiopia, and Mozambique, is supplied by Cuba, with the Soviet Union supplying large amounts of equipment, logistical support and financing, and the East Europeans providing additional technical skills and equipment.[32]

Following the Angolan and Ethiopian wars, Moscow and Havana continued other cooperative activities in Africa. Both provided support for military operations against the MPLA's rival liberation group in Angola, UNITA (National Liberation for the Total Independence of Angola) and advisers for the Mozambican military. Meanwhile, the Soviets and East Europeans concentrated on support to ZAPU (Zimbabwe African People's Union) where Cuba continued to train both ZAPU and ZANU (Zimbabwe African National Union). And in the late 1970s, both countries stepped up their Middle Eastern activities in South Yemen, and continued their support for the Palestinian Liberation Organization.

One special aspect of the Soviet–Cuban connection should be noted in the cases of Africa and the Middle East. The Cuban dimension should be considered not only as a surrogate force for the USSR, so frequently cited in studies of the affair, but also as an independent response to Cuba's own revolutionary impulses denied to Havana in Latin America. As a lesser-developed country with a history of resistance to U.S. imperialism, Cuba's activities in Africa undoubtedly were more acceptable than a unilateral Soviet military action could have been. Cuba's prior contacts with Angola and other countries in Africa, dating back to the early 1960s, gave it legitimacy that Moscow's great power status could not achieve. Cuban medical teams (990 in Algeria, Iraq and Libya, and approximately 900 in Angola alone in 1978; 100 in Nicaragua in 1979), technical assistance (approximately 1,300 Cubans in Angola during 1977 with more coming in thereafter) and educational training (1,500 Ethiopian and 1,200 Mozambican children in Cuba in 1978) generate added legitimacy to Cuba's African presence as a country dedicated to Third-World problems.[33] By associating with the Cuban presence, then, Soviet activities achieved the benefit of added respectability and legitimate presence—a feature of the relationship going substantially beyond the Cubans simply acting as surrogate mercenaries fighting Soviet battles by proxy.

Soviet and Cuban policies converged to some extent also within the nonaligned movement. Within this group of countries, made up of the developing countries of Africa, Asia, and Latin America, Castro set about to raise Cuba's status as a leader, exemplified by his extended tour of the Middle East, North Africa, and Black African states around Rhodesia in March 1977. He simultaneously pressed home the thesis that Moscow must be envisioned as a "natural ally" of the Third-World states. To the extent Cuba gained substantial support as friend and patron of Third-World countries, the Soviet Union would benefit by Castro's per-formance. Thus, from mid-1975 until about mid-1978, most African countries appeared to support Cuba's military assistance on the continent, just as Cuban support for the Palestine Libera-tion Organization encouraged friends in the Middle East. But, as events were to unfold by the end of 1978, the Cuban and Soviet presence in Africa were coming under increasing criticism by a number of African states. This antagonism toward Cuba in the Soviet context became clear at the Belgrade Conference of non-aligned countries in July 1978, followed by the Sixth Summit Meeting of Nonaligned States in August 1979, held in Havana itself.

INDEPENDENT ASPECTS OF CUBAN FOREIGN POLICY

When interviewed by CBS correspondent, Dan Rather, in September, 1979, Fidel Castro was asked what he was doing in Africa if not "just being a mercenary army for the Soviets."[34] Castro lashed back that Cuba was its own master—in Africa and elsewhere. In his words: "The Sixth Summit [of nonaligned countries] and the tremendous support our country received at the Sixth Summit is the clearest indication that the peoples know that Cuba has its own policy."[35] "At times," he said, referring to the Soviets, "we coincide. We don't always coincide."[36] The pattern of Cuba's foreign policy under Fidel Castro clearly tends to support this prognosis. To probe all the nooks and crannies behind this thesis is beyond the limits of space here, yet the broad outline of independence within the context of Cuba's need for Soviet economic and military resources can be drawn. Such an outline helps indicate not only just where, when and how Cuban policies serve the ends pursued by Moscow. For it also suggests Cuba's use of the Soviet Union to pursue its own policy ends and just how Cuban diplomacy operates by its own unique dictates. And to the degree we can highlight the motivating factors behind and nature of Cuba's own foreign policy impera-tives, we at least can focus on a more useful starting point to examine the Soviet–Cuban relationship in its meaning for the U.S.

Cuban foreign policy is in part shaped by traditional interests pursued by states in an international setting marked by the absence of guaranteed security and acceptable standards of econ-omic life. And like other countries—communist and non-com-munist alike—the island must maximize its power in quest of these physical security and economic development goals. While its options vary, events of the early 1960s and 1970s when the sugar harvest failed to meet expected targets indicated that ties with Moscow would guarantee Havana the economic and military power required to survive as a soverign country in the adversarial international arena. Not unnaturally, then, Havana shifted its "armed struggle" thesis in Latin America, designed to bring to power governments in sympathy with Cuba's revolutionary beliefs but failing to do so, toward a more peaceful posture in line with the Soviets, and found new outlets for its revolutionary tendencies in Africa. To seek Soviet economic and military support is simply a pragmatic response to Cuban state interests, one that Havana closely followed throughout the 1970s and into the 1980s.[37]

Unlike states that have not experienced a colonial past fol-lowed by a revolutionary movement, however, Cuban foreign-policy pragmatism is conditioned also by its colonial and revolutionary heritage. It is one peculiarly sensitive to past dom-inance by foreign powers, weakness in the world political and economic arena, internal fragmentation as a people, and struggle for economic and political independence, first from Spain, then from the U.S., Castro's brand of foreign policy is marked, there-fore, by its links to this historic legacy. It results in a drive to forge a new Cuban identity, one of national dignity in the global setting, close to home in the Caribbean and Central America, in the more distant but culturally related lands of Africa, and within the very heart of other excolonial countries, the nonaligned movement itself.[38] This thrust toward defining a new national image of Cuba—for Cubans at home and abroad and in the eyes of the world—forms another set of attitudes behind Havana's expanded state-to-state relations with Latin American governments in the 1970s, matched by technical aid, teachers, medical teams, and trade with leftist governments in the Caribbean and Central America, military action in Africa, and the drive for leadership of the nonaligned movement which Castro achieved in September 1979 when he was elected as new chairman of the movement for a three-year period.

Still a third set of *Cuban* as opposed to *Soviet* motivations in Havana's foreign policy stem from Cuba's revolutionary past and adoption of Marxism–Leninism as its guiding ideology. Castro's past revolutionary movement which overthrew Fulgencio Batista in 1959, the leaders of which continued to guide Cuban foreign policy twenty years later, leads quite naturally to a foreign policy in support of revolutionary movements elsewhere. This posture serves to improve Cuba's status position in world affairs, and with that comes new options for an improved security network and economic future. This support of struggles against imperialism, colonialism and neocolonialism—rooted in Cuba's own revolutionary past, is amplified through the prism of Marxist-Leninist ideology which was adopted by the *fidelistas* after 1959. Marxist-Leninism brought with it the continued perception of North America as leader of the imperialist camp, plus the concepts of struggle, self-sacrifice and work toward communism at home and abroad for an economically improved Cuba and a more just international world order in Cuba's perspective. Marxism–Leninism inspired, as well, notions of inevitable progress and victory for the Cuban cause as the correlation of world forces between socialism and communism, on the one hand, and capitalism/imperialism on the other shifted toward the former.

As to techniques of influence, Cuba clearly has developed its own apart from the USSR, although aided in their development through Moscow's economic and military support. A strong military establishment capable of waging conventional and guerrilla warfare is one major instrument of power. The Cuban military—amounting to approximately 117,000 individuals in the late 1970s and one of the three largest military establishments in Latin America (second only to Brazil and about equal to Argentina)—became increasingly more competent and technically trained in the mid-1970s. When coupled with the efforts to institutionalize and strengthen the civilian administration during this period, and in light of USSR-U.S. detente relations which reduced the North American threat, Cuba's army found natural outlets in Africa in pursuit of Havana's foreign policy objectives, albeit greatly supported by Moscow. The first application of military power came in defense of Angola's MPLA in 1975, a regime with which Cuba had established its own contracts early in the 1960s. Fighting on behalf of the Ethiopian central government followed, with more Cuban troops sent elsewhere in Africa and the Middle East.

The Cuban military is by no means the only instrument of Cuban foreign policy. Havana developed its own brand of foreign aid, one highly amenable to Third-World countries, and one not excessively expensive. These are the personnel that form Cuba's medical teams, technical assistants, construction workers and teachers sent to Jamaica, Guyana, Grenada, Panama, Nicaragua, Angola, Ethiopia and elsewhere during the 1970s. Cuba is moving very strongly toward training of medical students for international service, with 1,000 students to be graduated every year from 1981 onward. Consider, too, the Cuban work in international organizations as vehicles to further its foreign policy objectives: in the Latin American Economic System (SELA; excluding the United States), the joint Caribbean Shipping Company (NAMUCAR), the United Nations, where its work on the Decolonization Committee projected Puerto Rico into the limelight as a U.S. "colony," and of course in the nonaligned movement of Third-World countries. Throughout many of these organizations runs the personal diplomacy of Fidel Castro himself, *lider maximo* on the island and extremely persuasive within international organizations. Especially important among Cuba's policy instruments is its extraordinary growth in maritime strength, not least of which is the fishing fleet operations on which it can draw for technical assistance in maritime matters.

The projection of these techniques into Cuban foreign policy produced a number of benefits for Cuba, as well as for the USSR, throughout the 1970s. In Caribbean and Central American international affairs, Cuba's presence had expanded broadly, which must have enhanced Havana's sense of physical security and revolutionary status compared to a Cuba more isolated and threatened in its own backyard during the 1960s when it pursued armed struggle tactics. Heads of states and high level ministers traveling between Cuba and Guyana, Jamaica, Trinidad and Tobago, and Panama during the mid-1970s could only drive home this "success" interpretation of Cuban foreign policy goals, as did the aid, scientific, technical, educational, cultural, and trade accords signed with these countries during the period.[39] And consider the Sixth Summit meeting of nonaligned countries in September, 1979, where these Caribbean and Central American countries, along with Grenada, Nicaragua, Surinam, and a representative of the Puerto Rican Independence Movement sung the praises of Cuban foreign policy. Meanwhile, Costa Rica, Dominica, and St. Lucia were brought into the movement as observers, while the conference as a whole expressed support for other Cuban neighbors in the Caribbean—Belize, Guadalupe, Martinique, and French Guiana, all locked in anticolonial struggles.[40] By September, 1979, the number of Caribbean and Latin American members and observers of the nonaligned movement over which Castro governed as chairman had grown to 24. This multiplying of Cuba's friends through Havana's independent efforts undoubtedly not only reduced the threatening Washington shadow. It also indicated the uniqueness and flexibility of Cuban economic and diplomatic power in regions close to its own shores. Should Moscow's economic and military support to Cuba begin to dry up in the future, then these regional ties could be of benefit to Cuba.

Elsewhere in Latin America, Cuba gained acceptance by a number of other countries to add to its sense of physical security in the hostile environment created by Cuban–U.S. adversarial relations since 1959. Diplomatic relations with Argentina, Colombia, Mexico, Peru, and Venezuela improved and became part of this successful record, as did Venezuela's agreement to supply crude oil to Cuba in exchange for Soviet oil to Venezuelan customers in Western Europe and Colombia's agreement to repair Cuban ships in Cartagena in the late 1970s. And while some South American countries, e.g., Chile, Uruguay, and Paraguay, still look unfavorably upon Cuba, others from Mexico to Argentina perceive the island not as a Soviet proxy but as a country that has defied U.S. pressures since 1959. Moreover, the *Sandinista* guerrilla struggle in Nicaragua, depicted in the United States as Cuban intervention, brought no direct military Cuban involvement, but produced, instead, open money and arms from Venezuela, Panama, and Costa Rica. The extent of Central and South American support in that affair, despite the geographic presence of Communist Cuba, illustrates again the extent to which Cuba had been accepted back into the family of Latin American states by the late 1970s as an independent actor rather than as a surrogate of the USSR.

Cuban support for African and Middle Eastern regimes also produced benefits for Havana as an independent actor in world affairs. While the presence of 38,650 Cuban troops in underdeveloped countries, principally Africa, in 1978 did not meet with total Third-World acceptance, examined below, Havana's presence was welcomed in an impressively large number of countries compared to the decade of the 1960s. These included three North African countries (Algeria, Morocco, Libya), eight Sub-Saharan African states (Angola, Equatorial Africa, Ethiopia, Guinea, Guinea-Bissau, Mali, and Mozambique) and two Middle Eastern countries (Iraq and South Yemen)—measured in military presence alone. And to be sure, the Belgrade Conference of nonaligned countries in July, 1978, and the Sixth Summit meeting of nonaligned states in 1979 generated opposition to Cuba's military posture. But Castro nevertheless was elected chairman of the nonaligned movement for three years in 1979, the final document of the conference reflected many of Cuban perspectives, and not surprisingly, Moscow greatly lauded Cuba's role in the nonaligned movement.

This brief overview of the independent thrust in Cuban foreign policy suggests three key points. First, Cuba is winning friends (and some enemies) with its independent activities—in the Caribbean, Central America, South America, Africa, and the Middle East. Second, in accomplishing this goal, Havana creates independent lines of action amenable to its own quest for leverage in a rapidly changing and insecure international arena which could be used not only to advance the revolutionary causes within the underdeveloped world with which it so closely identifies, but also to pursue alternative options to advance Cuban physical security and continued economic growth. Third, given the facts of global energy and natural resources problems and future potential constraints on Soviet capability to support Cuba along with its other client states, these independent aspects of Cuban foreign policy may become increasingly critical for Havana in the future. It undoubtedly is the same line of thought that drives Cuba into economic links also with Western European countries and Japan, and continues to attract it to future economic ties with the United States. Just how strong the independent thread in Cuban foreign policy will become in the future is difficult to say, but it undoubtedly will turn in part upon Cuba's bilateral relations with the U.S. in terms of how far they move toward normalized economic ties.

LIMITS TO SOVIET AND CUBAN INFLUENCE IN THIRD WORLD SETTINGS

A major aspect of Soviet-Cuban relations is the extent to which their converging policy techniques and objectives are constrained in actual influence. The expanding shadow of Moscow and Havana over Africa, Latin America, and parts of the Middle East is one thing; the degree of real power exerted in the present and future is another. A balanced perspective of the relationship, then, requires not only delineating the nature of Cuba's convergence with Soviet diplomacy, but as well the obstacles to influence that lie in the path of each country's activities abroad. These constraints operate within the domestic realm of both Moscow and Havana, in the nature of their bilateral relations and, of course, through forces at work in the Third World.

Economic difficulties faced by the USSR and Cuba pose one set of constraints. They impede each state's capacity to extend more economic assistance abroad, reduce their image as a model of successful economic growth and make each country dependent on outside help. Best known are Soviet economic problems that captured news headlines during the 1970s: agricultural deficiencies, increasing labor and energy shortages, problems in consumer production, and continued need for external supply of raw materials, markets, and high-level technology. Combine these features with Soviet trade imbalances with many developing countries, its nonparticipation in the dominant international economic organizations, e.g., World Bank and International Monetary Fund, and the large number of credits which go undrawn with developing states, and the picture of a very limited economic actor quickly emerges.

On the Cuban side of the equation lies another economy undergoing severe strains by the late 1970s. Tentatively held together by the estimated $9-million-per-day support from the USSR—which, incidentally, weakens Soviet capacity to extend the same kind of treatment broadly throughout the Third World—Havana entered the 1980s plagued by productivity difficulties, indiscipline, irresponsibility, complacency, worker apathy, and other serious problems.[41] These beset the sugar industry, food production, transportation, foreign trade, and industrial development. Cuban economic problems in light of the $9-million-per-day Soviet support illuminate not only the economic dependence of Cuba on the Soviet Union and Havana's economic weakness relative to its foreign-policy goals, but also the costs experienced by Moscow in pursuing its Cuban adventure.

Soviet and Cuban military capability, admittedly extensive as their African campaigns from the mid-1970s onward demonstrate, nevertheless should be put into perspective. Students of Soviet military power, for example, argue that Moscow's activities in Africa, or the January, 1980, Afghanistan invasion, should not be projected as military action replicated easily in every Third-World country. Major difficulties face the Soviets in more distant operations, especially when required to support a large invasion force by sea. The ability of Moscow's large blue-water navy to fight a protracted war is questionable, given the logistical problems of supplies and replacements, the nature of Soviet naval capabilities and practices, and the narrow straits and waterways through which Moscow's ships must pass in coming and going to home ports. All of these difficulties weigh not only upon future Soviet capability and intent, but also upon the Cubans, given their own reliance on the USSR for logistical support to get to and fight in distant locations.

The Cuban military, on which the Soviets came to rely so heavily in Angola and Somalia campaigns, is meanwhile still another question as to future cooperation with Moscow. The impact of military activities abroad on the Cuban economy is diffficult to measure, but decline in Cuban economic growth appears to be one consequence of the Angolan War—as indeed may be other subjective problems noted by Castro in his complaints about worker-productivity in December, 1979. As one student of this situation notes, "Cuba is still an underdeveloped country, with limited trained personnel. To win wars, it must commit its best people overseas, who are thus taken away from productive and social activities at home."[42] Should these responses increase, given their economic and social fallouts, the future use of Cuban troops abroad in support of revolutionary objectives may have to be revised into alternate sources of external influence. In any case, the economic costs of military victories are not strangers in Cuba today—not to the Cubans and certainly not to the Soviets.

Global interdependence—by which is meant the dependence of states on external commodities and resources; linked to consequent vulnerabilities—conditions both the USSR and Cuba in their capacity to influence events abroad. Soviet food vulnerability, for example, weakens the USSR's ability to respond to Third-World food needs, rather causing it to purchase grain on the world food market that reduces available food supplies and drives up prices for lesser-developed food-deficit countries. But the big issue is oil, where Soviet oil production may not be sufficient to meet Moscow's East European and Cuban client demands in the future. Moscow's export of four nuclear reactors to Cuba, scheduled to go on line in the mid-1980s, is designed to offset this eventuality, but it may be insufficient as Cuba's industrial growth places upward demands on Soviet oil. Cuba, meanwhile, continues to be vulnerable owing to its dependence on external capital, Western technology, and markets. Just what the future holds for changes in Cuban foreign policy due to these external dependencies is difficult to measure, but one could foresee new opportunities for U.S.-Cuban rapprochement, especially should events unfold along specific lines: (1) constrained Soviet economic deliveries, (2) unacceptable costs associated with Cuban military adventures in Africa, or (3) unbearable Third-World pressures on Cuba for its Soviet relationship.

Both Moscow and Havana are outmatched by Western capitalist lending institutions. Neither countries participate in the World Bank nor in the International Monetary Fund (IMF), as noted above, and both of these international organizations continue to be sought out as sources of capital within the Third World. Private foreign investment, meanwhile, continues to be invited into many a Third-World country, despite both Moscow and Havana's brave talk about the crisis of capitalism and the shift in world "correlation of forces" between socialism and capitalism/imperialism toward the former.[43] While this is exceptionally true of Latin America and the Caribbean, the attraction to Western capital is strong also in parts of Africa, the Middle East, and Southeast Asia. And it is true even in countries noted to be "leftist" in nature, such as Jamaica and Mexico. An international economic system dominated by Western capitalist institutions, then, continues to impede Soviet and Cuban influence in foreign policy toward the Third World.

Nationalism remains high throughout the Third World and constantly conditions Soviet and Cuban successes and failures. The Soviet record, despite the attention to its expanded presence and power projection during the 1970s, is not all that favorable in Third-World regions. It lost power in a number of countries over the years—Egypt, Somalia, Ghana, Indonesia, Iran, and even China, as the Sino–Soviet rift gathered steam. And as 1970 ended, Moscow's invasion of Afghanistan inflamed Third-World nationalist sentiments, bringing censure against the Kremlin for its Afghanistan adventure through a momentous United Nations General Assembly vote and later when 36 foreign ministers attending the Islamic Conference in Islamabad, Pakistan, took Moscow to task in two separate resolutions dealing with its activities in Afghanistan and in the Horn of Africa.[44] Previously, a number of African states had become especially displeased with both Moscow and Havana for their military activities, as expressed in the 1978 Belgrade Conference of Nonaligned Countries and within the Organization of African States (OAU).[45]

Negative nationalist reactions against Cuba and the Soviets are not restricted to African countries. Within the Caribbean, Central, and South America, a number of states are not sanguine about Havana's expanding presence. Haiti and the Dominican Republic, traditionally fearful of Cuba, given its proximity and greater size, are two cases in point. El Salvador, Guatemala, and Honduras also fear Cuban involvement with leftist forces there, and Cuban–Brazilian relations were strained by the end of the 1970s. Neither Chile, Paraguay, or Uruguay are close friends with Havana. Despite Havana's generally broader acceptance into the family of Latin

American countries, then, several states continue to resist this trend, and strong Latin American support, not surprisingly, helped to prevent Cuba acquiring a Security Council seat in the UN in January, 1980.[46] Third-World nationalism runs in a variety of directions, and rivers once flowing with Cuban policies can quickly be rerouted.

Havana's close links with Moscow produce negative as well as positive political outcomes in the eyes of Cuba's Third-World colleagues. And, as the 1980s began, the negative results seemed to be on the rise. Certainly Cuba earned the chairmanship of the non-aligned movement for a three-year period beginning in 1979, as the Sixth Summit Meeting of Nonaligned Countries came to a close in Havana. But it came at a time of growing strains between Cuba and many of its lesser-developed allies in the nonaligned movement which eventually resulted in Cuba's losing its bid for a Security Council seat in the UN. And Moscow's invasion of Afghanistan in January, 1980, did not help Cuba's nonaligned posture, not only due to Moscow's violation of Afghanistan's sovereignty. For the Afghanistan invasion raised the spectre of a Soviet Union heedless of Third-World interests and sensitivities, a military giant acting in its sphere of influence reminiscent of Washington's previous actions in the Caribbean, and as such, open game for criticism by the sovereignty-conscious Third-World states, with Cuba caught in the crossfire.

Cuba may suffer from its Soviet embrace from yet another perspective, as far as its Third-World nonaligned colleagues are concerned. Moscow has not demonstrated great capacity to respond to Third-World demands in nonmilitary global issues. In world conference after conference, Third-World states increasingly chastize the developed Socialist countries, including the USSR, for their ineffective attention to central global issues in the North–South dialogue on an economic development strategy for the 1980s. These issues include food, technology-transfer, more open and accessible markets, and available capital, the latter most often cited as a need for a minimum 0.7 percent of the developed country's gross national product (GNP). Moscow's claims that the blame for Third-World economic difficulties lay with the Western capitalist countries' past colonial policies, not with the USSR, simply had begun to fall upon inattentive ears by the late 1970s. As these global issues reach higher visibility and volatility in the 1980s, Cuba's close connection with an "irresponsible" USSR will not improve Havana's standing within the Third-World nonaligned movement.

CONCLUSION

Moscow's ties with Cuba, undoubtedly considered successful from Soviet perspectives, nevertheless continued to plague Soviet-U.S. ties and U.S.-Cuban relations. Interpreted in Washington circles as evidence of Cuban "surrogate" relations with the Kremlin, Havana's African military adventures became the key obstacle to improved U.S.-Cuban economic links and yet another obstacle in the path of ratifying the Strategic Arms Limitations Talks Treaty. Closer to home, the Soviet-Cuban relationship became translated into a direct hemispheric threat by several U.S. congressmen as *Sandinista* attacks on Nicaragua's Somoza were linked to a Soviet-Cuban shadow and as Soviet troops in Cuba became evidence of a threatening "brigade" in 1979. While Moscow might envision its Cuban partners as extremely beneficial to its Third-World objectives, costs of the relationship continued to be high from both Soviet and Cuban long-range interests with the United States.

From Washington's position, despite congressional reactions to the Soviet-Cuban "threat," the nature of Soviet-Cuban convergence and of independent Cuban motivations suggests much to be gained from closer economic ties—as a number of scholars have been urging for years. Given Cuba's dependence on outside energy sources, capital, and high-level technology, the evidence suggests that Cuba would be receptive to stronger overtures from Washington. Widened contacts with the U.S. would allow the independent nationalists threads of Cuban foreign policy to be strengthened, would reduce Cuba's dependence on the USSR, and would diffuse the image of Washington as Cuba's natural external adversary. But given Moscow's invasion of Afghanistan and rapidly deteriorating U.S.-Soviet relations as the 1980s began, it is unlikely that these are propitious conditions for renewed U.S. overtures to Cuba— ironically at precisely the time they might be welcome in Havana, given the shadow falling over Cuba's own relationship with a militant USSR from the point of view of its other Third-World colleagues.

The possibility of U.S. policy-makers reading too much power into the Soviet–Cuban relationship distinctly exists, and with it the probability of inappropriate policy responses. The misconception of Soviet aggressive military troops in Cuba in August, 1979, triggered quick military action in the Caribbean that undermined U.S. relations in the region. The belief that Moscow's shadow lay behind *Sandinista* nationalism in Nicaragua unleashed distorted U.S. congressional perceptions and responses that were distinctly against the tides of change in that country. And the notion of a Soviet threat through Cuba in effect eroded congressional enthusiasm for the SALT II treaty, which must have suggested to Soviet decision-makers that they had little to lose in their military gambit in Afghanistan. When diplomatic historians look back on the late 1970s and early 1980s, they may well reach the conclusion that Washington's misconceived Soviet and Cuban power led to exaggerating Moscow's strengths and underestimating its limits. This tendency, in part, may have led the Soviet Union to take risks that it mught not have done otherwise, resulting in even higher tension between the two countries, not only over the Cuban relationship, but also elsewhere in the Third World where superpower conflict had so centered in the 1970s.

FOOTNOTES

1. On early Soviet attitudes toward the developing countries, *see* Roger E. Kanet, "The Soviet Union and the Colonial Question, 1917–1953," ed. Kanet, *The Soviet Union and the Developing Nations* (Baltimore: The Johns Hopkins University Press, 1974), chap. 1. For background reading on the history of communism in Latin America, Rollie Poppino, *International Communism in Latin America; a History of the Movement, 1917–1963* (London: The Free Press of Glencoe, 1964). On the origin and nature of the Cuban Communist party before Castro's victory in 1959, see Andrés Suárez, *Cuba: Castroism and Communism, 1959–1966* (Cambridge: the M.I.T. Press, 1969).

2. The special role of Cuba in leading the forces of anticolonialism and anti-imperialism in the Caribbean and Latin America is regularly cited in key Soviet periodicals, such as *International Affairs* (Moscow), and on Soviet radio broadcasts dealing with Latin American issues.

3. *Communist Aid Activities in Non-Communist Less-Developed Countries 1978*, National Foreign Assessment Center, Central Intelligence Agency, September 1979, pp. 9–10.

4. *Ibid.*, pp. 7-10.

5. See Jorge I. Dominguez, "Cuban Foreign Policy," *Foreign Affairs*, 57(1) (Fall 1978): 90.

6. *Ibid.*

7. *Ibid.*

8. For examples, Suárez, *op. cit.*; Edward Gonzalez, *Cuba Under Castro: The Limits of Charisma* (Boston: Houghton Mifflin Co., 1974); and Jorge I. Dominguez, *Cuba: Order and Revolution* (Cambridge: Harvard University Press, 1978).

9. Gonzalez and Dominguez generally stress the independent strands in Cuban foreign policy; for an alternate view of Cuban-Soviet relations, see Leon Goure and Morris Rothenberg, *Soviet Penetration of Latin America* (Coral Gables: University of Miami Press, 1975), chap. 2.

10. Michael D. Davidchik and Robert B. Mahoney, Jr., "Soviet Civil Fleets and the Third World," *Soviet Naval Diplomacy*, eds. Bradford Dismukes and James McConnell (New York: Pergamon Press, 1979), pp. 317-335. On Soviet foreign policy objectives, see also *The Soviet Union and the Third World: A Watershed in Great Power Policy?* Report to the Committee on International Relations, House of Representatives (Washington: U.S. Government Printing Office, 1977; and *Strategic Survey 1978* (London: The International Institute for Strategic Studies (IISS), 1978), pp. 1-2, 4-8.

11. Communist Aid Activities in Non-Communist Less-Developed Countries 1978; *op. cit.*; *ibid.* for 1977.

12. S. Mishin, "Latin America: Two Trends of Development," *International Affairs* (Moscow), 6 (June 1976): 54; L. Klochkovsky, "The Struggle for Economic Emancipation in Latin America," *International Affairs* (Moscow), 4 (April 1979): 39-47.

13. Klochkovsky, *op. cit.*; A. Shulgovsky, "The Social and Political Development in Latin America," *International Affairs* (Moscow), 11 (November 1979): 52-61.

14. Viktor Volsky, "Relative Maturity, Absolute Dependence," *World Marxist Review* (June 1979): 40-45.

15. *Communist Aid Activities in Non-Communist Less-Developed Countries 1978, op. cit.*, pp. 14-15, 18.

16. S. Mishin, "Latin America: Two Trends of Development," *op. cit.*

17. *Ibid.* Also A. Shulgovsky, *op. cit.* and L. Klochkovsky, *op. cit.*

18. Davidchik and Mohoney, Jr., "Soviet Civil Fleets and the Third World," *op. cit.*, p. 329.

19. From the late 1960s onward the Latin American countries demonstrated escalating concern for control over state resources such as oil, copper, and tin in order to stimulate economic development. Latin American

commitment and duty to control their resources and process of development were enunciated at major meetings at Vina del Mar, Chile (1969) and Lima, Peru (1971).

20. See Mishin, *op. cit.*

21. Soviet analysts are quick to point out that the Havana conference of nonaligned countries is the first to be held in Latin America, no small achievement for Castro's Cuba. A. Klimov, "On the Havana Conference," *International Affairs* (Moscow), 9 (September 1979): 44.

22. See Goure and Rothenberg, *op. cit.*, pp. 1-7.

23. *Ibid.*

24. D. Lozinov, "The Liberation Struggle in Latin America," *International Affairs*, 8 (August 1977): 39-45.

25. *Granma Weekly Review in English*, January 13, 1980.

26. These policies include inviting American businessmen into Cuba, hosting Cuban exiles in Havana, and releasing Cuban prisoners to go to the United States. See *The Christian Science Monitor*, November 17, 1978.

27. *Communist Aid Activities in Non-Communist Less-Developed Countries 1978, op. cit.*, p. 4.

28. Dominguez, "Cuban Foreign Policy," *op. cit.*, p. 96.

29. *Keesings Contemporary Archives*, May 26, 1978, pp. 28989-28995. David D. Newsom, "Communism in Africa," *Africa Report* (January-February 1980), pp. 41-48.

30. Dominguez, "Cuban Foreign Policy," *op. cit.*, p. 101.

31. Newson, "Communism in Africa," p. 45.

32. *Ibid.*;

33. Cuba's medical teams deserve special attention. In November, 1979, Havana radio announced that more than 1,000 medical students will be graduating every year from 1981 onward; they will allow Cuba to increase its international medical aid. Havana radio noted that 11,000 students were in medical training as of 1979, plus another 1,000 in stomatology and another 1,400 were student nurses. Cuba provided medical help to 20 developing countries in Africa, Asia, Latin America and the Caribbean through its 2,400 doctors, nurses, and medical technicians abroad. *Havana International Radio Service*, November 28, 1979.

34. *Granma*, October 7, 1979, p. 4.

35. *Ibid.*

36. *Ibid.*

37. On Cuban foreign policy during the 1970s, see Edward Gonzalez, "Cuban Foreign Policy," *Problems of Communism*, 26 (November-December 1977): 1-15.

38. By 1976, Fidel Castro had begun to speak of Cuba as a "Latin-African" people—"enemies of colonialism, neocolonialism, racism and apartheid, which Yankee imperialism aids and protects." *Granma*, May 2, 1976, p. 3.

39. Cuba and Jamaica, for example, signed an agreement whereby Cuba expected to import goods from Jamaica worth U.S. $14 million in 1980. See *Latin America Weekly Report*, December 14, 1979, p. 4.

40. *Granma*, September 16, 1979, p. 16.

41. *Granma*, December 9, 1979, pp. 2-3.

42. Dominguez, "Cuban Foreign Policy," p. 104.

43. *Ibid.*

44. *Christian Science Monitor*, January 30, 1980, p. 1. The United Nations vote was 104-18 to "deplore" Soviet moves in Afghanistan and to demand a troop withdrawal. Previously the USSR had used its veto power to kill a similar resolution in the Security Council. Cuba voted against the resolution, along with 17 other countries, including Grenada in the Caribbean. *New York Times*, January 15, 1980.

45. *Keesings Contemporary Archives*, October 27, 1978, pp. 29281-29283.

46. *Christian Science Monitor*, January 11, 1980.

CHAPTER SIX

OIL AND SOVIET POLICY IN THE PERSIAN GULF

David Lynn Price

Turbulence and violent change characterized the Persian Gulf during much of 1978 and 1979. Each crisis in the area threatened the regional *status quo* and most political groups and governments opposed to the *status quo* felt drawn, for one reason or another, toward closer association with the Soviet Union. In Ethiopia, Lieutenant Colonel Mengistu Haile Mariam relied heavily on Cuban and Soviet military aid in his counter-offensive against and victory over Somalia's ill-conceived adventures in the Ogaden; and in the second half of the year, he launched a similar Ethiopian–Cuban–Soviet tripartite offensive against Eritrean separatist movements in his country's northern coastal province on the Red Sea. Elsewhere, a savage *coup d'etat* in April brought a pronouncedly Marxist regime to power under Nur Mohammed Taraki in Afghanistan. Then, in June and July, the leading political figures of the Yemen Arab Republic (YAR) to the north and the People's Democratic Republic of Yemen (PDRY) to the south were assassinated, provoking serious border clashes between the two strategically located states and bringing to power in the PDRY radical pro-Soviet elements which made the PDRY the first professed Marxist republic in Arabia. Under the leadership of Abd al-Fattah Isma'il, Secretary General of the Yemen Socialist

Party, and Ali Nasir Muhammad al-Hasani, Chairman of the Council of Ministers, South Yemeni forces penetrated deep inside North Yemen in March, 1979, before withdrawing their troops in the aftermath of strong international reaction against their advance. Finally, in Iran, after 18 months of protracted crisis and political violence, Shah Mohammed Reza Pahlavi was forced to leave the country in January, 1979, by a loose but popular movement—which included some leftist forces—spearheaded by the Shi'ite Muslim leader Ayatollah Ruhollah Khomeyni.

The cumulative effects of these changes are still being assessed by the states of the region, in particular, Iraq, Saudi Arabia, and Kuwait. From the regional perspective and what happened indeed seems alarming. The Soviet position appears to have improved spectacularly and with unexpected ease and speed. Conversely, the Western position seems irretrievable. But is this evaluation accurate? The answer depends to a very large degree on how one interprets Soviet behavior in the region.

THE ORIGINS OF SOVIET BEHAVIOR

Currently, two theories are popular for explaining Soviet behavior in the Persian Gulf. The first is that Moscow's policy is determined by a "grand design," a classic combination of strategy and tactics in which long-term and short-term aims merge to promote Soviet communism, to establish pro-Soviet regimes, to erode Western and Chinese presence, and to use the Gulf (or any other region, for that matter) as a springboard for later achievements elsewhere.[1] This theory is based on the hypothesis that Soviet foreign policy is evolutionary and historical, and certainly there is evidence of long-term Soviet interest in the Gulf region. In November, 1940, for example, while German–Soviet relations were still determined by the Nazi–Soviet nonaggression pact signed in August in 1939, V. M. Molotov told Hitler's Ambassador in Moscow that the Soviet government was prepared ". . . to accept the text of the Four-Power Pact . . . provided that the area south of Tatum and Baku in the general direction of the Persian Gulf is recognized as the center of the aspirations of the Soviet Union."[2] Later in August, 1941, after the German invasion of the USSR, Soviet and British troops occupied Iran and, as in World War I, divided it into Russian and British zones, with the

USSR controlling the northern provinces. Iran was an important corridor for the shipment of U.S. supplies to the Soviet Union during the war, and once the war ended the USSR was extremely reluctant to leave. Soviet forces remained in the country and in December, 1945, established the Autonomous Republic of Azerbaydzhan and the Kurdish People's Republic in their zone. When Western allied pressure eventually compelled the USSR to withdraw its troops however, both republics collapsed.

On the face of things, then, there is some substantive basis for asserting the existence of a Soviet grand design. But if such design does truly exist, Moscow has not pursued it with any vigor for more than 30 years. Had the USSR carried out a sustained vigorous, and coherent policy toward the Gulf during the postwar period, political changes in the region would surely have reflected it, for the Soviet Union has had ample opportunities to supplant the West. The destruction in Iraq of one branch of the Hashemite dynasty in 1958 sharply curtailed British influence in the area and damaged the Central Treaty Organization (CENTO). But no Soviet-oriented alliance system displaced it and, when the British withdrew entirely from the Gulf between 1968 and 1971, the vacuum they left was filled not by the USSR but by a loose regional security understanding between Saudi Arabia and Iran. Later, in 1975, the Soviet-backed Marxist revolt by the Popular Front for the Liberation of Oman (PFLO) in Oman's Dhofar Province was successfully put down.[3] And even the 15-year treaty of friendship and cooperation signed in 1972 by the USSR and Iraq has not deterred the Baghdad government from persecuting local Communists and seeking Western development aid.

In short, few pro-Soviet governments have been installed in the Gulf over the last 30 years, and between 1973 and 1978, the only objective factor favoring the USSR in the region appeared to be the independence exercised by the Organization of Petroleum Exporting Countries (OPEC), which, to protect its own interests, was prepared to propose and apply economic policies damaging to the West. Moscow accepts this gain from the oil-producing states without any ideological reservations, despite the fact that the OPEC membership on the whole favors the capitalist system.

That the USSR has missed—or chosen to miss—its opportunities in the Gulf over the last three decades probably explains the popularity and credibility of the second theory which has been proposed to explain Soviet behavior, i.e., the "muddle" theory. According to this hypothesis, the Gulf has been of only peripheral interest to Moscow, coming after Europe, China, the Middle East, and the Indian Ocean region on the list of major Soviet concerns. Consequently, the USSR has not had any set policy for dealing with the Gulf and has relied on expediency and opportunism as the basis of its behavior, trying to take advantage of each opportunity for short- or long-term Soviet gain which has presented itself.[4] Soviet policy in the region, in other words, has been essentially reactive. But the political events of 1978 and 1979 in the Gulf weakened the Western position and, as a result, were objective factors which seemed to be fulfilling the Soviet aim of eroding the Western position in the region.

SOVIET ENERGY NEEDS

In early 1979, Soviet diplomatic overtures to Saudi Arabia were intensified in an attempt to fully exploit the opportunities presented by the change of regime in Iran and by Arab resentment at the U.S. role in the Egyptian–Israeli accord. But the Soviet leaders were not only seeking to expand their own political influence in the Middle East (at the expense of the West). They rather were laying the foundations for future economic cooperation with the major Arab oil producers as energy demands in the USSR and Eastern Europe become acute.

Until 1967, Soviet interest in Arab oil was not pronounced, though when it became so it was expressed as a principle of economic warfare against the West. At the Khartoum Summit Conference in August, 1967, Arab states met and, *inter alia* ended the Arab oil oil embargo that followed the Six-Day War. As the summit conference approached, Radio Moscow's domestic service affirmed (25 August) ". . . the Arabs rightly assume that a blow against the oil interests of the West will accelerate the elimination of the consequences of aggression."[5]

But this does not in any way imply that OPEC is a Soviet instrument nor that it is likely to become so. Recent Soviet interest in oil imports has placed more emphasis on oil imports as a commercial necessity. If all that were involved were Soviet domestic requirements, Soviet reserves are more than adequate for the forseeable future. But the Soviet Union has commitments to other Communist states. At present some 70-75 percent of the oil imports of COMECON states are supplied by the Soviet Union; in the period 1976-1980, some 354-million tons of oil products were delivered to other COMECON members. The trouble is that between 1970-1990 the energy requirements of COMECON (excluding the USSR) are expected to grow by 250 percent. "At the same time the main centers of extraction and production in the Soviet Union are moving more and more to eastern regions which involves a significant rise in costs."[6] At this rate the cost of East Siberian oil will be so high as to be prohibitive. Saudi oil, therefore, is a much more attractive proposition—but it must be paid for in hard currency. Saudi Arabia has no desire to purchase nonconvertible rubles which can only be spent in the USSR.

It is possible for the East European states to negotiate separately with Gulf states for oil supplies, e.g., Yugoslavia and Romania, but again, the problem of noncovertible currencies has first to be solved. The Russians face another obstacle in negotiating Arab oil imports and that is the competition they present to the petrochemical industries of the Arab oil states. The Gulf states of Iran, Iraq, Saudi Arabia, Kuwait, and Qatar, have petrochemical plants in operation and such plants are meant to provide an alternate source of income for these states which will enable them to reduce their dependence on oil exports. But competitive Soviet ammonia sales could average 3.1-million tons a year in 1978-87 and it is unlikely that this quantity can be absorbed by world markets.[7] In recent years world ammonia exports have averaged only slightly more than 3-million tons—at a time when prices and profits have been depressed. So if Russia seeks to import Arab oil, the Arab states are entitled for a reduction in Soviet-petrochemical production to allow the Arabs to enter the market. The prospects for the Soviet Union of negotiating Arab oil on favorable terms are slim. For the foreseeable future the oil market will be a seller's market; the pressure is for conservation and cut-backs. The Soviet Union cannot at the moment, offer realistic barter terms to Saudi Arabia, the only oil producer with long-term surplus production capacity. The range of Soviet barter goods is restricted to cultural exchanges, arms, timber products, and technical assistance—all of which the West provides at a higher quality on straight commercial terms.

Therefore, what option does the Soviet Union have in dealing with Saudi Arabia? The only solution which would fully satisfy Soviet requirements would be for a pro-Moscow regime to take over Saudi Arabia, make it a "people's republic" and join COMECON. But this is to presuppose that Soviet economic interest in the Gulf would predominate over the more classical interests of Soviet policy in the region, namely, strategic, political, and ideological. The diplomatic history of Soviet foreign policy does not provide a single piece of evidence of such behavior. If the Soviet Union were to conspire for the Finlandization of Saudi Arabia—or for that matter, any of the states of the region— it would be as a result of a wide range of complex factors.

Until recently, authenticated Soviet concern on oil supplies was difficult to obtain. What information was available was confined to strong denial of Western assessments of Soviet energy reserves, prepared mainly by the Central Intelligence Agency (CIA). The Kremlin's unease at the deteriorating energy situation was revealed in a decree issued by the Communist Party Central Committee and the Council of Ministers in June, 1979.[8] The decree stressed the need to bring quickly into operation several new projects in the fuel sector of the economy. A "save-it" campaign was launched in which the thrifty were praised and the wasteful criticized.

This fuel-saving campaign appeared to confirm CIA projections that Soviet oil production would start declining in 1980 or 1981. A CIA report of July 1979 quoted U.S. Congressman Les Aspin who said that, ". . . a murderously steep decline is expected to set in after 1982." This would mean that instead of exporting some 150-million tons of oil annually, as in recent years, the Soviet Union will have to import tens of millions of tons to maintain supplies to the economies of the Soviet bloc.

There is a school of thought which believes that the Soviet could force the USSR to move into the Gulf and seize the oil fields. U.S. Air Force Secretary Thomas C. Reed predicted that the USSR will be compelled to act in the Gulf and take over the oil fields even at the risk of nuclear confrontation with the U.S. "They (the USSR) will not be able to produce oil and having no hard currencies acceptable to the OPEC exporters, they cannot buy oil . . . it is unlikely the Soviet will allow this situation to develop."[9]

STRATEGIC INTERESTS

Until 1954, Soviet strategic interest in the Gulf was expressed in the desire for secure borders and for the creation, if possible, of pro-Soviet regimes adjacent to those borders.

But between 1954 and the late 1960s, Soviet staategic interests in the Middle East were confined to the Arab–Israeli conflict and the opportunities it presented to unbalance the U.S. In the nuclear era, however, more complex strategic interests have come to dominate Soviet behavior in the area. In 1968, the U.S. deployed Polaris and Poseidon missiles—with a range of about 2,800 nautical miles—in the Indian Ocean which meant that the Soviet Union's industrial areas were within range of the missiles. The same year, the British government decided to withdraw militarily from the lower Gulf which led to a still unresolved debate about a "power vacuum" in the region. Two years earlier, in December 1966, Britain and the U.S. agreed on the construction of an American naval facility on the Indian Ocean island of Diego Garcia. Within the Soviet Union the doctrines of Soviet Admiral Sergei Gorshkov shifted the emphasis of Soviet naval strategy to a more forward deployment, aircraft carriers, submarines, anti-submarine warfare, and on-shore facilities for the Soviet fleet. In addition, the Soviet Union sought air bases for the protection and operation of the fleet. In his writings, Admiral Gorshkov has supported the expansion of the Soviet navy not only for military strategic reasons, but also in terms of its ability to serve foreign policy goals and increase Soviet influence and prestige.[10] What Soviet–Indian Ocean naval deployment means is that in any negotiations about the Indian Ocean, the Soviet Union will have a place at the conference table.

After 1968, Soviet–Indian Ocean naval units visited the ports of a number of littoral states, concentrating primarily on countries in the north-west segment of the Indian Ocean. At various times the Soviet Union has enjoyed facilities at Aden, Berbera, Socotra, Visakhapatnam and Umm Qars but this is far from saying that these are bases. Military facilities are determined by the state of political relations between the Soviet Union and the host country. They can be highly vulnerable. In 1975, relations between Somalia and the Soviet Union were close enough to allow the latter to build a runway and missile storage compounds at

Berbera. But within two years, a territorial dispute between Somalia and Ethiopia led to a rupture in Soviet–Somali relations and the Soviet facilities at Berbera were terminated. "Nowhere does it (the USSR) have access to full-service installations that can compare to the United States Navy facilities at Subic Bay in the Philippines, Yokosuka in Japan or Rota in Spain. United States bases, moreover, are usually secured by treaty and defended by American forces, whereas many of the ports now used by Moscow would be closed to Soviet vessels in the event of hostilities."[11]

Some analysts have raised the possibility of Soviet attempts to interfere with Western shipping in the sea lanes leading from the Gulf and Indian Ocean. But it is unclear what benefits the Soviet Union would gain from piracy. Moreover, any interference with the oil supply routes would amount to a declaration of war and there would be no guarantee for the Soviet Union that the conflict would be localized.

Within the Gulf, Soviet vessels have visited the Iraqi port at Umm Qasr but in military terms it had been of little or no advantage. Geographically, the Gulf is a *cul-de-sac*, the waters are shallow and useless for submarines; all the littoral states have adequate shore-based artillery or naval firepower and strike aircraft. In addition, Moscow's relations with Baghdad have been erratic and difficult.

Where the Soviet Union has been involved in indirect military intervention as in Afghanistan and the People's Democratic Republic of Yemen (PDRY), the short-term gains have not yet permitted the Soviet Union to prepare a long-term political strategy for the region. When the Khalq (People's) Party seized power violently in Afghanistan in April 1978, the party's strongman and the new foreign minister, Hafizullah Amin, stated that the ultimate goal of his party was to create a modern, socialist society, and it soon became evident that the new government was willing to use Soviet aid to achieve that goal. In addition to the party's estimated hardcore membership of about 2,000,[12] the party relied on the support of approximately 5,000 Soviet civilian and military advisers; Afghanistan even signed a friendship treaty with the USSR in December, 1978.

The government itself is fighting Islamic guerrilla movements in the north and east and has provoked violent local clashes with its land reform and literacy policies. In January, 1979, the government moved against some of the country's main religious leaders after months of trying to win them over. Since then, about 70 people have been arrested in two coordinated sweeps against the clergy and the government has emphasized that ". . . those who use religion as a means to serve the enemies of the people will face repercussions."[13] Until recently, the opposition was scattered and uncoordinated and an easy target for the government. But even if sullen and passive, it has shared a common discontent with and distrust of the left-wing regime, and in March there were signs that a coordinated Islamic opposition movement was being planned. Three groups—*Hizbe Islami* (Islamic Party), *Muyn Inqlabe Islami* (Movement for Islamic Revolution), and *Jamatei-Islami* (Islamic Society) met in exile in Islamabad, Pakistan, and stated that they were ". . . . engaged in a struggle to remove the present government."[14] The land reform program seemed well-intentioned at first, but the redistribution, which is being handled by 100 separate party committees, has been turned into a reward system for individuals who show the greatest loyalty to the party.

Every recent Afghan government has been extremely protective of Soviet interests in Afghanistan, and the *Khalq* regime has done little to enhance the Soviet physical presence in the country. The Russians were embarrassed in Afghanistan, in fact, by the murder in February 1979, of U.S. Ambassador to Kabul Adolph Dubs, which brought them into unwelcome conflict with the U.S. and gave the impression that they were supporting a savage and callous Afghan regime. The real potential gains for Moscow lie in the tribal frontier regions of Iran and Pakistan. But all depends on the stability of the *Khalq* regime, and recent turbulence indicates that it may be undone unless concessions are made to the Islamic movement. If they are, though, Soviet freedom to maneuver is likely to be restricted.

Unlike the *Khalq* party in Afghanistan, the ruling Yemen Socialist Party (YSP), which declared the PDRY the first Marxist republic on the Arabian peninsula in 1978, is closely modeled on the CPSU and clearly pro-Soviet. In fact, Soviet-Cuban-East German presence is probably more extensive in the PDRY than anywhere else in the Gulf. Currently, there are 700 Cubans, 116 East Germans, and more than 1,000 Soviet citizens in the country, all serving either as military advisers or as instructors in ideological training centers.

Cuban involvement in the PDRY began in 1973 as a direct result of the continuing Sino–Soviet conflict within the communist world. Since 1967, the Soviet Union had been losing its revolutionary credibility among Middle Eastern leftist guerrilla movements, especially among those which had come under Chinese influence. In an attempt to stop the ideological shift in the region away from the Moscow line, Moscow arranged for Cuban paramilitary advisers to go to the PDRY. The first 150 arrived in early 1973, and apart from instructing PDRY forces, they were also involved in training Popular Front for the Liberation of Oman (PFLO) guerrillas at Hauf, Mukalla, and al-Gheidha on the Gulf of Aden. Some of the Cubans flew MIG aircraft along the PDRY–Oman border, and in late 1974, it could be seen that PDRY/PFLO artillery positions across the border in South Yemen were manned and directed by Cubans. Although the PFLO insurgency was defeated in 1975, the Cubans have remained in the PDRY as a result of the increased Soviet commitment generally in southern Arabia and the Horn of Africa. In the event of hostilities breaking out in the future between the PDRY and Saudi Arabia, the Yemen Arab Republic, or Oman, the Cubans can be expected to play a direct role, as they did in Angola in 1975 and the Ogaden region of Ethiopia in 1978.

As for the Soviet personnel in the PDRY, they are by no means less active than the Cubans militarily though they may be less visible. They already have port facilities in the country at Aden and on the strategic island of Socotra at the mouth of the Gulf of Aden; and they are extending the port of Aden to accommodate vessels up to 12,000 dwt. This will give them a strategic advantage in the Bab el Mandeb area. Gorshkov visited Aden in May, 1978. His visit followed by only two months the signing of a protocol worked out by delegates of the CPSU and YSP ideological sections regarding cadre training and the exchange of party experience. The Soviet delegate at the signing on March 15, and during the working sessions held in March and April related to the protocol, was Yevgeniy Tyazhel'nikov, member of the CPSU Central Committee and the director of its publicity and information departments.

But the pervasive Soviet presence in the PDRY has not yet turned the country into a monolithic state (though it may have been more successful in creating a police state). For while there is is a strong faction within the ruling hierarchy that wants to set ideological purity above economic pragmatism, there have also been repeated indications that Aden is not yet ready to abandon its willingness to maintain close relations with the conservative regimes of the Arabian peninsula. How realistic this willingness is, to be sure, is open to question, for it has seldom been reciprocated. The regime is greatly distrusted by the Yemen Arab Republic to the north and indeed, between October 1977, and March 1979, leadership assassinations, border clashes, and finally conventional warfare have marred relations beteeen the two. In addition, the mere existence of the Marxist PDRY unsettles countries like Saudi Arabia, Kuwait, and Oman, which voice their opposition (and fears) in statements such as the following ". . . the Communist ideology is not a beloved form of government in the area. The Aden ideology may be good for . . . South Yemen, but it cannot be imposed on North Yemenis or Saudis." [15]

Apparently, the "Aden ideology" is not all that good for South Yemen either, as there are continuing signs of serious discontent. In July, 1978, a bus carrying Cuban advisers was blown up by a land mine, and nine Cubans died. By October, an unreported full-scale civil war was being fought between supporters of the late President Rabay'i Ali and the Cuban-organized People's Militia, which supports his successors. As a result of the conflict, there have been mass movements of South Yemenis to North Yemen and Saudi Arabia, and some 15,000 of them are currently receiving military training in Saudi Arabia alone.

In strategic terms, the usefulness of the PDRY to the Soviet Union is as a toehold—it is no more than that at present—at the Bab el Mandeb Strait in the northwest segment of the Indian Ocean. The security of the toehold will depend on the Aden regime's ability to stay in power in the face of civil war and the large exile armies currently being marshalled across the PDRY's borders.

In October, 1979, PDRY President Abdul Fattah Ismail visited Moscow and signed a friendship treaty with the Soviet Union. It contained 16 points of which the most significant was the one on defense. Stripped of the Marxist-Leninist verbiage, it provides for military cooperation and for mutual consultation in case of war or the threat of war. The PDRY treaty is identical to that signed on Nobember 20, 1978, between Ethiopia and the Soviet Union.

It also meant that the PDRY is the only Indian Ocean state which allows Soviet maritime reconnaissance flights from its territory.

Arab reaction to the Aden–Moscow treaty was uncertain. Some Arab states impressed by conspiracy theories, believed that U.S. policy had forced Aden to turn to Moscow but this was too simplistic. What the treaty did illustrate was that combined Arab and Western pressure on the PDRY had been less successful than that of the Soviet Union. But the treaty has also allowed the West to play the Soviet card against the Gulf states; and the treaty has also dispelled any prospect of unity between the two Yemens for some time to come.

POLITICS AND IDEOLOGY

Until now there has been no lasting example in the Middle East of any Soviet success in converting military agreements into political influence. Attempts to do so by means of friendship treaties and support for local communist parties have been strikingly unsuccessful. The casualty list is impressive; Egypt, Sudan, Somalia, Iraq, and possibly Afghanistan. In the past, the Soviet Union has sacrificed local Communists in the interests of maintaining or improving normal state-to-state relations.

The Iranian Communist Party (*Tudeh*) was proscribed in 1954 but that has not really impeded conventional, even cordial, diplomatic and trade relations between the Soviet Union and Iran. But since the revolution in Iran forced the Shah to abdicate in January, 1979, the Tudeh party's prospects have improved. It was allowed to operate openly in November, 1979, by the regime of Ayatollah Khomeini and immediately professed support for the Islamic program of the Ayatollah. In the political confusion that disfigured Iran in 1979, there were signs that the Tudeh Party had begun to rally its supporters and to present a potential challenge to the Shia theocracy. But the Tudeh Party is challenged by a cluster of about 10 Marxist–Leninist factions which have, in some cases, far more authentic revolutionary credentials. Shortly after the Shah was deposed, Tudeh changed its policy at least three times in 18 months.[16] At first, it supported the united-front tactic; then it switched to a call for armed struggle; and since February, 1979, it had declared itself in favor of the creation of an Islamic republic. In the short-term, the tactical aims of the clerics and Tudeh are similar—nationalization of farm land, workers' committees, centralized economic planning. But the long-term aims of the Marxists and Shia radicals are irreconcilable. In traditional manner the Soviet Union will provide calculated and limited support until its planners decide where real power lies in Iran and then act.

On the surface, Iraq's relationship with the USSR seems much less ambiguous than that of Iran. Since 1972, Iraq and the Soviet Union have enjoyed a treaty of friendship and cooperation intended to remain in force for 15 years. For 20 years Moscow has supplied 90 percent of Iraq's defense hardware needs and recent Soviet sales of MIG-23 and TU-22 military aircraft and advanced SA-5 missiles to Iraq have totalled U.S. $2 billion in value. Among Iraq's trading partners, the Soviet Union ranks sixth as supplier and seventh as customer (nonoil).[17] Furthermore, there has been considerable Soviet involvement and assistance in the development of Iraq's Rumalia oilfields. The Communist Party of Iraq (CPI) was represented by the ruling government coalition dominated by the Ba'th Party, and Iraq's radical positions in international affairs—especially its stance in the Arab-Israeli conflict and its strident anti-American line—coincide with those of Moscow.

But in May, 1978, 21 members of the CPI were hanged for attempting to set up Communist cells within the armed forces. Those executed were all middle-level army officers, and the charges against them related to their activities in 1974-75. This was the largest single group of communists executed in Baghdad since 1968. As if to underscore the significance of the executions, the ruling Revolutionary Command Council (RCC) declared ". . . we do not consider the Communist Party as an adversary. But we will execute anyone who tries to engage in political activity inside the armed forces."[18]

The executions in May were clearly intended as a warning to anti-Ba'thist forces in the country not to attempt to disturb the *status quo*. But not all dissenting elements were intimidated. Less than a week after release of the first official accounts of the hangings, a bomb, for which no one ever claimed responsibility, exploded in Baghdad. In November, trouble erupted again between the CPI and the regime when Communists were discovered organizing within the civil service, especially in the education, information, and planning ministries. In late December, ten Arab Communist parties in other countries protested publicly when reports appeared that the Baghdad government had executed another 18 CPI members.

In fact, the relationship between the CPI and the Ba'thist regime in Iraq has always been one of "blood and vengence." The Ba'thists do not trust the Communists for three fundamental reasons: (1) because they could be competitors for power; (2) because they represent an alien ideology; and (3) because they are seen as tools of a superpower conspiracy. As a state with considerable regional influence, Iraq wants to preserve a free hand in implementing its own regional policy, and as an integral part of its policy, the government is anxious to turn Iraq into the granary of the Persian Gulf and has turned to Western agribusiness consultants for advice. The CPI has deplored this move, however, declaring that ". . . the agrarian revolution cannot make progress without a clear-cut class policy in the countryside expressing the interests of the rural poor and the middle poor."[19] To the extent that CPI aims differ from those of the ruling Ba'thists on this and other matters, the party is vulnerable. Already it is not consulted on major issues, and it is clear that the regime has the oil wealth, the political toughness, and the security system to destroy any incipient Communist plot if the party turns to violence. On July 17, 1979, a new government was formed in Baghdad and the most important change was the absence of Communists in the cabinet.

A CHINA CARD

It has been suggested in some circles that Gulf states, "play the China card" to offset—or halt—the Soviet advance. China is alarmed at the current level of Soviet activity in the Gulf and at what it sees as a Soviet desire to reach the Indian Ocean and gain direct access to Middle Eastern oilfields. As a result, the Chinese are anxious to revive the regional talks on Gulf security which have been stalled since November, 1976. But while Chinese Communist Party Chairman Hua Guofeng could warn, during his visit to Iran in August, 1978, against "hegemonism and expansionism by big powers," there is in fact little the Chinese can offer the

Gulf states in the way of direct military aid. Consequently, Gulf states are likely to be very circumspect about the China card. China, after all, was unable to deter Soviet-Cuban operations in the Horn of Africa in 1978, and any threat or decision to call in the Chinese might provoke the Soviets rather than frighten them. It could also create a problem for the United States, which might fear being drawn into a conflict with the USSR in the region by the Chinese.

CONCLUSIONS

The tactical gains for the Soviet Union in Afghanistan, Iran, and the PDRY, the setbacks in Iraq, the hostility of the conservative Arab states of the Gulf, the impending Soviet oil crisis and the commercial disadvantages it faces in buying Gulf oil and the superiority of the Western naval deployment in the Indian Ocean, would suggest that the Soviet position in the Gulf is precarious, even deteriorating. There may have even been a policy decision taken in the Kremlin to downgrade Soviet interest in the Middle East.

At the 62nd anniversary celebrations of the Bolshevik Revolution on November 6, 1979, Andrei Kirilenko, a senior Politburo member expressing nominal support for the Palestinians, drew attention to the changes taking place in Iran and Afghanistan but no Arab state was mentioned by name.[20] Since Egypt turned to the U.S. for a solution to the Arab-Israeli conflict, the Soviet Union has been compelled to ally with the disunited Arab front which is opposed to the Egyptian-Israeli peace treaty. It is conceivable that the Soviet Union was particularly disappointed that the brief display of Arab unity at the Baghdad Conference in November, 1978, failed to make any real impact on U.S.-Saudi relations. But Arab rejectionism proved too unstable a cause for Soviet purposes in the Middle East and the Gulf.

For the future, the pattern of events which unfolded in 1978-79 is an imperfect guide to Soviet policy in the area. The political changes in Afghanistan and the PDRY did indicate a measure of Soviet foreknowledge and involvement, suggesting that a more hardline policy has predominated in Moscow. Soviet policy in these countries has been aggressive. At the same time, Soviet influence is not fully established in either, and in Saudi Arabia and

Iran, where events are still evolving, the Soviets have undertaken initiatives that do not commit them to act in any way at all. With leadership changes imminent in the USSR, foreign policy may be an area where the struggle for power has already begun, with disagreements existing over what should be done. But whatever the rationale behind Soviet inaction, in Saudi Arabia and Iran, the USSR has much to gain and little to lose and can afford to watch and wait.

There is no reason to believe that Soviet interest in the Persian Gulf will decline in the future, but it still tends, on the whole, to follow events rather than to direct them. This could change if the left-leaning regimes or factions in the region were able to ensure themselves a few years in power. Security of tenure of the Left within the Gulf area might encourage the USSR to prepare a long-term political strategy for the region. The Soviet occupation of Afghanistan in December 1979, marked a new level of Soviet risk-taking that could become a pattern for Soviet behavior along the southern borders of the USSR. The view from Moscow to the south reveals political turmoil and decay in Turkey, Iraq, Iran, Afghanistan, and Pakistan. If that instability is prolonged, and if the United States and the West continue to vacillate, the Soviet regime may be encouraged to implement a long-term strategy sooner rather than later.

FOOTNOTES

1. For a recent discussion of this theory, see A. Yodfat and M. Abir, *In the Direction of the Gulf: The Soviet Union and the Persian Gulf* (London: Frank Cass and Co.), 1977.

2. *Nazi–Soviet Relations, 1939–1941: Documents from the Archives of the German Foreign Office* (Washington, D.C.: Department of State, 1948), p. 257.

3. On the Dhofar Rebellion, see D. L. Price, *Oman: Insurgency and Development* (Conflict Study No. 53) (London: Institute for the Study of Conflict, January 1975).

4. This view was expressed by Dr. Shahram Chubin of the International Institute for Strategic Studies, London, in an interview with the author in March 1979.

5. Quoted in *The USSR and the Middle East*, ed. M. Confino and S. Shamir (Jerusalem: Israel Universities Press, 1973).

6. *Ekonomicheskaya Gazeta*, (24), June 1979.

7. *Arab Oil and Economic Review*, Kuwait, November 1979.

8. *Pravda*, June 14, 1979.

9. *Aviation Weekly*, October 25, 1979.

10. S. G. Gorshkov, "The Navy in War and Peace," *Morskoy Sbornik*, Moscow, 12 (1972): 16.

11. Michael T. Klare, "Superpower Rivalry at Sea," *Foreign Policy*, 2 (Winter 1975-76): 165.

12. *Financial Times*, October 31, 1978.

13. *Ibid.*, March 6, 1979.

14. *Arab Times* (Kuwait), March 4, 1979.

15. *Al Seyassah* (Kuwait), March 11, 1978.

16. *Le Monde*, February 21, 1979.

17. The rankings are those of the Moscow Narodny Bank, London, June 1978.

18. Author's interview with Naim Hadda, Secretary-General of the National Progressive Front, Baghdad, June 1978.

19. On CPI agricultural policy, see Jasem Muhammed al Helawi, "Rural Iraqi Changes and Problems," *World Marxist Review* (London) (July 1978): 83-89.

20. *The Middle East* (London), December 1979.

PART THREE

ISSUES IN THE STUDY OF SOVIET-THIRD-WORLD RELATIONS

CHAPTER SEVEN

THIRD-WORLD MILITARY ELITES IN SOVIET PERSPECTIVE

Charles C. Petersen

The importance that military aid has assumed in Soviet dealings with Third-World governments has long been recognized by Western students of Soviet arms transfers, and a large number of monographs on the subject have been published in the last decade.[1] Even so, available treatments have been largely confined to statistical analyses of aggregate data on Soviet outlays for military assistance, tabulations of hardware deliveries, or case studies of bilateral aid relationships. But a systematic effort to uncover the system of political–military views that informs Soviet policy toward and dealings with the armed forces of the Third World has yet to be undertaken. For all the tactical opportunism of their behavior, the Soviets do possess such a system of views— views which have changed significantly over the years, and without an awareness of which no understanding of the Soviet military aid program would be complete.

These views are not, to be sure, set forth in Soviet writings that treat the subject directly—it is much too sensitive for that. But the Soviets do write about their clients, the military establishments of the Third World, and in particular about the role of these establishments in the societies of which they are members. And an understanding of Soviet perceptions of this role is the key, as will become clear in the following pages, to an understanding of the outlook that conditions Soviet military aid policy in the developing nations.*

THE POST-STALIN DECADE

In the classic Marxist–Leninist interpretation, the world's military machines are of two sorts: bourgeois and socialist. The former are an instrument of the ruling bourgeois class, charged with defending the capitalist order and keeping the working masses in a state of subjection. At the international level, the function of bourgeois armies is to "prepare and wage aggressive wars and enslave other peoples." Socialist armies, in contrast, are armies of a "new type," organs of the dictatorship of the proletariat, created to defend the socialist achievements of the working class against internal and external class enemies, and the Socialist Fatherland against the encroachments of imperialism. Though consequently the army, in Lenin's oft-quoted words, "cannot be, never has been and never will be [politically] neutral," it must not be regarded as an independent socio–political entity, an organization of like-minded individuals looking mainly after its own corporate interests. For, in the political arena, the army never acts on its own, but only at the behest and under the control of the ruling class it serves.[2]

With the decision by Stalin's epigones in the early 1950s to abandon his "two-camp" doctrine and seek ties with the nation-states of the developing world, however, it became clear that these views stood in need, if not of revision, at least of amplification. It was difficult to place Nehru's or Sukarno's armies, for example, in the category of those which "wage aggressive wars" and "enslave other peoples." The ruling class these armies served, to be sure, was still bourgeois because it promoted the capitalist system of development; but for all that, it was fighting against imperialism and colonialism; it was a "national" bourgeoisie.[3] The character of this ruling class in turn determined that of the armies that served it. In the words of a 1962 text, the armed forces of the new national states

---

*Soviet views on guerrilla liberation movements will not be mentioned.

differ fundamentally from the reactionary armies of the imperialist states in their political purpose and character. . . . Being at the disposal of the national bourgeoisie, they . . . are more closely tied to the people and to the general national interest of the formerly oppressed countries.[4]

It was not long after this work appeared, however, that the party line it reflected itself came under fire. It was wrong to think of the national bourgeoisie as the ruling class everywhere in the Third World, the revisionists argued, for in many countries it was "barely taking shape." Some such countries were ruled by a coalition of "bureaucrats, landowners, and profiteers" who were not only promoting capitalist development but consciously supporting the aims of imperialism as well. On the other hand, the rulers of countries such as Ghana, Guinea, Mali, the U.A.R., and Algeria, though of a far different political stripe, were equally difficult to describe as bourgeois. Rather, they were "representatives of the progressive intelligentsia, revolutionary democrats who understand the need for developing the anticolonial revolution into an anticapitalist one." The socialism to which these "revolutionary democrats" adhered, while not presently "scientific," could in time evolve in that direction, and with it the character of their regimes.[5]

When first advanced in February 1963, by some Soviet scholars—notably G. I. Mirskiy, of whom more will be said—these revisionist views were hotly contested;[6] but, before the year was out, Nikita Khrushchev, himself, had put an end to orthodox critical declamations by publicly endorsing the substance of Mirskiy's argument.[7]

This doctrinal change had the great merit of providing the Soviets with a theoretical answer to the annoying question of what the behavior of domestic communists *vis-à-vis* revolutionary-democratic regimes should be. Rather than work for their eventual overthrow as previous doctrine had prescribed, communists were now instructed to support their anticapitalist measures and encourage their evolution in Marxist-Leninist directions. What this entailed in practice, as Richard Lowenthal has said, was "nothing less than the deliberate renunciation of independent communist parties, publicly acting as such," in all one-party revolutionary-democratic states. Domestic communists were now to join the sole legal parties, and work to transform them into Marxist–Leninist parties from within their ranks. The Soviets hoped in this way to persuade the revolutionary democrats in power to cease persecuting communists and accept them as loyal allies and partners in the revolutionary cause.[8]

Although the military origins of a number of Third-World regimes did not escape Soviet notice at the time,[9] the classic view of the army as an instrument of the ruling social strata, even as applied to the Third World, remained fundamentally unchanged. The nature and composition of the classes wielding political and economic power was described differently, but the class relationship between them and the military elites was not. The possibility that some armies might possess a will of their own and be able to flout that of the politically and economically dominant social groups was never raised. Thus, if a country had "linked its destinies with imperialism" so *ipso facto* had its armed forces; and if, on the other hand, it had taken the "noncapitalist path" of development, its army became a bulwark of the revolution. Transforming an army into a force for progress seemed in Soviet eyes to require little more than freeing it from the control of "foreign generals and officers" occupying top-command and staff positions.[10]

With the wave of military coups that swept across Africa between November 1965, and January 1966, however, the analytical framework conditioning these views began to bend somewhat. In less than three months, President Kasavubu of the Congo (Leopoldville), President Congacou of Dahomey, President Dacko of the Central African Republic, President Yameogo of Upper Volta, and President Balewa of Nigeria were all toppled by military officers.

Attempting to explain these events, *Izvestiya's* Vladimir Kudryavtsev allowed, on the day Balewa was deposed, that African armies were "a more mobile force, capable of acting quickly" on the political stage because of the "weakly manifested" differentiation of African social classes.[11] This was a clear departure from previous orthodoxy, for it implied that some military establishments were more than just an armed extension of the will of the ruling classes. But that was as far as Kudryavtsev dared to go in accounting for what had happened. The latest coups, he asserted, had involved only capitalist-oriented countries, where economic conditions had changed little since colonial times. Ultimately, he suggested, these armies had acted, if not directly on behalf, then in the *interests* of the ruling bureaucratic-bourgeois cliques because they were trying to preserve the old order.[12] It did not occur to him, or to any other Soviet commentator then, that progressive regimes which had rejected the "capitalist alternative" might themselves be vulnerable to the depredations of military men who wished to restore the old order. For in countries which had taken the noncapitalist path, as another contemporary account had it, "the army is regarded as an inalienable part of the national political process," and "the ruling parties are in full control" of it.[13] The overthrow of Algeria's Ben Bella seven months before could only have reinforced this conviction, since the officers who replaced him soon showed they were just as committed to the revolution as he had been.

THE LESSONS OF NKRUMAH'S OVERTHROW

Proffered only weeks before the fall of Ghana's Nkrumah, these appraisals reflected the optimism that had infected Soviet thinking about the prospects for the spread of socialism in the developing world. The shock of the redeemer's almost effortless removal from office on February 24, 1966, by a group of patently "reactionary" army commanders was therefore as stunning as it was unexpected, for it demolished, in a single blow, the very foundations of Soviet confidence in the rapid forward progress of the "world revolutionary process" in general and the inherent stability of revolutionary democratic regimes in particular.[14] Almost overnight, the Soviets were compelled to recognize that the revolutionary process had not been "developing in a straight line, but in a more tortuous and contradictory way;"[15] that establishing a progressive regime and choosing the "correct" path of development "do not in themselves automatically solve complex internal problems;"[16] that the transition to socialism could take as long as "an entire historical epoch;"[17] and that the national liberation movement could not only enjoy "headlong surges," but also suffer "temporary failures."[18] And finally, that the attitude of the military was of critical importance to the fate of the revolution, for the army "is actively drawn into political life," and "often exerts a decisive influence on the development of events"[19]—a fact of Third-World political life which, as one writer conceded seven months after the coup, "has until recently escaped the attention of researchers."[20]

By late 1966 and early 1967, the main outlines of an authoritative explanation of the army's role had emerged in the Central party and government press organs, and involved—despite repeated disclaimers—fundamental changes in the old view of the armed forces as an instrument of domination by the ruling classes.

The "low level of socioeconomic development," "inadequate class differentiation," and "immaturity of social relationships" in many developing countries—so the explanation went—had led to a situation in which "no one social class can individually lead the revolutionary process." The working class, for one thing, was small, poorly organized, and politically immature; and the national bourgeoisie—where it actually could be said to exist—had proved unable when in power to "strengthen the economic and political stability" of the state.[21]

These weaknesses, moreover, were reflected in both the ruling parties and the state. The ruling parties, which incorporated forces "heterogeneous in the social, political, and ideological respects," more resembled "national fronts" than cohesive organizations expressing the will of a given class.[22] While these parties had been able to rally their countrymen when the issue was national independence,[23] they were proving inadequately prepared to deal with the "incomparably more complex tasks" that now faced their countries, and were showing themselves "incapable of exerting a decisive influence" on national development.[24] Similar flaws afflicted the state as a whole, since in most cases power was exercised not by a single class, but by a coalition of disparate petty-bourgeois, peasant, worker, and even feudal elements.[25] Only the army escaped the centrifugal effect of these forces:

> [When] progressive elements struggle against reactionary ones within the ruling party itself; when the party is inadequately (or not at all) linked to the revolutionary masses . . .; and when the functions of the state itself are still contradictory, its institutions also find themselves in a process of internal contradictions and organizational shaping. The army is frequently the only exception.[26]

The army, to be sure, also harbored class, tribal, regional, and ideological antagonisms; but unlike civilian institutions, it was "bound together by strict discipline," and the sense of belonging to a "formally established organization" was much stronger.[27] Hence, the military "frequently prove to be the best-organized force in public life"[28]—a force capable of exercising a considerable measure of independent political initiative. "The lessons of the military coups in a number of Asian and African countries," then,

> have shown that the army can play not only a progressive role in the national liberation movement, but easily becomes the instrument of reactionary forces if the influence of democratic ideas is weakened. In some instances the army acts to hasten progressive development . . . and in others . . . it retards that development. . . . The army is an institution in society where democratic ideas can get along quite peacefully with reactionary views, giving rise to the danger that individual bearers of these views might attempt to use the army or a part of it against the revolution.[29]

The revolution's deadliest enemy, in other words, could easily be the very same armed forces ostensibly charged with defending it. Much ink was expended, to be sure, in blaming the "intrigues of imperialism" for what had happened, and to some extent this concern was then (and remains today) genuine. But, at bottom, the Soviets understood that "it would be self-delusion . . . to imagine that imperialist intrigue alone was the main cause of the coup" in Ghana.[30]

WHAT IS TO BE DONE?

It would be wrong, however, to suppose that the Ghana debacle led to any flagging of Soviet preoccupation with or interest in the developing world. It is true, as Robert Legvold has said, that "by 1968 the Soviet Union had long since been disabused of its revolutionary vision of Africa;" but to suggest, as he does, a consequent "obvious loss of interest on the part of Soviet leaders in most of Black Africa,"[31] or in any other part of the Third World for that matter, is nonsense. This view is not only at variance with the facts of Soviet involvement in the Third World since the fall of Nkrumah, but also is prey to the logical error of confusing the act of identifying the problems afflicting the revolutionary process with that of conceding defeat by them. Nowhere is this more evident than in Soviet efforts to deal with the problem of politicians in epaulettes.

To the Soviets, the problem was not one of civil-military relations—at least not in the sense of a challenge to liberty, equality, and fraternity from the forces of infantry, cavalry, and artillery. The military's involvement in Third-World politics, in their jargon, was a *zakonomernoe yavlenie*—a fact of life, an "objective" phenomenon governed by immutable "laws of social development"—which would be channeled in certain desirable directions, but not in the circumstances suppressed. It was therefore pointless, in fact dangerous, to strive for an apolitical military establishment, for to regard it "as though it were a force which stands outside of politics can have grave consequences for the destinies of the national revolution."[32] What was worse, this view failed to take account of the positive aspects of the military's political bent. "The ideologues of imperialism," as one Soviet commentator put it in 1975,

> try to treat the problems connected with the participation of the young national armies in the sociopolitical life of their countries in a distorted way. Shielded by the hypocritical slogan of the army's "political neutrality," the social functions the armed forces perform in individual countries or groups of countries are persistently covered up, reactionary and progressive military regimes are put on the same level, and the positive role and patriotically- and democratically-minded army circles play in the developing countries is denied.[33]

Thus from the Soviet point of view, as these words suggest, the task was not to *remove* the armed forces from political involvement, but to transform the *character* of that involvement so as to ensure that their political initiatives served the cause of "social progress."

The officer corps, to begin with, must be thoroughly purged from top to bottom of all "reactionary elements." It would not do merely to dismiss officers of the former colonial *metropole* who had remained in key positions. Nkrumah's removal of British officers in 1961 from the Ghanian army's top command—an action which had once earned Soviet praise[34]—was not dismissed as purely cosmetic in effect, amounting to no more than a "change in guise" since the new army commanders, though Ghanian, had been "trained in British military educational establishments and had experienced the strong influence of imperialist ideology."[35] The loyalty of the military could not be assured, as Nkrumah's experience had shown, by "leaving them untouched, by not subjecting them to annoying 'loyalty checks,' or by refraining from politically-motivated campaigns to shift or remove officers."[36] Nor, for that matter, would expedients such as creating a people's militia "as a counterweight to the army" (a decision made by Nkrumah in 1965) accomplish anything but the "aggravation of relations between army and government" unless they were "backed up by serious preliminary organizational and ideological-political work in the army" *per se.*[37]

Moreover, the army's officers (or what remained of them after the purge) and rank and file must be "actively indoctrinated" in the "spirit of defending national interests and social progress."[38] This, again was something the Ghanian army had conspicuously failed to do, which resulted in its personnel being ignorant of the "essence of the [revolutionary] events which had been taking place" under Nkrumah,[39] and, in consequence, unwilling to defy the will of the reactionary officers who effected the coup.

Third, internal service regulations and manuals must be revamped to "conform to the objectives and practical tasks of training the army for antiimperialist struggle." In many of the Asian and African armies—including Ghana's own—military and psychological training was being conducted using the "regulations, manuals and instructions of the former colonial armies, that is, according to the canons of bourgeois armies."[40]

A fourth task advocated by the Soviets was to raise the low literacy levels prevailing in most of the young armies, in order to eliminate the "great difficulties" in the training and indoctrination of personnel occasioned by "high illiteracy rates in the population." Illiteracy not only hampered efforts at political indoctrination but was also "a serious obstacle in the way of mastering the fundamentals of modern combat and a nearly insurmountable impediment to the study and utilization of modern combat equipment"[41]

Finally, methods of manning the army's rank and file which had been instituted by the colonial authorities must be abandoned. The recommendation, like the others, was born of the Ghanian experience. The government of Ghana, as Soviet writers began to observe within months of the coup, had "failed to change radically" the methods of recruiting employed by the colonial administration. The Ghanian army command continued, like the British colonial command before it, to "orgaize special recruiting expeditions to [the country's] backward northern regions thereby furthering the preservation of the national army's previous character."[42] Like the colonial army, the national army was dominated by illiterate ethnic monorities which were "untouched by political ferment," "more receptive to discipline" than urban groups,[43] and attracted to military service not by notions of "duty, honor, country," but by expectations of privilege, perquisites, and high pay. "Valuing his privileged status," the Ghanian soldier "became an unquestioning executor of the officers' will,"[44] making it "extraordinarily easy" for the reactionaries to "exploit the army in carrying out the military coup."[45]

What was required to remedy these flaws, in the Soviet view, was a "permanent army which is manned by provision of a law on compulsory military service for all citizens of suitable ages."[46] An army thus manned, to be sure, would be "numerically large" and outlays for maintaining it "extraordinarily burdensome" for the people.

> But for the defense of the achievements of the national revolution and of its development along the path of progress ... the whole people must be prepared. Its physically and morally best-trained youth contingents, brought up in the spirit of responsibility for their country's destiny, are prepared [in the army] to serve, arms in hand, the cause of the national revolution. A system of compulsory military service can provide the army with trained reserves and expand the social framework of military formations; and the army as a whole will become a copy of society and will be made stronger as an army of the people.[47]

THE MILITARY AS AN ENGINE OF
REVOLUTIONARY DEVELOPMENT

The conviction that a "radical reorganization and democratization" of the armed forces was critically necessary to the continued survival of the revolution was only one outcome of Moscow's revised thinking about Third-World military elites after the Ghana debacle. Another result was the gradual emergence of the view—which seems to have acquired the backing of most of the top policy-making Soviet leadership—that the tortuous voyage along the "noncapitalist path" might well entail a lengthy period of military tutelage, with "democratic army circles" steering the ship of state while the socioeconomic ground for a successful transition to socialism matured. For if the events in Ghana forced the Soviets to take heed of what unfettered reactionary elements in the military fold could destroy, they also provided the occasion for a new look at what progressive elements in that same fold could achieve. Egypt's Nasser and Burma's Ne Win, it is true, had already been in power for a number of years, and both had long enjoyed Soviet esteem as two of the Third-World's most radical leaders. But it was not until after the coup that the Soviets began to appreciate the significance of these men as military officers, and to think of the governments they headed as military regimes.

The notion that military stewardship might be the only answer to the instability plaguing many of the "socialist-oriented" countries, however, was adopted with not a few misgivings, for it did no little violence to the belief, consecrated by a half-century of dogmatic reiteration, in the primacy of the party as the "vanguard" of the revolution. Thus, for a time after the Ghana coup, the Soviet leadership's position on this issue was somewhat ambivalent. "The character of any social movement," asserted an authoritative *Izvestiya* article in January 1967,[48] is determined not by who leads it, but by what the *objective* result of its development is and by what the purposes it *objectively* serves are."[49] The military flavor of a given regime, in other words, was less important than its political orientation; and yet the article states just a few paragraphs later that "military leaders who have come to power, thanks to the army, are beginning to understand that the army . . . cannot take the place of a party as the guiding force of society."[50]

On balance, however, the article came down on the military's side. Although it praised attempts which it claimed were being made to create "vanguard parties" which would "unite within their ranks the forces . . . most devoted to the cause of the revolution," it was revealingly silent about *where* such efforts were underway, and conceded that "this process is, for the time being, proceeding slowly, and efforts to hasten it are still very timid." As if to underscore the difficulties involved, the words of a perennial-favorite revolutionary democrat, General Ne Win, were adduced: "the Burmese Socialist Program party . . . which is to become the political leader of the people, is nevertheless unprepared, despite the four years of its existence, to perform the leadership role."[51]

In the final analysis, then, the most that could be demanded of these regimes was the leavening presence of some sort of progressive political organization, whose role would be to help the military rulers keep sight of the goals of the revolution and the "interests of the popular masses." A genuine vanguard party capable of taking charge of the social revolution must await the long-term future; until then, the military must fill the vacuum as guardians of the revolution.[52]

When a series of military coups in the late 1960s and early 1970s brought uniformed revolutionary democrats to power in several countries—including, for the first time, Latin America outside of Cuba*—this belief hardened into certainty, as can be seen from a number of changes in the way Soviet *publitsisty*— that is, apologists for and disseminators of the party line—wrote about progressive military regimes.

For one thing, the problem of creating vanguard parties was shelved, and no longer even mentioned by such writers. Nor, for that matter, did the vast majority of Soviet scholars—with one notable exception, the significance of which will be discussed

---

*General Ahmed Hasan al-Bakr seized power in Iraq in July 1968; Major Marien Ngouabi did so in the Congo (Brazzaville)—since renamed Congo People's Republic—the following month; General Juan Velasco Alvarado deposed the Peruvian president in October 1968; Major General Mohammed Siad Barre seized power in Somalia a year later, and Major (now Lieutenant Colonel) Mathieu Kerekou in Dahomey—now People's Republic of Benin— three years after that. And in 1974, a military junta headed by Colonel Megistu Haile Mariam toppled the centuries-old Ethiopian monarchy.

below—give the subject anything resembling the sort of attention it would have commanded had the leadership regarded it as really important. As late as 1976, in fact, an editorial in the Institute of Orientology's journal detailing the research tasks assigned to Soviet Third-World scholars by the Twenty-Fifth party Congress had nothing at all to say about it, directly or otherwise.[53]

Secondly, the positive aspects of military rule were discussed much more frankly, and defenses of it became much less elliptical. "The establishment of military regimes has been typical of many socialist-oriented countries," said a military writer in 1974. On the one hand, "this has had a negative effect" on the course of the revolution, since it "has objectively retarded the democratization of public life," "hampered the formation of political parties," and "shackled the initiative and activity of the popular masses." But on the other hand, he added, the "rise of such regimes . . . has become an objective necessity" because "political, social-class, and national institutions have remained weak in the face of a strong domestic and foreign reaction."[54]

More, indeed, than just a necessary evil, the military came to be viewed as an effective vehicle for launching and developing revolutions. "In contrast to the past, when military coups as a rule . . . possessed an openly-expressed antipopular bent," said a spokesman for the Soviet Armed Forces Main Political Administration in 1975, "in the current situation they can . . . serve the purposes of the struggle against reactionary regimes." Reflecting the "discontent of the broad popular masses with the proimperialist policy of the ruling classes," the initiatives of patriotic and democratic army circles "can accelerate the course of revolutionary development," making these circles one of "driving forces of national liberation revolutions." Another Soviet writer averred, in 1974, that the army's role of "vanguard of the nation"—a revealing choice of words—"is not infrequently expressed in its performing not only military, political, and administrative-police functions, but also important national—economic, ideological, and educational functions." Particularly if it has an insurgent background, the army "ordinarily participates in all mass campaigns of economic importance . . . pioneers many cultural undertakings" and "manages 'model farms'" that are also used to "educate cadres needed by the country." All these "essential social functions," this writer concluded, ennoble the army even more in the eyes of the population and contribute to the strengthening of its political influence and control over the masses. In many cases this turns the army into a more effective means than the civilian bureaucracy of linking the elite with the masses. What is more, the "politicization" of the army, its relative numerical strength, effectiveness, and discipline make it a political organization of sorts. This is why military regimes often make do without mass political organizations. . . .[56]

These views, all expressed by current or former spokesmen for the Soviet military establishment,[57] were echoed by writers who may be presumed to have been speaking for the CPSU leadership as a whole. "New forms of statehood are arising," wrote R. A. Ul'yanovskiy[58] in 1977, "with the armed forces taking a leadership role in [progressive] social development." Although in time such regimes "acquire a constitutional civilian form," the "'controlling shares of power' *still remain for a long time in the hands of the ruling military group.*" Hence the "curious phenomenon" of "antiimperialist bonapartism headed by the military intelligensia," which "assumes the role of hegemonic political force" in the young nation-states. "There can be no doubt," Ul'yanovskiy pointedly concluded, that

national revolutionary military figures who have come to power . . . to liquidate a feudal order and open the road to social progress are helped in every possible way by the socialist world, which not only gives them foreign policy support, but also serves as a convincing demonstration of the role and importance of a revolutionary dictatorship in the period of transition to a society of social progress.[59]

IMPLICATIONS FOR MILITARY TIES

The realization that the future of the revolution "to a large extent depends on the [political] position of the army,"[60] and the resulting belief that protracted military rule may be the only answer to the instability afflicting many revolutionary-democratic regimes appear to have affected Soviet relations with Third-World military elites in at least two ways.

First, the importance Moscow attaches to direct ties with these elites has risen, of which perhaps the clearest outward sign is the Soviet defense minister's practice—inaugurated two years after the Ghana coup—of sending his opposite number in most of the "socialist-oriented" countries an annual congratulatory message (usually printed on the front page of *Red Star*) on the occasion of the latter's armed forces anniversary. Algeria, Egypt, and Syria began receiving such messages in 1968, followed by Guinea, Iraq, and Sudan in 1969, the Congo People's Republic and Somalia in 1970, South Yemen in 1971, Guinea-Bissau in 1975, and Angola and Mali in 1976.[61]

This practice attests to the Soviet conviction that the armed forces of the Third World have become a critically important focus of East-West competition for influence. "The military-economic potential of the developing states is so weak," wrote a high-ranking reserve officer in 1974, "that their armies depend in full measure on the military–economic potential of the capitalist or the socialist states." And it was "on this very basis," he added, that "an acute and fundamental struggle" was underway between "the forces of progress and the forces of reaction" within the developing countries, and between "the forces of imperialism . . . and the forces of socialism" in the international arena.[62]

Second, the complex of political purposes that Soviet military aid is designed to serve has expanded. Until the mid-1960s, the central concern was to improve the "defense capability" of client armies, a concern which tallied with the conviction that only outside armed aggression by the imperialists or their "puppets" posed a real threat to progressive regimes. Thus, in early 1965, a *Red Star* commentator spoke of the imperialists' "criminal plans" to use "Asians to fight against Asians and Africans against Africans," and Latin American armies "for aggression against Cuba." But thanks to the military assistance of the socialist commonwealth, the new nations could "strengthen their defense capability" and create armed forces "that protect the independence they have won."[63]

The events in Ghana, however, showed that the defense of progressive regimes was "not just limited to the purely military sphere, but . . . directly tied to the solution of a whole series of exceptionally important moral–political problems."

> It is impossible not to see that no military organization, armament, or combat equipment whatever can by themselves ensure the execution of the tasks lying before the young armies if soldiers and officers have no clear or well-defined conception of their obligations in the defense of [their country's] independence ... and are unprepared to resolutely rebuff, if necessary, the intrigues of imperialism and internal reaction.[64]

The purpose of Soviet aid, then, is no longer merely to enable the young nations to "completely overcome the heritage of colonialism in the *military* sphere," but also to "place their armies at the service of national interests *as an instrument of progressive social development.*"[65]

In practical terms, this means that the training of personnel and the "replenishment of the officer corps with progressive elements, particularly persons who have graduated from military educational establishments in the socialist countries," has become decisively important in the Soviet military aid program, for *"the stability of the national democratic system depends to a large extent on the success of this work."*[66] "It is becoming increasingly obvious," in the words of another commentator,

> that the problem of training officer cadres of all ranks for the national armies of the developing states ... presents *the main* problem. ...
>
> The training of cadres of military specialists of all types ... is of fundamental military-political importance, and because of this a critical struggle is unfolding both in government circles and in the armies of these states, for this is a question not only of combat capability, but also of the army's future, its political orientation, and its social role.[67]

THE SKEPTICS

A few Soviet scholars, however, look upon military tutelage as a long-term evil—an ultimate dead end for the revolution— and in so doing have raised basic questions about the support Moscow has invested in recent years in left-wing military regimes.

The standard-bearer of these skeptics is Georgiy Mirskiy, a Third-World specialist at the Soviet Academy of Sciences' World

Economy and International Relations Institute (IMEMO) whom we earlier met as an advocate of doctrinal revision in the early 1960s.[68] Since 1968, when he published an article on the "Political Role of the Army in the Countries of Asia and Africa,"[69] he has expressed grave doubts about the progressive potential of Third-World military establishments in general, and revolutionary-democratic military regimes in particular. In 1970, he published the first full-length treatment of the topic in Soviet scholarship,[70] following this with another six years later.[71] Since all three publications follow basically the same line of argument, they may be considered here as a whole.

Mirskiy makes two main points to support his thesis. The first is that "progressive" military takeovers are infrequent, exceptional occurrences. As a rule, he argues, coups are carried out by senior armed forces commanders, officers who "have been brought up in a pro-Western, conservative bourgeois spirit,"[72] and aim only to rescue the existing order from "threats to the *status quo* under which they were a privileged stratum."[73] The odds against radical middle-ranking or junior officers attempting to seize power, on the other hand, are very high, for not only must they remove the government, but their own high command as well. The deaths of many organizers of such attempts, Mirskiy observes, "eloquently attest that officers who have come out not just against the government but also the high command can expect no mercy" if they fail.[74]

Secondly, in the unlikely even that radical officers of any rank do succeed in seizing power, their willingness to carry through really fundamental changes in the existing social order is doubtful. Not only are they members of an elite social group;[75] they also have corporate interests which they feel impelled to protect. Both of these factors have a dampening effect on revolutionary ardor which very few military officers can resist. Thus, although the military are capable of playing a progressive role during the fight for national independence, "conservative, antidemocratic tendencies, conditioned by their . . . corporate interests" become apparent among some officers when the time comes for the "profound social revolution." Thus, "to consider the army as the leading force of the anticapitalist revolution and as the leader of society in the socialist-oriented countries *would be a serious error.*"[76]

To commit this error, Mirskiy strongly suggests, is to play into the hands of the imperialists, who "reckon that the corporate interests of the privileged military elite will make it an opponent of radical trends, and that ties with foreign capital . . . will hamper the influence of world socialism"[77] Only a "vanguard party that upholds the positions of scientific socialism," Mirskiy concludes, "will ensure genuinely democratic, progressive development."[78]

Mirskiy is not, to be sure, the only Soviet writer to have observed flaws which are peculiar to revolutionary-democratic military regimes.[79] But, unlike his colleagues, Mirskiy is alone in his unrelieved pessimism. "The very nature of economically backward countries" he asserts in his 1970 monograph, "promotes the conversion of a professional army into a bureaucratic corporation with conservative views."[80] Nor, in his opinion, are the prospects for creating a vanguard party—the only agency capable of preventing this—any brighter, as he made clear during a 1977 conference on the political role of the military in Latin America.[81] Speaking on "the lessons of Peru"—where, as the result of a change in the military government in 1975, the revolution began to "tilt" in a decidedly conservative direction—Mirskiy stated that the development of events there was "extremely distressing" to those "who had hoped that a force had finally appeared which even in the absence of a mass communist party and of a powerful people's movement" could "determine a progressive path of development with an orientation on socialism."[82] But rather than offer solutions, Mirskiy spoke of a "vicious circle:" on the one hand, it was "perfectly clear" that without the army's support "it is today impossible to accomplish a revolution;" yet on the other, the military will not likely tolerate any force—such as a vanguard party—under whose influence the revolution might escape their control. "The way out of this vicious circle," said Mirskiy, "can be found only by answering the principal and most difficult question . . . how is the army to be influenced?" "No one," he concluded, "has until now been able to propose anything concrete." "Nor am I able," he added, "to offer any prescriptions."[83]

Mirskiy's views have been greeted with considerable hostility by spokesmen and apologists for the policy-making establishment, for what is ultimately at stake is nothing less than the Soviet

Union's heavy political and material investment in revolutionary-democratic military regimes. "G. I. Mirskiy paints a picture which is pessimistic in the extreme; what results is a downright hopeless situation," fumed B. G. Sapozhnikov, a conference participant, in a disjointed rebuttal that suggested he had been provoked into setting aside a prepared text. Mirskiy, he suggested, had all but abandoned ship because of "negative results," and "isolated failures of the revolutionary movement."[84]

A reviewer of Mirskiy's 1976 book was even more to the point in *Kommunist Vooruzhennykh Sil*, the ideological journal of the Army and Navy Main Political Administration. Mirskiy, he charged, had failed to highlight the "fundamental difference between progressive and reactionary military coups and the regimes established as a result of them." In "a number of instances" Mirskiy "either uses generalizing assessments on the irresolute, conservative character of the majority of military coups, or confines himself, as is obvious from the examples adduced in the book, to simply establishing the fact itself of a military coup . . . without penetrating to the essence of the given occurrence at all."[85]

Nor did Mirskiy's insistence on a vanguard party escape this reviewer's censure:

> One also cannot accept without reservations the author's categorical assertion that it would be a serious error to regard the army as the leader of society in the socialist-oriented countries. In Burma, for instance, where a program of radical transformations was proclaimed as long ago as 1962, the army retains even today its leadership role in the state. In Somalia, a vanguard party was established only in 1976, that is, almost six years after the proclamation of a socialist orientation [i.e., six years after embarking on the noncapitalist path]. Consequently, in concrete conditions *there can be a relatively prolonged period during which leadership of the revolutionary process in this or that country can be exercised directly by revolutionary-democratic representatives of the armed forces.*[86]

But what seems to have annoyed the reviewer most about this "on the whole unsatisfactory book" was its implicit attack on Soviet military-aid policy. In the concluding paragraphs of the review, for example, he condmned Mirskiy's treatment of "certain key questions of military development in the liberated countries" as "slipshod."[87]

> In the first place, it is bewildering that the author should state that many national states of Asia, Africa, and Latin America "do not need an army at all as an instrument of defense against the external enemy" and that an army is necessary only as a "symbol of sovereignty."[88] To put the question that way, whether the author wants to or not, is to cast doubt on the need to strengthen the defense capability of the young states in the face of colonialists who are armed to the teeth. . . .
>
> Noting the young states' difficulties in the realm of military development and dwelling in this connection on external sources of aid, the author stresses that without the latter "there is no other way to create national armed forces."[89] But he says not one word about Soviet military supplies. . . .

That academic critics like Mirskiy are given the freedom to mount thinly-veiled attacks on the Kremlin's backing of tutelary military regimes is eloquent evidence of its greater willingness in recent years to permit what Jerry Hough has called "far-ranging public discussion of policy questions."[90] But there may be more to Mirskiy's freedom to criticize the policy-making establishment than just the sanction of relaxed censorship. For there is evidence to suggest that he has enjoyed the protection of a few in the leadership who themselves oppose Moscow's heavy investment in left-wing military regimes, and who are strong enough, if not to speak for themselves, then at least to provide him with opportunities to state his case beyond those normally available to other Third-World scholars. In 1968, for example, he wrote that the example of the Egyptian revolution showed the army to be "capable of playing a progressive role" during "the struggle for independence and for the liquidation of feudal sway," but that during the "profound social revolution" which follows "conservative tendencies nearly always become apparent" in it, thereby promoting its "transformation into a bureaucratic corporation " that "strives to preserve its privileges" and "opposes radical social changes." Had this formulation appeared in a limited-circulation scholarly periodical such as *Narody Azii i Afriki*[91] or *Latinskaya Amerika*,[92] it would have escaped the attention of all but a small circle of specialists; but it appeared instead in *Kommunist*, the Central Committee's mass-circulation (600,000–700,000 copies) ideological journal, the Party leadership's principal means of disseminating its views on "theoretical" questions to the rank and file.[93]

The unusually large printing of Mirskiy's *"Tretiy mir:" obshchestvo, vlast', armiya* is equally suggestive. Izdatel'stvo "Nauka," which issued the book, is the Soviet Union's chief publisher of scholarly treatises on Third World subjects.[94] In a typical press run, "Nauka" prints between 1,000 and 5,000 copies of such titles.[95] Mirskiy's earlier book on the army and politics, *Armiya i politika v razvivayushchikhsya stranakh*, was issued in 4,000 copies. *"Tretiy mir,"* however, was favored with a press run more than three times as large—23,000 copies.

EFFECTS OF RECENT DEVELOPMENTS

Ultimately, of course, the criticism of scholars like Mirskiy, or of a minority faction in the Politburo, will not have a major impact on Soviet policy unless events themselves are seen to strengthen the critics' opposition. And, in fact, there is evidence to suggest that their opposition has recently been bolstered, perhaps because of the sudden *volte-face* of Siad Barre, until 1977 one of the most staunchly pro-Soviet of Third-World military rulers. This may well account for the return in late 1977—after an absence of several years—of an emphasis on the need for vanguard parties in the popular press and in other texts which may be presumed to bear the Soviet government's imprimatur.

Thus, a recent book on war and the armed forces, signed to press in November 1977, and recommended as a "textbook for the Marxist-Leninist schooling" of Soviet military officers, notes that the army "can play an active role" in overthrowing reactionary regimes and in "creating favorable political conditions for the manifestation of the popular masses' revolutionary creative work," but "is not capable of playing the role of an advanced, conscious, and organized vanguard of the working class," or of performing the mission of "political and ideological leader of the working class and its allies."[96] An April 1978 article in *Red Star* echoes this theme. "Life itself suggests the need . . . to strengthen or create vanguard parties" in countries under progressive military rule, writes the author, who had himself attacked Mirskiy less than two years earlier for insisting on this very same point.[97] The "military methods of rule" employed in "a number of countries" with "patriotic military regimes" are "a substantial hindrance," he adds, "even though it is perfectly obvious that the army alone cannot substitute for the state's democratic institutions."[98]

The theme has also been picked up by the Soviet broadcast media. "What must guarantee the formation of a people's army?" asked Radio Moscow in an English-language commentary beamed to Africa in April 1978. The answer might have been written by Mirskiy himself: a "vanguard party that expresses the interests of the masses of people and adheres to scientific socialism. This party alone can turn the army into a genuine people's army. . . ."[99]

OLD WINE IN NEW BOTTLES

When all is said and done, however, the facts of political life in the developing world will probably discourage any really fundamental change in the Soviet approach to revolutionary–democratic military regimes. For all their recent talk of vanguard parties, the Soviets remain profoundly aware that the "army occupies a special place in the liberated countries"[100] and that it often "plays a decisive role in political transformations and in the formation and conduct of state policy."[101] Nor is Moscow likely to have forgotten that much of its success in courting these armies has resulted as much from its willingness to defer to their claim to pride of place in the revolutionary process as it has from its support of their revolutionary goals. If it now insists too loudly, after years of silence, on the primacy of the party in that process it might well invite their resentment for seeming to cast doubt on their revolutionary credentials. Surely the Soviets have at least this much in mind when they concede, as they still do, that the problems involved in setting up vanguard parties are "complex" and that "time is not infrequently required for their solution."[102]

We must not be misled, then, into taking Soviet calls for the "purposeful political leadership . . . of a vanguard revolutionary party"[103] as more than a reaffirmation of first principles whose realization, however desirable, must await the more or less long-term future. For the present, it is clear that the Soviets are willing to live with something short of this ideal:

It is true that in the socialist-oriented countries there are contradictions between the social and political aspects of democracy. But the main criterion of democracy is not the number of parties, or the holding of elections, or the presence or absence of representative institutions. . . . The main criterion [is] . . . : who is served by this or that form of democracy or this or that regime—the exploiter minority or the working majority. . . . In the socialist-oriented countries the state authority and revolutionary-democratic parties are conducting a policy which accords with the interests of the majority and are establishing the preconditions for the future building of a socialist society. *This is why the national-democratic regime is a democratic regime, even though it sometimes resorts to military or quasi-military methods of governing*, [methods] which are most often occasioned by the acuteness of the class struggle and by the striving of internal reaction and international imperialism to push the liberated peoples off the socialist-oriented path.[104]

CONCLUSIONS

In most of the countries of the developing world, the professional soldier has long played a vital role in domestic political affairs. In Latin America the armed forces have vied for power with civilian politicians for well over a century and a half, and in Africa and Asia for more than a generation. More often than not, politicians are not in the running at all, and the struggle for national leadership is waged entirely within the military establishment itself.

Until little more than a decade ago, Soviet ignorance of these processes was profound. The army, it was held (in classic Marxist fashion), was merely an instrument of the ruling classes, acting on their behalf. That it could play an independent and often decisive part in shaping the destinies of backward countries was consequently thought impossible. In fact, the subject of the army's role in society was rarely discussed at all.

The overthrow of Ghana's Nkrumah—a "progressive" civilian ruler—by a "reactionary" military junta, therefore, came as something of a shock to the Soviet government, deprived as it had been of any advice, sound or otherwise, on how to defend revolutionary gains from the depredations of professional soldiers. The fall of Nkrumah led to a substantial reevaluation of Soviet views of Third-World political processes, a reevaluation which profoundly affected Soviet attitudes toward the relations with the Third World's armed forces.

The armed forces became in Soviet eyes the center of a critical struggle between progressive and reactionary ideologies, a struggle whose outcome could be of decisive consequence to a nation's political, social, and economic future. Later, as radical officers seized power in a number of countries, Soviet hopes came to rest on left-wing military rule not only for the political stability it seemed to guarantee, but also for the momentum it seemed to import to the revolutionary process. Military stewardship came to be viewed as an often inevitable stage along the path to a socialist order.

The exact role that this change in outlook has played in increasing Soviet military aid levels to Third-World countries in the last decade cannot be determined without further research. But it is certain from the evidence of Soviet writings that the relative importance of military cooperation as an instrument of policy has grown in the measure that Third World military elites have become a leading focus of Soviet attention. Neither the warnings of those who insist on the dangers of prolonged military rule, nor the seeming confirmation of these warnings in the recent deflection of Somalia from the fraternity of socialist-oriented countries, are likely to make for significant changes in this state of affairs as long as the Soviets remain persuaded that soldiers play a decisive role in the domestic affairs of Third-World countries.

None of this augurs well for current American efforts to limit the international arms trade with the developing nations, for Moscow's dealings with these nations' military establishments are governed in considerable measure by considerations having little or nothing to do with the behavior of Western suppliers, and a lot to do with the political stability of client regimes. In the Conventional Arms Transfer (CAT) talks now underway, the Soviets accordingly seem less interested in the sorts of blanket restrictions the U.S. would like to impose than in gaining legal enshrinement of their own military aid practices. Hence, their insistence that "the aggressor and the victim of aggression cannot be put on the same level,"[105] and that "rational and precise political and international legal criteria must be elaborated which would define the situations in which, and the recipients to which, arms deliveries are justified and permissible, and those in which they should be prohibited or sharply restricted."[106] If the record of their public statements is any indication, the Soviets have not budged from this position since the CAT talks began in December 1977,[107] and are unlikely to do so in the foreseeable future.

FOOTNOTES

1. Wynfred Joshua and Stephen P. Gilbert, *Arms for the Third World: Soviet Military Aid Deiplomay* (Baltimore: Johns Hopkins University Press, 1969); Uri R'anan, *The USSR Arms and the Third World* (Cambridge, Massachusetts: M.I.T. Press, 1969); Stockholm International Peace Research Institute (SIPRI), *The Arms Trade With the Third World* (New York: Humanities Press, 1971); Jon D. Glassman, *Arms for the Arabs: The Soviet Union and War in the Middle East* (Baltimore: Johns Hopkins University Press, 1976); eds. Uri Ra'anan, Robert L. Pfaltzgraff, Jr., Geoffrey Kemp, *Arms Transfers to the Third World: The Military Buildup in Less Industrial Countries* (Boulder, Colorado: Westview Press, 1979).

2. *Sovetskaya voennaya entsiklopediya*, 1 (Moscow: Voenizdat, 1976), s.v. "Armiya," pp. 248-255.

3. For an authoritative view on the "national bourgeoisie" in the early 1960s, see Boris Ponomarev, "O gosudarstve natsional'noy demokratii," *Kommunist*, 8 (May 1961): 33-48.

4. *Marksizm-leninizm o voyne i armii*, 3rd. ed. (Moscow: Voenizdat, 1962): 197.

5. G. I. Mirskiy, "Tvorcheskiy marksizm i problemy natsional'no-osvobod-itel'nykh revolutsiy," *Mirovaya ekonomika i mezhdunarodyne otnosheniya* (henceforward *MEiMO*), 2 (1963): 65-66.

6. In the very same journal, apparently at the behest of influential party figures. See R. Avakov and L. Stepanov, "Sotsial'nye problemy natsional' no-osvoboditel'noy revolyutsii," *MEiMO*, 5 (1963); 46-54.

7. Interview with Ghanian, Algerian and Burmese correspondents, published in *Pravda* and *Izvestiya*, December 22, 1963, pp. 1-2. Uri Ra'anan's "Moscow and the 'Third World'," in *Problems of Communism* (January-February 1965): pp. 22-31, remains the best summary treatment of this policy debate.

8. Richard Lowenthal, "Russia, the One-Party System, and the Third World," *Survey*, 58 (January 1966): 43-58.

9. See Mirskiy, "Tvorcheskiy marksizm i problemy natsional'no-osvoboditel'nykh revolyutsiy," p. 65.

10. Ye. I. Dolgopolov, "Rozhdennye v bor'be za nezavisi-most': ob armiyakh molodykh natsional'nykh gosudarstv," *Krasnaya zvezda* (Henceforward *KZ*) (February 1, 1964): 5; Dolgopolov, "Armii svobodnoy Afriki," *KZ* (September 25, 1965): 3.

11. Vladimir Kudryavtsev, "Afrikanskie potryaseniya," *Izvestiya* (January 15, 1966): 2.

12. In the Central African case, for instance, the army had been "forced to reckon with the sentiments of the masses in order to avoid falling by the board of political life along with the corrupt leadership clique." *Ibid.*

13. Boris Pavel'tsev, "The Military Corps in Africa," *The New Times*, 4 (January 26, 1966): 12.

14. The sense of alarm aroused in Moscow by the coup is difficult to exaggerate. The events in Ghana, said Vladimir Kudryavtsev eleven days after the coup, were not a "purely domestic affair," for the coup was "directed against all independent Africa and against the national-liberation struggle" The fate of Ghana, he continued, "is closely tied to the fate of the entire African continent," and particularly (or so he implied by referring to Egypt, Guinea, Mali, and Tanzania) with that of other revolutionary-democratic regimes. But even in those countries which remained in the thrall of the "neocolonialist hypnosis," claimed Kudryavtsev, the "broad public" was "alarmed at the events in Ghana." See "Nakal bor'by v Afrike," *Izvestiya* (March 6, 1966): 3.

15. K. Brutents, "Afrikanskaya revolyutsiya: zavoevaniya i problemy," *Mezhdunarodnaya zhizn'*, 1 (January 1967): 21.

16. A. Iskenderov, G. Starushenko, "Proiski imperializma v Afrike," *Pravda* (August 14, 1966): 4.

17. A. Iskenderov, "Armiya, politika, narod," *Izvestiya* (January 27, 1967): 2.

18. Iskenderov, Starushenko, "Proiski imperializma v Afrike."

19. Iskenderov, "Armiya, politika, narod."

20. V. Vasil'ev, "Armiya i sotsial'nyy progress," *Aziya i Afrika segodnya* (henceforward *AAS*), 9 (September 1966): 5. It was no accident, indeed, that the year that followed the Ghana coup witnessed an outpouring of treatments of the military's role in Third World societies that was altogether unprecedented in Soviet scholarship on the developing areas. Within twelve months of the coup, the following articles, devoted wholly or partly to a discussion of that role, had appeared in Soviet newspapers

and periodicals: T. Kolesnichenko, "Armiya i politika," *Pravda* (November 2, 1966): 5; A. Iskenderov, G. Starushenko, "Proiski imperializma v Afrike;" A. Iskenderov, "Armiya, politika, narod;" K. Brutents, "Afrikanskaya revolyutsiya: zavoevaniya i problemy;" V. Vasil'ev, "Armiya i sotsial'nyy progress;" V. Kudryavtsev, "Nakal bor'by v Afrike;" Lutfi el-Kholi, "Antiimperialisticheskaya bor'ba v Afrike na sovremennom etape," *Problemy mira i sotsializma*, 1 (January 1976): 11-19; "Soldat v nezavisimoy Afrike," *AAS*, 9 (September 1966): 8-9; "Armiya i osvoboditel'noye dvizheniye," *ibid*., pp. 2-4. In addition, a special session of the seminar on "Africa—national and social revolution," held in Cairo in late October 1966 and sponsored jointly by *Problemy mira i sotsializma* and At-Talia *(the Egyptian communist* organ) was devoted to "The Role of the Army in African Political Life" (see *Problemy mira i sotsializma*, 1 (January 1967): 59-60. The conference venue, ironically, had been moved from Accra to Cairo because of the coup. See Robert Legvold, *Soviet Policy in West Africa* Cambridge, Massachusetts: Harvard University Press, 1970), pp. 278-279.

21. Iskenderov, "Armiya, politika, narod."

22. *Ibid.*

23. Kolesnichenko, "Armiya i politika."

24. Iskanderov, "Armiya, politika, narod."

25. Kolesnichenko, "Armiya i politika."

26. *Ibid.*

27. *Ibid.*

28. *Ibid.*

29. Iskenderov, "Armiya, politika, narod."

30. Lutfi el-Kholi, "Antiimperialisticheskaya bor'ba va Afrike na sovremennom etape," p. 17. El-Kholi, a pro-Moscow Egyptian communist, was the editor-in-chief of *At-Talia*. A plot to overthrow Egypt's President Nasser, uncovered after the Six-Day War and headed by Nasser's own vice president, Field Marshal Abdal Hakim Amer (who together with Nasser₊had been awarded the title of Hero of the Soviet Union in 1964), showed that threats to progressive development might issue even from revolutionary democrats who had fallen by the wayside. "It would be wrong," wrote Karen Brutents in 1968, "to believe that political evolution is possible in only *one*—a *progressive*—direction for all who are in the ranks of revolutionary democracy. This is far from being so, if one takes account of the heterogeneity of the forces formerly gathered in the revolutionary democrats' political boat as well as their socially-conditioned [i.e., petty-bourgeois] inclination to political vacillation, which can engender serious zigzags even in those who become radicalized." See "O revolyutsion-noy demokratti," *MEiMO*, 4 (April 1968): 27.

31. Legvold, *Soviet Policy in West Africa*, p. 335.

32. Iskenderov, "Armiya, politika, narod."

33. Dolgopolov, "Armii razvivayushchikhsya stran i politika," *Kommunist Vooruzhennykh Sil* (henceforward KVS), 6 (March 1975): 76. The "notorious burgeois principle" that the army should keep out of politics has become a special target of Soviet invective. See Iskenderov, "Armiya, politika, narod;" Dolgopolov, *Natsional'no-osvoboditel'nye voyny na sovremennom etape* (Moscow: Voenizdat, 1977), p. 91; B. G. Sapozhnikov, "Klassy i armiya v razvivayushchikhsya stranakh," *Leninizm, klassy i klassovaya bor'ba v stranakh sovremennogo Vostoka*, ed. B. G. Gafurov et al. (Moscow: Izdatel.stvo "Nauka," 1973), p. 252.

34. Dolgopolov, "Rozhdennye v bor'be za nezavisimost.'"

35. Dolgopolov, "Vooruzhennye sily razvivayushchikhsya stran," *KZ* (May 31, 1969): 5.

36. G. I. Mirskiy, *Armiya i politika v stranakh Azii i Afriki* (Moscow: Izdatel' stvo "Nauka," 1970), p. 265.

37. A. V. Kiva, "Afrika: nekotorye aspekty politicheskoy nestabil'nosti," *Narody Azzi i Afriki* (henceforward *NAA*), 4 (July–August 1972): 38.

38. Dolgopolov, "Armii osvobodivshikhsya stran," *KZ* (May 19, 1968): 3.

39. Dolgopolov, "Vooruzhennye sily razvivayushchikhsya stran."

40. Sapozhnikov, "Klassy i armiya v razvivayushchikhsya stranakh," p. 247.

41. Sapozhnikov, "Rol' armii v gosudarstvakh Azii i Afriki," in *Zarubezhnyy Vostok i sovremennost': osnovnye zakonomernosti i spetsifika razvitiya osvobodivskikhsya stran*, vol. 1 (Moscow: Izdatel'stvo "Nauka," 1974), pp. 446–447. The book was edited by an "editorial collective" headed by B. G. Gafurov.

42. V. B. Iordanskiy, "O kharaktere voennykh diktatur v tropicheskoy Afrike," *NAA*, 4 (July–August 1967): 27.

43. Ibid., p. 26.

44. *Ibid.*

45. *Ibid.*, p. 27.

46. Sapozhnikov, "Rol' armii v gosudarstvakh Azii i Afriki," p. 445.

47. *Ibid.*, p. 453.

48. Iskenderov, "Armiya, politika, narod." The article is introduced by the following words, set off from the text and apparently supplied by *Izvestiya's* editorial board: "The fact that recently the army has found itself in the forefront of political events in many of the young national states of Asia and Africa has brought out a number of problems whose theoretical elaboration is acquiring great practical importance for the elaboration of ways, forms, and methods of uniting progressive forces in the struggle against imperialist and internal reaction and for social

progress. Among them in particular belong questions concerning the role and place of the army in the national-liberation movement, its influence on the political life of the developing countries, and the importance of the struggle of the popular masses and their organizations."

49. *Ibid.*

50. *Ibid.*

51. *Ibid.*

52. The article concluded with a call for something more modest than a vanguard party: "It would be wrong to generalize from the experience of one or a few countries and mechanically transfer it to other countries. But regardless of how the masses are organized politically, the main thing is that building a new society is impossible if the popular masses do not take an active part. As the experience of the UAR, Burma, Algeria, Syria [all of them military regimes] and some other countries attest, the army has an important role to play in the national liberation movement.... But [it] ... will not be able to perform its mission unless it serves the interests of the people, correctly determines its place in society, and sensibly assesses its potentialities in directing the complex processes of the economic, social and political development of the liberated states." *Ibid.*

53. "XXV s'ezd KPSS i zadachi sovetskikh vostokovedov i afrikanistov," *NAA*, 5 (September–October 1976): 3-14. Although the concept of vanguard parties "has entered the scientific terminology of research devoted to revolutionary–democratic parties," allowed G. I. Shitarev in 1976, "[its] content . . . is still being defined in the most general way. . . . So far, the vanguard party is emerging only as a potentiality, as a problem of the more or less remote future; and the question of what the distinction between it and existing organizations consists in is being broached more on the theoretical plane than at the concrete political level." Shitarev's ideas of what a vanguard party should be are of interest. First, it must have "a clear goal—socialism" and "know the laws of social development;" second, scientific socialism must be "the ideological basis" of its activity, with only minor "deviations" on "nonessential theoretical points;" third, it must enjoy paramountcy "over all other mass unions," organizationally as well as ideologically; fourth, it must "represent the progressive classes and social groups" of the country; fifth, its membership must be restricted to those who are "capable of assuming all the obligations which belonging to the vanguard detachment of society entails;" and finally, it must combine "in all its internal life democracy with centralism, personal initiative with firm discipline . . . , with the obligatory subordination of the minority to the majority, and of the lower organizations to the higher ones." (G. I. Shitarev, "Nekotorye problemy evolyutsii revolyutsionno-demokraticheskikh organizatsiy v napravlenii partii avangarda," *NAA* (March–April 1976): 39.

54. Yu. G. Sumbatyan, "Armii v politicheskoy strukture stran sotsialisti-cheskoy orientatsii," *AAS*, 4 (April 1974): 18.

55. Dolgopolov, "Armii razvivayushchikhsya stran i politika," p. 78.

56. Sapozhnikov, "Rol' armii v gosudarstvakh Azii i Afriki," pp. 436–437.

57. Sumbatyan and Dolgopolov are both Soviet Army colonels, and both have Candidate degrees in "Philosophical Sciences"—that is, Marxism-Leninism—which suggests they are representatives of the Soviet Army and Navy Main Political Administration, the CPSU Central Committee's arm in the Soviet military. Sumbatyan is assigned to the V.V. Kuybyshev Military Engineering Academy in Moscow. Dolgopolov is a frequent contributor to *Krasnaya zvezda* and *Kommunist Vooruzhennykh Sil* (the Main Political Administration's ideological journal) on Third-World armies. (Some of Dolgopolov's articles in the latter periodical are explicitly addressed "to leaders of political study groups" in the Armed Forces, which is further testimony to his association with the Main Political Administration: see his "Razvivayushchiesya strany Azii, Afriki i Latinskoy Ameriki," *KVS*, 16 (August 1973): 72-79, which outlines a course of instruction to be conducted by "propagandists"—political officers—for the edification of Soviet military personnel on Moscow's policy in the developing world.) Sumbatyan may well be a purveyor of the "party line" at the Military Engineering Academy to Soviet officers destined for advisory duties in Third-World armies.

Sapozhnikov, now a major general in the Reserves, has had an association with the Main Political Administration which dates back to 1935, when he was graduated from the V. I. Lenin Military-Political Academy, the institution charged with training political officers for the Armed Forces. He returned as an instructor in the late 1930s and early 1940s, and in the early 1950s taught at the Frunze Military Academy (1941) and the General Staff Academy (1951). After retiring from the Soviet Army in 1958, he joined the Academy of Sciences' Institute of Orientology. (S. D. Miliband, *Bibliograficheskiy slovar' sovetskikh vostokovedov* (Moscow: Izdatel'stvo "Nauka," 1975), pp. 231-232.

58. Rostislav Aleksandrovich Ul'yanovskiy was until recently a deputy director of the CPSU Central Committee's International Department, which is headed by Politburo Candidate Member and Central Committee Secretary Boris Ponomarey. (Ul'yanovskiy's departure from that position may have something to do with his advanced age—73 years in 1977.) The International Department is responsible, among other things, for relations with nonruling communist parties and ruling revolutionary-democratic parties. For a discussion of the International Department, see Leonard Schapiro, "The International Department of the CPSU: Key to Soviet Policy," *International Journal*, 32(1) (Winter 1976-1977): 41-55.

59. Ul'yanovskiy, "Idei Velikogo Oktyabrya i sovremennye problemy natsional'no-osvoboditel'nogo dvizheniya," *Novaya i noveyshay istoriya,* 3 (May–June 1977): 6.
60. Boris Ponomarev, "Aktual'nye problemy teorii mirovogo revolyutsionnogo protsessa," *Kommunist,* 15 (October 1971): 62.
61. The Foreign Broadcast Information Service.
62. Sapozhnikov, "Rol' armii v gosudarstvakh Azii i Afriki," p. 451.
63. Dolgopolov, "Tikhoy sapoy: kolonizatory v mundirakh voennykh sovetnikov," *KZ* (January 9, 1965): p.
64. Dolgopolov, "Armii osvobodivshikhsya stran."
65. Dolgopolov, "Armii razvivayushchikhsya stran i politika," p. 81. (Emphasis mine.)
66. L. M. Entin, MMMesto partii v gosudarstev," in *Afrika: problemy sotsialisticheskoy orientatsii,* ed. N. I. Gavrilov, G. B. Starushenko, et al. (Moscow: Izdatel' stvo "Kauka," 1976), p. 316. (Emphasis mine.)
67. Sapozhnikov, "Rol' armii v gosudarstvakh Azii i Afriki," pp. 45-453.
68. A capsule career biography of Mirskiy appears in *Bibliograficheskiy slovar' sovetskikh vostokovedov,* pp. 361-362, 66.
69. "Politcheskaya rol' armii v stranakh Azii i Afriki," *NAA,* 6 (November-December 1968): 2-14.
70. *Armiya i politka v stranakh Azii i Afriki.*
71. *"Tretiy mir": obshchestvo, vlast', armiya* (Moscow: Izdatel'stvo "Nauka," 1976).
72. *"Tretiy mir,"* p. 170. *See* also "politicheskaya rol'," p. 8; *Armiya i politka,* p. 300.
73. *"Tretiy mir,"* p. 66.
74. *Ibid.,* pp. 172-173; *see* also "Politicheskaya rol'," p. 9; *Armiya i politika,* pp. 301-302.
75. "Nowhere'" Mirskiy avers, "have the military resorted to a coup because they believed themselves to be a deprived or discriminated-against social group." *"Tretiy mir,"* p. 66.
76. *Ibid.,* p. 385; *see* also *Armiya i politika,* p. 336. (Emphasis author.)
77. *Ibid.,* p. 378.
78. *Ibid.,* p. 385; *see* also *Armiya i politika,* p. 336.
79. *See* R. E. Sevoryyan, "Armiya i obshchestvo v molodom gosudarstev," *MEiMO,* 6 (June 1970): 105; *Armiya v politicheskom rezhime stran sovremennogo Vostoka* (Moscow: Izdatel'stvo "Nauka," 1973), pp. 115-122; "O politicheskoy roli ofitserstva v stranakh sovremennogo Vostoka," ed. V. F. Li, *Srednie sloi gorodskogo obshchestva v stranakh Vostoka* (Moscow: Izdate'lstvo "Nauka," 1975), pp. 60-62.

80. *Armiya i politka* , p. 334; *see* also *"Tretiy mir"* , p. 378. Compare Sevortyan's viess: "Military bureaucratic rule," he wrote in 1970, "is a frequent trait of army governments," but is only "a temporary phase in the life of a young state;" for there are "a number of circumstances" that "force the military to define their class orientation" and "dictate a transition to "a new political system" based on mass political support. Among the "circumstances" Sevortyan lists are (1) the military's experience under previous governments, which "graphically showed that, devoid of mass support, they were doomed to failure;" (2) the new functions that the military must perform upon seizing political power—"functions which are far from peculiar to them"; and (3) the military's knowledge "from their own experience" of "the strength and importance of ideology." "Armiya i obshchestvo v molodom gosudarstev," pp. 105-106. Much the same point is made with reference to the Egyptian revolution in Sevortyan's *Armiya v politicheskom rezhime stran sovremonnogo Vostoka:* "The experience of the Egyptian revolution shows that the moment comes when . . . the military leaders arrive at an understanding of the limitations of military dictatorial methods of governing, and of the need for a transition to a new political organization of society," p. 130.

81. An apparent transcript of this conference, sponsored jointly by the Academy of Sciences' Latin America Institute and its journal, *Latinskaya Amerika*, was printed *ibid.*, 3 (May–June 1977): 49-85, and 4 (July–August 1977): 113-148.

82. *Latinskaya Amerika*, 3 (May–June 1977): 69-70.

83. *Ibid.*, pp. 70-71.

84. *Ibid.*, pp. 74-75. The conference chairman, A. F. Shul'govskiy, Director of the Latin American Institute's Department of Socio-Political Problems, also criticized Mirskiy's emphasis on the "corporate character" of the military. "I do not deny any importance to the investigation of questions connected with the corporate-mindedness, elitism, and militarism which occur in the armed forces," said Shul'govskiy, whom Sapozhnikov had earlier commended for his "optimistic" keynote report. "But it is my profound conviction that the study of these elements is not at this point in time the most fruitful for promising [research] activity, above all for the struggle of progressive forces for the army." *Ibid.*, 4 (July–August 1977): 148.

85. Dolgopolov, "Molodye armii i sotsial'nyy progress," *KVS*, 21 (November 1976): 91.

86. *Ibid.*, p. 92. (Emphasis author.) While not of itself heretical—no Soviet writer has ever claimed that the actual *transition* to socialism can be effected without a vanguard party—Mirskiy's point is that military rule is

also incompatible with non-capitalist development, or the period of anti-capitalist measures that paves the way for that transition.

87. *Ibid.*

88. *"Tretiy mir,"* p. 7.

89. *Ibid.*, p. 366.

90. Jerry F. Hough, *The Soviet Union and Social Science Theory* (Cambridge, Massachusetts: Harvard University Press, 1977), p. 25. On this subject, *see* also pp. 26–28, 190–202.

91. Circulation 4,500.

92. Circulation 7,500.

93. "O kharaktere sotsial'nykh sil v Azii i Afriki," *Kommunist*, 17 (November 1968): 96.

94. The publishing house's Main Editorial Office of Eastern Literature (Glavnaya redaktsiya vostochnoy literatury) oversees the publication of studies dealing with the developing countries.

95. In a sampling by the author of 27 titles, published between 1967 and 1977 and dealing with general Third-World problems, the mean press-run was 3,300 copies. Press-runs of 5,000 copies or less accounted for 93 percent of the sample. None of the titles was issued in more than 6,300 copies.

96. *Vayna i armiya* (Moscow: Voenizdat, 1977 [signed to press November 17, 1977]), pp. 334–335.

97. *Ibid.*, p. 30.

98. Dolgopolov, "Vazhnyy politicheskiy faktor: o roli armiy v razvivayushchikhsya stranakh," *KZ* (April 21, 1978): 3.

99. Radio Moscow in English to Africa, 1630 GMT April 13, 1978, transcribed in Foreign Broadcast Information Service *Daily Report*, vol. 3, *Soviet Union* (April 14, 1978): H2–H3.

100. *Voyna i armiya*, p. 328.

101. *Ibid.*, p. 326.

102. V. Ye. Chirkin, "Idei Velikogo Oktyabrya i revolyutsionnoe preobrazovanie politicheskoy sistemy v stranakh sotsialisticheskoy orientatsii," *NAA*, 5 (September–October 1978): 10.

103. S. P. Nemanov, "Partii avangardnogo tipa v afrikanskikh stranakh sotsialisticheskoy orientatsii," *NAA*, 2 (March–April 1979): 16.

104. Chirkin, "Idei Velikogo Oktyakrya i revolyutsionnoe preobrazovanie," pp. 15–16.

105. From speech delivered by Soviet Foreign Minister Andrey Gromyko before the United Nations General Assembly Special Session on Disarmament, May 26, 1978; for text, see *Pravda*, May 27, 1978, p. 4.

106. "O prakticheskikh putyakh k prekrashcheniyu gonki vooruzhenity" (Soviet disarmament proposals presented to the U.N. General Assembly Special Session on Disarmament in May 1978), *Pravda*, May 31, 1978, p. 4.

107. The above phraseology has been repeated, almost word for word, in every subsequently published Soviet discussion of the CAT talks. *See* V. Kravtsov, "A Promising Avenue," *New Times* (August 18, 1978): 18-19; A. Nikonov, "Problema, kotoruyu nado reshat," *Pravda* (January 27, 1979): 4; A. Kemov, "Osnovoy ogranicheniya torgovli oruzhiem," *Mezhdunarodnaya zhizn'*, 2 (February 1979): 128; P. Tarabaev, N. Shishkin, "Prodazhi i postavki vooruzheniy v strategii imperializma," *MEiMO*, 3 (March 1979): 44.

CHAPTER EIGHT

TRENDS IN SOVIET RESEARCH ON THE DEVELOPING COUNTRIES

Elizabeth Kridl Valkenier

Since 1956, Soviet studies of the developing countries have been evolving from a narrow and simplistic ideological basis to a more objective and pluralistic approach. Within that steady evolution, in which factual material and inductive analysis modify or replace superficial schemes and deductive reasoning, one can observe two phases.

Roughly speaking, for the first fifteen years research was conducted within a deterministic framework. That approach interpreted the disintegration of the colonial system, the emergence of the newly independent states, the class origins of the ruling elites as well as the character of their policies, and the expanding relations of these states with the USSR through the prism of "national liberation revolution" which was said to be a component of the worldwide socialist revolution. In that scheme, the primary purpose of research was to determine which class and policies, and to what degree, were in step with the inevitable advent of socialism.

The tone for these investigations was set by the jettisoning of the Stalinist formula that had relegated all the former colonies to the imperialist camp, dubbed the national leaders as bourgeois puppets of the metropoles, and credited only the Communists with the ability to affect genuine progress. At the 20th CPSU Congress in 1956, Khrushchev asserted that the newly independent states formed a "vast zone of peace" and gave a positive evaluation to the middle-class nationalist governments. At the same gathering, Anastas Mikoyan charged that the learned institutions concerned with research on the East "slumbered" while the contemporary world passed them by.

No such dramatic pronouncements marked the emergence of the second phase around 1970. But it is characterized by changes as significant as the one that took place after 1956. With the focus shifting from politics and class analysis to economics, the Third World is now increasingly examined not as an integral part of the advancing socialist revolution but as a participant in the world economy, facing certain global and specific problems. In addition, the former normative assumptions are being undermined through an incremental process of refining and redefining Marxist methodology. And third, it is the academic community, not the party, that is primarily responsible for changing the tenor and content of research.

Mikoyan's criticism of the somnabulent profession was followed by the First All-Union Conference of Orientalists in June 1957, at which scholars were again enjoined to readjust their focus from the past to the present. To make this possible, the venerable and prestigious Institute of Oriental Studies, charged with research on the East (the traditional appellation for all the non-European areas), was refurbished. It was renamed the Institute of the Peoples of Asia, and separate institutes for the study of Africa and Latin America were formed in 1959 and 1961, respectively. The Institute of World Economy and International Relations was set up in 1956 to deal exclusively with contemporary issues, one of its sections being charged with studying the "liberated and dependent countries."

At the outset, there were plans to publish three scholarly journals separately devoted to Asia, Africa, and Latin America. Thus far, however, only one bimonthly, *Narody Azii i Afriki*, covers the first two continents, and another bimonthly, *Latinskaya Amerika*, deals with the South American continent. Both print articles on current affairs as well as on history and culture. But the monthly organ of the Institute of World Economy and

International Relations, *Mirovaya ekonomika i mezhdunarodnye otnosheniya*, deals solely with current events throughout the world. In addition, a popular illustrated monthly, *Aziya i Afrika segodnia* (first called *Sovremennyi Vostok*), began publication in 1957. Rather inconsequential at first, it has of late been printing a number of substantive articles and discussions, reflecting the general rise in professional standards.[1]

The reawakening of the profession was guided by the reformulation of Marxist terminology. The December 1960 meeting in Moscow of the communist parties made an attempt to find a common language with the nationalist leaders of the newly independent countries by devising the formulas of the "national democratic state" and the "noncapitalist path of development" as patterns for the transition to socialism and for overcoming backwardness. Both slogans acknowledged a role for the national bourgeoisie; it could undertake some measure of the revolutionary task hitherto reserved to the proletariat and its party. The communists, however, were explicitly designated as the leading force of the liberation revolution. But the 22nd CPSU Congress, held in October 1961, no longer tried to tread the middle ground between the Chinese insistence that communists lead the democratic phase of the liberation revolution and the Soviet preference to let the middle classes carry on for a while with communist support. It dropped all references to communist hegemony in a united front, insisting instead on the cooperation of all the progressive forces. From then on, until Khrushchev's fall in October 1964, Soviet policy and theory moved closer and closer to identifying the radical nationalist leaders and their programs with some sort of a proto-socialist phase in the progression of the national liberation revolution.

Against this background of a creeping modification in Marxist theory on the course and leadership of the national liberation revolution, the academic community shifted to a more differentiated class analysis. The goal of research and writing was to identify the bearers of progressive ideas among classes formerly dismissed as the "national bourgeoisie" whose rule had to be superseded by that of the working class in order to result in genuine progress. This is how the situation looked in 1960-61, before a more tolerant approach was adopted:

A prevalent notion among our writers was that in most former colonies or semicolonies the national bourgeoisie was firmly in power. No distinction was made . . . , the term "national bourgeoisie" embraced the medium and even the big industrial bourgeoisie, along with the petty and medium-trading bourgeoisie and even the petty bourgeois intelligentsia. The deduction was drawn that these countries were ripe for an accelerated development of capitalism, and that only working-class leadership of the movement could make possible further advances of the revolution. These authors considered that where there was no working class hegemony it must be fought for. . . . [They] rejected the possibility of intermediate stages in the development of the national democratic revolution and denied the possibility of its deepening under the leadership of nonproletarian strata of the population—revolutionary democrats, the progressive intelligentsia, and others.[2]

By 1964, these "schematic attitudes" had been overcome. Soviet scholars gave up concentrating on the limitations the class origins imposed on the policies of various bourgeois regimes and on keeping a clear distinction between the democratic and the socialist revolutions. They came to accept that the socialist and the general democratic tasks were interwoven in the national liberation revolution and that the middle-class leaders were in effect "radical democrats" who were either very close to or on the point of going over to the position of the working class. Accordingly, much research and publication became centered on minute class analyses designating which social groups in which country, continent, or the entire postcolonial world were capable of carrying out the liberation revolution to the threshold of, or even into, the initial stages of Socialism.[3]

Three publications can be cited as fairly typical products of the first phase in Soviet research on the postcolonial world.[4]

V. Tiagunenko's *Problems of Contemporary National Liberation Revolution* is representative of the work done by the middle-generation of scholars, born in the 1920s.[5] Their studies began appearing in the 1960s and more readily reflected the ideological adjustments that accompanied the post-Stalin rapprochment with the newly independent countries than did the publications of the older generation of scholars whose training and outlook were shaped before World War II—men like I. Potekhin (b. 1903), the first director of the Africa Institute, and F. Gafurov (b. 1909), the first director of the Institute of the Peoples of Asia, or his deputy R. Ulianovsky (b. 1904).[6]

Tiagunenko's book looked at all the developments in the newly independent countries through the prism of worldwide Socialist revolution. Given this refraction, there was the sanguine assumption that the predominant tendency in the postcolonial world was the growing anticapitalist trend in both the economic and sociopolitical life of the new nations. Tiagunenko confidently asserted that the "transition to socialism was possible for any country, independently of its level of development." On the political side, due to the existence of the world socialist system, Marxist-Leninist leadership did not have to be provided by a strong working-class party but appropriate leadership could be supplied by other progressive forces representing the interests of the whole nation. On the economic side, things looked equally promising. The elimination of foreign and local exploiters, though it might lead to a temporary decline in production, was essential for "deepening" the revolution and was bound to result "very soon" in economic advance. Though published after Khrushchev's fall and after the first of the several collapses of radical regimes (beginning with Ben Bella's in 1965), the book exuded the former Soviet leader's optimism in history being on the side of socialism and the USSR. It also retained his reinterpretation that, because of the current third stage in the collapse of capitalism and the emergence of the world socialist system, the national liberation revolutions were substantially different from the bourgeois revolutions of the past and could afford to take various shortcuts on the way to socialism.

Classes and Class Struggle in the Developing Countries, a three-volume work compiled by the research staff of the Institute of World Economy, was cast in a similar deterministic framework.[7] Despite all the factual material it provided which might suggest other alternatives, it treated all issues of political, social, and economic development from the viewpoint of these countries' impending or eventual transition to socialism. The volume on class structure, despite many tables that clearly showed the contrary, stressed the growth of the working class. The volume on economic development, though it discussed the importance of the domestic accumulation of capital resources, extolled Ghana, Guinea, Mali, Burma, and the UAR for their radical reforms of economic institutions. The final volume, though it analyzed the entire spectrum of the existing regimes, nevertheless posited that only the choice of the noncapitalist path of development offered sure prospects for attaining both general democratic goals and speedy economic progress.

A similar optimistic tone permeated the three-volume work of the Institutes of the Peoples of Asia and of Africa: *The National Liberation Movement in Asia and Africa.*[8] The first volume traced the history of the opposition to colonial expansion from the 16th to the 20th centuries. The second analyzed the rising tide of the liberation movement during 1917–1945 in terms of the influence exerted first by the October Revolution and later by Soviet diplomacy. And the last described the policies of the liberated states in the context of the competition between the capitalist world and the socialist bloc for their political allegiance and economic cooperation.

During the first phase of research comparatively little attention was paid to economic matters. As noted above, what preoccupied most Soviet scholars was class analysis to determine the role of each group in either advancing or hindering progress. But Soviet economic aid to the non-Socialist regimes had to be justified. Hence, the concern of research was not genuine economic issues but whether state capitalism in the newly independent countries could qualify as a progressive phenomenon.

A conference held in 1958 at the Institute of Oriental Studies decided that state capitalism in the Third World, unlike its counterpart in the industrially developed countries, could be a progressive force when it was "harmful to the interests of imperialism."[9] Although the conference was organized by the economic section of the Institute, the discussion was coached almost exclusively in political terms. Only a few participants (for example, A. Levkovsky) talked about the "progressiveness" of state capitalism in terms of the impetus it gave to economic development. The majority (among whom R. Ulianovsky was most prominent) challenged this view, claiming that the progressiveness of state capitalism in the Third World was determined by the degree of its anticapitalist direction.

In this scheme, economic planning in India, Egypt, Indonesia, and Burma (all of them recipients of Soviet aid) was bound to succeed since the planning was said to be directed at gaining economic independence from the West. Conversely, the endeavors of the governments in Pakistan, the Philippines, and Turkey were scorned since these countries were said to be under the domination of monopoly capital and of imperialism. What either set of policies might contribute to the actual development of production was not under intensive study at the time. The overriding concern was to prove that state capitalism among Moscow's economic clients could eliminate capitalist relations and serve as a transition to socialist institutions.

Having found an ideological justification for the state sector, Soviet Third-World specialists turned their attention not to its performance but to its size. Until 1964–65, investigation centered almost exclusively on the ways to expand public ownership. Industrialization was regarded as the best means of assuring a regime its strong position in the national economy. Only by owning the means of production could the central government exercise direct control over the economic life of the country. Thus, Soviet experts attending the first UN conference on programming for economic development, held in Dehli in the fall of 1961, were highly critical of its working papers, which largely saw the public sector in the role of providing the impetus.[10]

Nationalization of foreign and domestic private property was another method favored by the Russians in this period. Direct state ownership was believed to be the best way of diverting the enormous funds, which the foreign companies were said to be syphoning off as profits, into investment for development. At times, more moderate voices would suggest that the state could increase domestic resources of capital accumulation by taxing foreign companies more heavily and limiting the profits they could take.[11] The prevalent mood, however, was to encourage such methods as nationalization without compensation to increase the level of savings. Expropriation decrees promulgated by radical regimes were loudly applauded in the daily and the academic press.

The third method of enhancing the position of the state sector was the expansion of economic relations with the Soviet bloc. Western aid was denigrated because it tended to promote

"capitalist relations" and safeguard ties with Western markets—
which both perpetuated backwardness and dependence. Conversely, Soviet assistance was extolled for strengthening the
public sector through the construction of industrial enterprises.[12]

After Khrushchev's removal, the party did not promulgate any
significant changes in theory, even though it switched to much
more pragmatic policies in the Third World.[13] The less rigid
attitude toward what constitutes a progressive political course
has been retained: to this day the revolutionary democrats are
accepted as a progressive force, although Soviet spokesmen on
ideological matters now credit disciplined "vanguard parties,"
instead of the amorphous "united fronts" or "mass parties," as
being the proper vehicles for effecting substantive change. However, the facile optimism about the future has been considerably
moderated by the recognition of realities. Among the more
striking signs of that change in official quarters was the abandonment of Khrushchev's faith in the primacy of politics over
economics. Accordingly, at the 1967 celebrations of the 50th
anniversary of the October Revolution, the customary paeans
to the influence of Russian events on the awakening of the East
were replaced by sober lectures on how "constant efforts to
advance the economy" were essential for progress.

A transition to a more pragmatic approach took place among
scholars as well, although, unlike a decade earlier, there was no
public prodding from the party. The first consequent inquiry into
the former assumptions appeared in December 1966.[14] It ques-
tioned the logic of assuming that all the national liberation movements were nothing but one huge revolutionary wave. After all,
out of more than 50 newly independent states of Asia and Africa
only 7 had chosen the noncapitalist path. "In all other countries
there has been an evolution—fairly rapid in some and slow in
others—along the capitalist path." Hence, it was incorrect to
argue that "growing into Socialism" was either the "dominant"
or the "general tendency" in the Third World. While strongly
questioning the "inevitability" theory that assumed the obso-
lescence of capitalism for the LDCs, the author also objected to
tampering with the basic Marxist scheme of political–social development by merging the tasks of the national with the socialist
revolutions. The processes taking place in Africa and Asia were
not that much different from historical evolution in Europe.

Therefore, for evolution to occur, there also had to be a class displacement; the existence of the socialist bloc was not enough by itself to eliminate the need for the working-class leadership of a Socialist revolution.[15]

A collective stock-taking took place at a conference convened in 1968 to discusss the three-volume work *Classes and Class Struggle in the Developing Countries,* issued by the Institute of World Economy.[16] (Like the parallel publication of the Institutes of the Peoples of Asia and of Africa on the national liberation movements, it was intended as a synthesis of the first decade of post-Stalinist scholarship. Though researched and written during the Khrushchev era, both works were published after his downfall. Thus, their reception indicated the transition to the new phase, motivated by different perceptions and interests.)

The participants directed their criticism at the excessive reliance on wishful thinking at the expense of ignoring demonstrable realities. There were objections to the basic assumption underlying the whole enterprise, i.e., the prospects of the noncapitalist path becoming the predominant trend. As for more specific issues, there was frank discussion of the paucity or absence of actual achievement in the radical states, as opposed to their grandiose programmatic claims. There was considerable concern about the transformation of revolutionary democrats into a bureaucratic élite that made use of the state sector for personal advantage rather than for the economic transformation of the country. And doubts were expressed that backward states could expect quick economic advancement by importing and utilizing the most advanced techniques to avoid wasting time on developing the necessary intermediate technology.

Under such questioning the post-Stalinist conceptual framework for Soviet studies of the newly independent countries began to crumble. What has emerged is a far more sober look at the realities of the Third World. As a result, the former concentration on the components of political progress has been to a large extent superseded by a close analysis of the factors contributing to economic development. At first, the shift was signaled by studies of the efficiency of the public sector, a distinct step forward from the former concern with its size.[17] But it soon broadened into the consideration of alternate policies that could contribute to economic advancement, such as the utilization of foreign investment, the fostering of domestic entrepreneurship, and participation in the capitalist world market.

By 1970, there were definite signs that a new outlook was taking shape. Among the most portentious was the publication in the November and December 1970 issues of *MEMO* of the preliminary findings of a new study group at the Institute of World Economy concerning the economic indicators of the level of development in nonsocialist states. The need for introducing a uniform system of analysis for 76 selected countries of Europe, Asia, Oceania, and Africa must have been pressing to justify publication in a preliminary form.[18] Here, for the first time, were comparative data on national income, the structure of the economy, population make-up, employment patterns, and literacy levels applied under the same rubrics to capitalist and developing countries alike.

Elementary as the study may seem, it heralded a basic shift in Soviet studies of the Third World. Its publication marked a decisive departure from seeing the world as divided into the antagonistic capitalist and socialist systems, and the LDCs as a unit with common problems and a common destiny resulting from that bifurcation. Henceforth, the best minds in the profession addressed their research on the developing countries not in terms of the socialist–capitalist competition for their political allegiance and economic cooperation but in terms of their actual position in world economy and domestic potentials. Furthermore, instead of treating Third-World countries as a uniform entity, all equally dependent and exploited, Soviet scholars began to study their heterogeneity.

Naturally, the old, normative judgments have not disappeared altogether. They persist to this day, though often in a much more attenuated form, for reasons of political convenience and habit, and because of their tenacious hold on the older members of the profession. But the old concepts no longer determine the innovative and creative research pursued mainly by the younger generation of scholars.

Just as in 1967–68, the publication of the two collective works by the two research institutes marked the conclusion of the first phase in Soviet Third-World studies, so the appearance of similar collective volumes in 1974 signaled the end of the transition and legitimized the current, next phase with its quite different focus and conceptual apparatus. The two works were entitled *The Developing Countries: Regularities, Tendencies, Perspectives*, and *The East Beyond Our Borders and Contemporary Times.*[19] As stated in their introductions, both were intended as correctives to the former, one-dimensional investigations centering on the newly independent countries' transition to Socialism.

In addition to posing new questions, the books also made a point of stressing the lack of consensus among the contributors and the unresolved nature of many issues. The variety of possible interpretations was further underscored in that each work discussed the Third World from a different perspective. *The Developing Countries*, produced by the research staff of the Institute of World Economy, treated Asia, Africa, and Latin America as a unit, subject to global processes. In contrast, *The East Beyond Our Borders*, published by the Institute of Oriental Studies, the current name of the Institute of the Peoples of Asia, took a more differentiated approach predicated on the particularities of domestic processes in Asian and the Near Eastern countries. Both made tentative departures from seeing the development process in terms of preventing capitalist take-over, and from regarding backwardness as the counterpart to the affluence of the industrial West. The simultaneous appearance of two such works infused the field with new life. In stirring up discussion (and disagreement) on the respective merits of the global and the particularistic approaches, they opened up vistas for a less politicized study of development issues at the time when the tremendous changes in the wake of the fuel crisis presented both the industrialized states and the LDCs with very different sets of problems from those that had marked the initial postcolonial period.

The post-1970 phase in Soviet Third-World studies is characterized by the emergence of three changed attitudes. This has resulted in quite a thorough-going cognitive reorientation. The focus is changed; new theories are being formulated and old ones revised.

First, there is the acceptance of extensive economic differentiation among the newly independent countries, which calls into question the former theory of unrelieved imperialist exploitation. Second, recognition of the functioning of a single world economy in responses to forces that transcend any specific political framework permits analysis of development strategies in terms other than economic liberation. Third, a coming to grips with the fluid, multilevel nature of Third-World societies and economies permits scholars to study the complexity and specificity of the LDCs with greater attention to their diversity and less adherence to a preordained uniformity.

An objective economic typology has gained legitimacy; it exists alongside and is completely unrelated to the political classification that divides the LDCs into capitalist- and socialist-oriented states. The 1974 collective work issued by the Institute of World Economy objected to the habit of treating the entire Third World as an undifferentiated unit. It proposed a more extensive and rigorous use of statistical data to "separate that gigantic mass of Asian, African, and Latin American countries into smaller groups and subgroups"[20] and to make possible a comparative analysis of economic development. The publication two years later of the volume on the economic typology of the nonsocialist states (resulting from the researches of the study group at the same institute first made public in 1970) gave substance to this proposal. At present, four basic groups are recognized: the poorest land-locked countries (mostly in Tropical Africa), the relatively advanced countries of North Africa and Asia, the oil-rich states, and Latin America.

There is no agreement on what constitutes the most reliable system of indicators for including a country in one or another economic grouping. While most of the disagreements concern the components of development—for example, the relative importance of income per capita as against the well-rounded integration of an entire economy—the discussions range farther than that. They do not stop with the static system of classification proposed by the 1976 volume on typology but touch upon the dynamics of development or, more specifically, what degree of progress can be acknowledged and what accounts for it.

On this topic the most lively disputes concern the characterization of capitalist development. The more traditional interpretations hold that the Third World can develop only within the framework of "dependent" capitalism, while the innovators want to dispense with political categories altogether and press for the recognition of "semideveloped capitalism"[21] With recourse to statistics and logic, they argue that objective indicators show the more backward areas of Europe (i.e., Portugal, Greece, Southern

Italy) to be on the same level as the more developed countries of Latin America (i.e., Mexico or Brazil) and should be grouped together as countries that have reached a level of semideveloped capitalism.

Since 1974, the theory of a single world economy that consists of two subsystems, the socialist and the capitalist world economies, has gained wide acceptance. Unaccompanied by any dramatic doctrinal pronouncements, it has considerably diluted, if not altogether replaced, the Stalinist version of the globe divided into two antagonistic world economies. Here, too, there is no uniform, agreed-upon interpretation of the new concept. The conservative academics accept cooperation between the two subsystems within the overarching framework to the extent of urging common action on global problems, such as the environment or ocean resources, but they hold that this cooperation cannot and should not alter each subsystem's specific mode of production and obliterate for the LDCs the choice of different paths of development.[22]

The liberal economists have a very different interpretation. They see the operations of the world economy as resulting from the scientific-technological revolution that has internationalized all economic processes. They are apt to downplay the significance of the two subsystems and to concentrate on the objective demands and opportunities the new situation poses for all countries. In their view, the world economy operates as "a sum total of all the separate national economies finding themselves in a complex interaction and mutual interdependence." Moreover, "the progress of each country is inseparable from its participation in a broad exchange of material and spiritual goods."[23]

The intransigent complexity of the Third World's social and economic structures has at last found a theory that does not force them into diluted Marxist categories. From the early 1970s, the concept of multistructuralism (*mnogoukladnost'*) has been increasingly used to cope with the demonstrable diversity. But again, while it has gained acceptance it is subject to different interpretations. The traditionalists interpret *mnogoukladnost'* as in no way deflecting from the predestined course of history from one economic order dominated by a single class and mode of production to another, i.e., as "an organic part of the evolution within the system of formations." Hence, they direct their research and analysis at locating the leading economic structures that will determine the evolution of a given country toward the capitalist or the socialist formation.[24]

A. I. Levkovsky, the leading exponent of an open-ended interpretation of *mnogoukladnost'*, argues that social and economic diversity is so endemic to the Third World that it is counterproductive to try to figure out at present toward which of the Marxist formations the LDCs are moving. They are passing through a separate "interformation" period of extremely long duration and deserve objective studies of their autochthonous, unique features.[25] While the conservatives object to Levkovsky's theories as deviations from historical materialism,[26] liberal scholars welcome them as new analytical tools that "rescue" the field from "oversimplifications" which crammed the development of the Afro–Asian countries "into a strictly deterministic . . . linear construction obligatory for all."[27]

Because of the cognitive reorientation in recent years, the development issues are now discussed in an entirely new framework. Although the ideologies of academe, like R. Ulianovsky, still maintain that all the problems of underdevelopment can be solved only through a decisive break with the capitalist system of exchange and production,[28] this spirit no longer guides those doing research in the practical aspects of development. These experts propose a development strategy cast within the framework of global interdependence, not of irreconcilable competition; of incremental change, not of decisive breaks.

The international division of labor is the key concept in the new development strategy. V. Tiagunenko gave it a full theoretical formulation in a book published in 1976. The book's thesis was the impossibility of studying the "preconditions, nature, and consequences of concrete social and economic changes" without taking into account "worldwide forces with which these processes are closely connected and intertwined."[29] Previously, the original Soviet model base on import-substitution industrialization had been somewhat modified by several less prominent specialists who discussed the practical advantages to be derived from adjusting production to international trade.[30] But a book by the "dean" of Third-World studies and a corresponding member of the Academy of Sciences redefining the relationship between development and participation in the world economy carried different weight. And indeed, it was hailed as a novel synthesis, enabling Soviet scholarship to advance to a new stage. As a result, the need of the LDCs to intertwine with the world market is by now generally accepted.

While some specialists still dwell on the costs of dependence, all deplore autarchic tendencies. There are alarmist articles about the recent trend among the LDCs to form closed regional economic groupings.[31] And Samir Amin's theories advocating economic isolationism from the industrial world as the best method for the developing countries to overcome backwardness has been severely criticized in Soviet scholarly publications.[32]

An important spin-off from the current Soviet advocacy of participation in the international division of labor is the admission that the Western presence is necessary and salutary for development. (This approach, be it noted, in no way contravenes Marx, who recognized the progressive role of the colonial powers in introducing advanced production methods to their dependencies.)

Many specialists, especially younger ones, openly state that the study of development in the Third World cannot be encompassed by denunciation of foreign domination, and they investigate the changes and advances resulting from the penetration, diffusion, and interaction of Western capital. Most frequently mentioned among its positive aspects are: the undermining of ossified social relations, the initiation of speedy development in some sectors of the economy, the contribution to the capital accumulation process, and the inclusion in the world market. Significantly, those authors who take a positive view of the Western presence maintain that the old colonial-type subordination is being replaced by a new relationship based on partnership and mixed enterprise.[33]

Nowadays, all economists who do substantive work on development strategy consider the utilization of Western capital know-how, and technology as an absolute necessity. Nothing demonstrates the reversal of Soviet views on the Western presence more graphically than the changing perceptions of the multinationals. Ye. Primankov, the director of the Oriental Studies Institute, has written that during the past decade they had divested themselves of complete control over local operations. A member of his staff, A. Volkova, has pointed out that the Third World is by no means the main theater of their operations; in fact, the extent to which the transnationals are active in these parts helps to integrate them into the world economy.[34] And I. Ivanov, from the Institute of World Economy, has stated at a roundtable conference that "it would be wrong to deny, while taking a realistic view, that the multinationals are in principle incapable of making a contribution to development."[35]

It is another matter that there is considerable disagreement about the measure of local control over foreign investment and operations which is deemed necessary and desirable. The conservatives assuage their conscience by urging stringent curbs; the liberal-minded modernists urge a reasonable dialogue resulting in mutually acceptable regulations.[36] Despite the persisting differences of opinion, there definitely has been an evolution in Soviet views on the Western presence: the export of capital is no longer equated with the export of capitalist production relations (i.e., of the capitalist system).[37] This theoretical formulation places the discussion of Western investment outside the systemic framework, permitting objective research on its contribution to economic growth.

The reinterpretation of the Soviet model of development also reflects changed perceptions. Recently, some scholars have resuscitated the idea of the New Economic Policy (NEP) as being more relevant to the LDCs than the construction of "socialism in one country" based on a forced industrialization drive. Introduced by Lenin in 1921, the New Economic Policy left the state in control of the "commanding heights"—heavy industry, banking, and foreign trade—while permitting small-scale private enterprise, private agriculture, and foreign concessions.

L. Reisner's study of the theory of economic growth contains the most detailed discussion of specific NEP policies that could be useful today: i.e., considering agriculture the basis for capital formation; promoting light industry to provide employment and income for the peasantry; undertaking measures to end agrarian overpopulation; building up labor-intensive industries; balancing consumption with accumulation; creating a domestic industrial complex; engaging in extensive economic and technical cooperation with the advanced states. More than that, Reisner ascribed the success of Western development theories in gaining acceptance among the LDCs to the fact that this valuable early Soviet experience has been "over-shadowed" by the subsequent Soviet policy which posited "forced industrialization as the only basis, method, and strategy for overcoming backwardness."[38]

The importance Moscow attaches to popularizing this new model can be gleaned from the fact that two recent works on the NEP are being translated into English: Y. Abramtsumov's *How Socialism Began: Russia under Lenin's Leadership, 1917-23* and A. Ugriumov's *Lenin's Plan for Building Socialism in the USSR, 1917-25.*[39] Both books stress the flexibility and moderation of Lenin's policies, his rejection of "infantile leftism," and reliance on compromise regarding foreign technicians and investment, as well as the local entrepreneurs and traders, in order to construct socialism without excessive losses and sacrifices.

The development strategy that is now strongly favored is one that will ensure political and social stability. Class struggle is no longer deemed essential for the establishment of proper production relations that will in turn instigate progress. (This is another point of contention the Soviets have with the Chinese and Third-World radicals.) Part of the reason why heavy industry and rapid industrialization are now deemphasized while processing industries and productive agriculture are considered essential for balanced development, is that, being labor-intensive, the latter contribute to the solution of unemployment. The massive growth of a *lumpenproletariat* is a source of considerable worry to Soviet Third-World experts.[40] The rapidly growing urban population is no longer considered as "hot material" for revolution but as a dangerously volatile element that is easy prey to reactionary or leftist extremism. Franz Fanon's theories about the revolutionary mission of the pauperized masses are in disfavor. And A. I. Levkovsky, the leading theorist on class structures at the Institute of Oriental Studies, has written that "excessive exaggeration of the role of de-classed social layers in the revolutionary movement inevitably leads to politically dangerous 'leaps' (*pereskoki*)"[41]

To prevent "disorderly" progression, wherein politics outrun the economic basis, Soviet scholars devote much time now to defining the proper relationship between the two. Ever since the serial collapse of radical regimes, beginning with Ben Bella's in 1965, Soviet scholars have been wary of economic "extremism." However, their *post mortems* on these reversals remained scattered in separate articles or chapters, and never examined the issue in a systematic manner. Finally, in 1975, N. Simoniya published a book pinpointing the reason for the failure of numerous national liberation movements in Africa and Asia—namely, the economic preconditions for success were inadequately established. He argued congently that a correct reading of the Marxist–Leninist classics demonstrated that progressive and lasting political change derives from a properly matured economic basis. Marx saw economic and political development as firmly sequential: socialism had to be the product of a developed and advanced economic system. Should revolution occur in a "weak link," as it had in Russia, then the situation demanded special attention to economic policies to bring industrial production, managerial skills, and labor discipline up to par with the requirements of the advanced political system. More specifically, Simoniya argued, such a regime had to rely on and develop the economic institutions left by the predecessor in order to create a firm foundation for its own survival. It could not abolish them forthwith and replace them with socialist production relations until capitalist production relations had developed sufficiently to make this possible.[42]

With all this rethinking of development strategy, what do the Soviet scholars now see as the best workable system for the Third World? Unquestionably, there is a common thread in their deliberations: to one degree or another, openly or indirectly, free enterprise and foreign investment are acknowledged to be necessary components of economic growth. The answer inescapably points to a mixed economy.

As yet, that term is not widely used; most economists refer to it obliquely by arguing that capitalism has not yet exhausted its potential for generating growth. But, surprisingly enough, the mixed economy is mentioned most often in discussions of the appropriate policies for countries of socialist orientation. It is the program the Soviets now propose to spare these states the costly and counterproductive excesses of premature socialist measures.

The concept of socialist orientation came into use in the late 1960s to denote states whose path of development offered a "socialist perspective." (Although it was meant to replace the concept of noncapitalist development, the two terms are now used interchangeably, and there is no agreement on what, if anything, differentiates them.) At the outset, the formula called for radical political reforms, an anti-Western foreign policy, crippling restrictions on local entrepreneurs and foreign investment, as well as active economic cooperation with the Soviet Bloc (involving elements of a socialist division of labor).[43] At present, the Soviet stance on domestic politics and diplomacy remains basically unchanged, but the interpretation of economic policies suitable for countries of socialist orientation has been altered substantially.

To begin with, it is recognized that both the capitalist- and the socialist-oriented countries remain in the world capitalist market, and no one seriously considers integration with the Soviet Bloc as a precondition for the noncapitalist path. "A specific feature of the development of [these] countries . . . is that even after their choice of the noncapitalist way they are still in the orbit of the world capitalist system."[44] On the domestic level, the survival of capitalist relations is also recognized: "All economically backward countries, including those which politically adhere to the most advanced and progressive positions, pass through some phase of capitalist development."[45]

When the economic malfunctioning of the radical states first became the subject of published commentary, most authors blamed the burgeoning bureaucracy for excessive costs and poor administration. At present, specialists increasingly advise more moderate policies on local free enterprise, foreign aid, and Western investment. Separately and together, all three are seen as indispensible to provide further stimulus to national efforts, introduce the needed technology and specialists, increase employment, improve services, and expand the food supply.[46]

Significantly, no specific set of economic policies is now regarded as essential for a socialist orientation, other than the vague enough theory about the state being the controlling agent. This is as much as "socialist" doctrine as it is an acceptance of what actually prevails in the Third World anyway. The more orthodox specialists like to dwell on what state power in these countries can accomplish:

> A mixed economy in the countries of socialist orientation . . . permits the utilization of capitalist elements [*uklady*] for the development of the production forces under state control in ways that prevent the transformation of these elements into the ruling capitalist system but create the preconditions for the victory of the state and cooperative sectors.[47]

217

Those specialists who concentrate more on economic performance than on political labels envision the operations of a mixed economy in less manipulative terms. Recognizing the weakness of the state apparatus, they speak about the "coexistence" of state and private sectors and quote from Engels that the state can successfully manage economic development only when it does not act as the sole agent but relies on the private sector.[48]

As for foreign capital, again realities are recognized. It is admitted that the West provides as much as 70 percent of the aid and credits to any radical regimes,[49] and no one urges the doctrinaire nationalization or exclusion of Western investment. On the contrary, even orthodox specialists argue that the socialist-oriented states should attract foreign capital and work out "such system of regulations . . . as will guarantee the interests of the radical regimes and grant sufficient advantages to foreign investors to attract them."[50]

What are the academic, ideological, and political implications to the reassessment of development issues? Some of the implications are more marked than others; still others are quite tentative.

In scholarship, the new trends denote an abandonment of the rigid deductive methodology and deterministic schemes. What interests many innovating specialists is not merely the refinement of analytical tools but the principle of open-ended inquiry. Sometimes they plead that "one should not limit oneself in advance to some obligatory framework [for], the world of the '80s will be more complex than the world of the '70s, and the world of the '90s more so than that of the '80s."[51] At other times and in other context, they accept the indeterminate nature of research, as did L. Reisner when he prefaced his book on the theory of development with reference to Niel Bohr's principle of complementarity.[52] This spirit, having already enriched the field with solid research in new subjects and a variety of challenging interpretations, offers prospects of much more to come.

New theoretical constructs and new fields of research have a bearing on ideology as well. To regard science and technology as the motive force of progress, to advise the LDCs to integrate with the world market, to acknowledge the private enterprise and foreign investment contribute much to development, to investigate the undefined yet distinct nature of Third-World economies—

all these arguments modify the traditional Marxist–Leninist assumptions about the ubiquitously maleficent role of imperialism and capitalism. They take into consideration the changing configuration of forces in the world economy, the general advance in knowledge, and the indigenous processes in the LDCs. The updated and realistic outlook among scholars should chasten our conventional wisdom that all Soviet analysis is purely political and views the economic problems of the LDCs as the consequence of an imperialist plot.

And, finally, there is evidence of a parallel evolution in the Soviet policy on international economic relations. When the LDC demands for a new international economic order were first made, Moscow welcomed them as another contribution to the struggle against Western imperialism. But more recently, Soviet statements at international forums have offered the novel suggestion that the LDCs give up confrontation and turn to cooperation. Kosygin's message to the IV UNCTAD, for example, stressed that conditions were now favorable for a "constructive discussion of international trade and development."[53] Similarly, at a discussion group on the national liberation movements, set up by the *World Marxist Review*, the Soviet delegate argued that it was no longer true that "imperialist exploitation could be limited only through the transition to the construction of socialism." It could be "curbed" even before the "abolition of the capitalist system."[54]

Thus, current Soviet thinking on development issues bears little resemblance to the formulation of the CPSU Program adopted in 1961 and left unchanged to this day:

> The young sovereign states . . . constitute that part of the world which is still being exploited by the capitalist monopolies. As long as they do not put an end to their economic dependence on imperialism, they will be playing the role of a "world countryside," and will remain objects of semicolonial exploitation.[55]

Both on academic and official levels, Soviet's views on development strategy are cast nowadays in terms of participation in a worldwide division of labor.

FOOTNOTES

1. For a more detailed description of these several Institutes of the Academy of Sciences, as well as of various faculties at the universities, and of other periodicals, see the very informative introduction in P. Berton, A. Rubinstein, *Soviet World on South East Asia: A Bibliography of Non-Periodical Literature, 1946-1965* (Los Angeles, Univ. of Southern California, 1967). See also N. A. Kuznetsova, L. M. Kulagina, *Iz istorii sovetskogo vostokovedeniya, 1917-1967* [From the History of Soviet Oriental Studies] (Moscow, Nauka, 1970; Yu. Illyn, et al., "African Studies in the USSR: the 1960s and 1970s," *Social Sciences* (Moscow), No. 4 (1979): 64-69.

2. *Mirovaya ekonomika i mezhdunarodyne otnosheniya*, 6 (1964): 81. (Henceforth cited as *MEiMO*.)

3. A clear sense of progression in readjustment can be obtained from reading the following materials: the report on the early 1962 conference held at the Institute of World Economy to discuss the new research priorities in the light of the decisions reached by the 22nd CPSU Congress, MEiMO, 3 (1962): 3-19; the six articles written by the leading experts on the newly independent states—V. Tiagunenko, R. Avakov, R. Andreasian, I. Farizov, Ye. Bragina, V. Kondrat'ev, G. Starushenko—for the September 1962 issue of the *Kommunist*, 13, 89-109; and the report on the 1964 conference at the Institute of World Economy at which the parameters of the new, "common point of view" were expounded, *MEiMO*, 4 and 6 (1964): 116-131 and 62-81.

4. Of course, a uniformity of interpretation has never characterized the discipline. Different emphases, novel approaches, a high level of scholarship have marked many individual works. My concern here, however, is not to evaluate the scholarly achievements of Soviet studies of the Third World, but to analyze prevailing trends.

5. *Problemy sovremennykh natsional'no-osvoboditel'nykh revoliutsii* (Moscow, Nauka, 1966). It was reissued in a revised edition in 1969 that shed some of the by-then outdated views.

6. The differences between generations may not have been as much apparent in the 1960s, since the tone was set by the Party. But they certainly became pronounced in the 1970s when the changing interpretations began to originate within the academic community.

7. *Klassy i klassovaya bor'ba v razvivayushchikhsia stranakh* (Moscow, Mysl', 1967-68).

8. *Natsional'no-sovoboditel'noe dvizhenie v Azii i Afrike* (Moscow, Nauka, 1967-68).

9. *Sovetskoe vostokovedenie*, 4 (1958): 213-215.

10. *Planovoe khoziaistvo*, 2 (1962): 91-95.

11. *Prolemy industrializatsii suverennykh slaborazvitykh stran Azii* [Industrialization Problems in the Soverign Underdeveloped Asian Countries] (Moscow, Iz. Akademii Nauk SSSR), 1960, pp. 52-53.

12. V. Rymalov, "Soviet Assistance to Underdeveloped Countries," *International Affairs*, 9 (1959): 25.

13. For one, the 1961 CPSU Program its formulations on the situation in the Third World remain unchanged to this day.

14. N. Simoniya, "O kharaktere natsional'no-osvoboditel'noi revoliutsi [On the Nature of the National Liberation Revolution], *Narody Azii i Afriki*, 6 (1966): 3-21.

15. Simoniya's arguments on the need to slow down the revolutionary timetable must have carried some weight for the article was expanded into a pamphlet and reissued in 1968 under the title *Ob osobennostiakh natsional'no-osvoboditel'noi revoliutsii* [On the Peculiar Features of the National Liberation Revolution].

16. *NEiMO*, 5 and 8, 70-104, 82-96.

17. See the *Narody Azii i Afriki* editorial in the December 1967 issue specifically calling for detailed analysis of the results of public ownership.

18. *MEiMO*, 11 and 12 (1970): 151-157, 142-149. The complete results were published six years later, *Tipologiya nesotsialisticheskikh stran* [Typology of the Non-Socialist States] (Moscow, Nauka, 1976).

19. *Razvivayushchiesia strany: zakonomernosti, tendentsii, perspektivy* (Moscow, Mys'l, 1974); *Zarubezhnyi Vostok i sovremennost'* (Moscow, Nauka, 1974).

20. *Razvivayushchiesia strany: zakonomernosti*, p. 133. *Zarubezhnyi Vostok* also called for detailed statistical studies of different regions and separate countries to introduce greater precision, p. 256.

21. There are many contributions to this dispute. The concept was outlined by V. Sheinis in "Strany srednego kapitalizma" [Countries of Middle-Level Capitalist Development], *MEiMO*, 9 (1977): 105-124. It was subject to public discussion and criticism at an academic conference in June 1978, *Latinskaya Amerika*, 1 (1979): 53-100.

22. See for example, Moskovskii Gosudarstvennyi Institut Mezhdunarodnykh Otnoshenii, *Mirovaya ekonomika* [The World Economy] (Moscow, Mezhdunarodnye Otnosheniya, 1978), p. 11.

23. M. Maksimova, *SSSR i mezhdunarodnoe ekonomicheskoe sotrudnichestov* [The USSR and International Economic Corporation] (Moscow, Mysl', 1977), p. 12. N. Shmelev, "Sotsializm i vsemirnoe khoziaistvo" [Socialism and World Economy], *MEiMO*, 10 (1976): 5.

24. S. Tiul'panov, "Obshchestvo perekhodnogo tipa" [Transitional Society], *MEiMO*, 1 (1979): 144-146.

25. For his early formulation, consult *Tret'ii mir v sovremennom mire* [The Third World in the Contemporary World] (Moscow, Nauka, 1970); and for the latest, *Sotsial'naya struktura razvivayushchikhsia stran* [Social Structure of the Developing Countries] (Moscow, Mysl', 1978).

26. A. Roslaev, "Eshche raz o teorii 'mnogoukladnosti' v stranakh tret'ego mira" [Once Again About the Multi-Structural Theory in the Countries of the Third World], *Rabochii klass i sovremennyi mir*, 1 (1977): 136-145.

27. V. Maksimenko's untitled review of A. Levkovsky's *Sotsial'naya struktura Narody Azii i Afriki*, 1 (1979), 208-214.

28. *Sovremennye problemy Azii i Afriki* [Contemporary Problems of Asia and Africa] (Moscow, Nauka, 1978), p. 230.

29. *Mezhdunarodnoe razdelenie truda i razvivayushchiesia strany* [International Division of Labor and the Developing Countries] (Moscow, Nauka, 1976), pp. 9-10.

30. E. Obminsky, *Razvivayushchisia strany i mezhdunarodnoe razdelenie truda* [The Developing Countries and the International Division of Labor] (Moscow, Mezhdunarodnye Otnosheniya, 1974).

31. L. Zevin, "novye kontseptsii ekonomicheskogo razvitiya i mezhdunarodnogo sotrudnichestva stran tret'ego mira" [New Concepts of Economic Development and International Cooperation in the Third World Countries], *Voprosy ekonomiki*, 1 (1978): 97-105.

32. See, for example, N. Gavrilov's review of Amin's *L'Agriculture africaine et le capitalisme, Narody Azii i Afriki*, 4 (1977): 231-232.

33. L. Gavrilov's *Eksport kapitala v razvivayushchiesia strany* [The Export of Capital into the Developing Countries] (Moscow, Nauka, 1976) was the first work to take an objective look at the role of foreign capital. He backed up his contentions with facts; since then, others have been much more outspoken: ed. A. I. Dinkevich, *Razvivayushchiesia strany: Problemy ekonomicheskogo razvitiya* [The Developing Countries: Problems of Economic Development] (Moscow, Nauka, 1978); ed. A. I. Levkovsky, *Inostrannyi kapital i inostrannoe predprinimatel'stvo v stranakh Azii i Severnoi Afriki* [Foreign Capital and Foreign Enterprise in the Countries of Asia and North Africa] (Moscow, Nauka, 1977).

34. "Nekotorye problemy razvivayushchikhsia stran" [Some Problems of the Developing Countries], *Kommunist*, 11 (1978): 81-91. "Nekotorye aspekty deyatel'nosti mnogonatsional'nykh korporatsii v razvivayush-chikhsia stranakh" [Some Aspects of the Activities of the Multinationals in the Developing Countries], in ed. A. I. Levkovsky (fn. 33), pp. 52-65.

35. "Multinationals: What Kind of a 'New World'." *World Marxist Review*, 7 (1978): 124.

36. Compare R. Ulianovsky's "The Developing Countries: Economic Front," *New Yimes*, 34 (1976): 12-20, with N. Simoniya's "Syr'evaya problema sovremennogo kapitalizma" [The Raw-Material Problem of Contemporary Capitalism], *MEiMO*, 3 (1978): 85-100.

37. This was pecitically stated by L. Goncharov in his review of V. Gavriliuk's *Gosudarstvenno-monopolisticheskii vyvoz kapitala v razvivayushchiesia strany* (Minsk, 1976); *Narody Azii i Afriki*, 2 (1979): 198-202.

38. *Razvivayushchiesia straya: ocherk teorii ekonomicheskogo rosta* [The Developing Countries: Outline of the Economic Growth Theory] (Moscow, Nauka, 1976), pp. 51-72, 321.

39. Published in Moscow by Progress (1977) and by Novosti (1976), respectively.

40. See the report on the round table conference on class struggle and egalitarian concepts, *Nardoy Azii i Afriki*, 6 (1978): 3-19.

41. A. I. Levkovsky, *Melkaya bourzhuaziya: oblik i sud'by klassa* (Moscow, Nauka, 1978), p. 137.

42. *Strany Vostoka: puti razvitiya* [Countries of the East: Paths of Development] (Moscow, Nauka, 1975).

43. V. Tiagunenko, *Problemy sovremennykh natsional'no-osvoboditel'nykh revoliutsii* [Problems of Present-Day National Liberation Revolutions] (Moscow, Nauka, 1969), pp. 187-188.

44. V. Solodovnikov, "Elimination of the Colonial System, an Expression of the General Crisis of Capitalism" *International Affairs*, 8 (1976): 24.

45. "The Revolutionary Process in the Socialist Oriented Countries of Africa," *World Marxist Review*, 1 (1978): 92.

46. A. V. Kiva, *Strany sotsialisticheskoi orientatsii. Osnovnye tendentsii razvitiya* [Countries of Socialist Orientation. Basic Tendencies of Development] (Moscow, Nauka, 1978), pp. 176-187.

47. G. B. Starushenko, *Sotsialisticheskaya orientatsiya v razvivayushchikhsia stranakh* [Socialist Orientation in the Developing Countries] (Moscow, Izd. politicheskoi litetatury, 1977), pp. 51-52.

48. V. Yashkin, "Gosudarstvennyi uklad v mnogoukladnoi ekonomike" [The State Sector in Multi-Sectoral Economy], *Aziya i Afrika segodnia*, 3 (1979): 41.

49. A. V. Kiva (fn. 46), p. 28.

50. G. B. Starushenko (fn. 47), p. 51.

51. "Kat otsenivat' osobennosti i uroven' razvitiya kapitalizma v Latinskoi Amerike" [How to Interpret the Traits and Level of Capitalist Development in Latin America], *Latinskaya Amerika*, 1 (1979), 69-70.

52. *Ekonomika razvivayushchikhsia stran. Teorii i metody issledovaniya*, p. 6.
53. *Vneshiniaya torgovlia*, 7 (1976): 2.
54. *World Marxist Review*, 5 (1979): 44.
55. *Materialy XXII S'ezda KPSS* [Proceedings of the 22nd Congress of the CPSU] (Moscow, Izd. Politicheskoi Literatury, 1961), p. 352.

CHAPTER NINE

DETENTE AND AMERICAN-SOVIET COMPETITION IN DEVELOPING COUNTRIES

Fred Warner Neal

Nowhere is the American-Soviet relationship which affects so vitally the future of mankind as delicate as in the vast areas of what we call the Third World. Competition between the two countries for influence in developing nations is fueled by the fact that so many of them are extremely unstable politically. The instability, exacerbated in turn by the competition, involves the possibility of ideological change and, this in turn, is seen by both Washington and Moscow as involving strategic geopolitical significance. In an age of ecological priorities, the resources of the underdeveloped areas are important to both countries—to the United States, especially as surrogate for its allies, doubtless more than to the USSR—and, as always, economic motives, no matter how veiled, are intertwined with ideological and strategic ambitions. Nevertheless, the military aspects of the U.S.-Soviet adversary relationship bulk so large that jockeying for global strategic position has become a goal in itself. As a result, the competition has a high military component even when armed forces are not actually employed.

As we shall see, in the early postwar period, the Soviet Union more or less ignored the developing nations. When, in the mid-1950s, the USSR began to compete in terms of economic and military assistance, there was a tendency in the West to interpret this as "intervention." Of course, assistance from either superpower constituted a form of "intervention," since it could not help but have an impact on internal affairs. It is not always easy to distinguish between economic and military assistance as far as "intervention," in this sense, is concerned, although obviously relationships involving military bases and armed forces are clearly different from those in which these components are not present.

The competition is thus a form of conflict, or potential conflict, between the superpowers. The Third World came to be an arena where much of it, in one form or another, takes place. The great danger is that such conflict could lead to military confrontation and thus to thermonuclear war.

Given the conflicting views of the world held by the United States and the Soviet Union, there is no way this competition, or conflict, can be eliminated. The need, therefore, is to make sure it does not result in military confrontation. This was one of the great hopes—and failures—of American-Soviet detente. It was not competition for influence in the developing countries which destroyed detente, but there is no question that such competition seriously contributed to its difficulties. The issue is one of the most important at the heart of differing concepts of detente. What we are concerened with here is the nature of that competition, its relation to the concept—and practice—of the detente of the 1970s and how the absence or presence of a new reconstructed detente relationships might affect international stability and the risks of superpower confrontation.

While the idea of detente can be thought of as a general relaxing of tensions, even on a worldwide basis, here we are talking primarily about detente as defined by Secretary of State Kissinger in 1974. "It is," he said, "the search for a more constructive relationship with the Soviet Union. . . . It is a continuing process, not a final condition that has or can be realized at any one time."[1] Detente did not envisage an end to American-Soviet competition but rather restrained it to avoid military confrontation and increased tensions. Detente is important for developing countries because they comprise the arena where such confrontation is most likely—and also, of course, because the fate of these countries, like that of all others, may ultimately be determined by the success or failure of achieving such restraint.

Like much of international politics, the American–Soviet competition in the developing countries had had about it something of an aura of unreality. In the first place it tended to see these countries as objects, having no interests and determination of their own, or at least none different from those of one or the other of the superpowers. If this were ever the case, it rapidly became less so. While the need for outside assistance remained, insistence on independent foreign policies could be seen in the nonaligned movement, and drive to reduce economic independence was reflected in Third-World enthusiasm for a "New International Economic Order." In both of these developments, the bulk of the new nations made small distinction, if any, between the United States and the Soviet Union.

Consequently, the American–Soviet competition was less than the zero-sum game it was often thought to be in Washington and Moscow. Both sides have "lost" developing countries to the other and, then sometimes, have "gained them back."[2] In virtually no developing countries identified at one time or another with Moscow or Washington was the position of either superpower wholly secure. As Prof. O. M. Smolansky has observed about the Middle East, "political 'successes' . . . are usually preludes to "failures' (and vice versa)."[3] It was not always clear who was seeking influence with whom.

Nevertheless, the competition goes on, spurred by the ideologies and materialistic drives of the United States and the Soviet Union—the one trying to maintain an unmaintainable *status quo*, the other trying to foster ties of internationalism in societies which are increasingly nationalistic, and both professing concern with peace and human welfare while loading on their "clients" vast amounts of armaments. In the irrationalism and neoanarchy which characterize the international system, the absence of some kind of detente relationship between the United States and the Soviet Union to defuse their competition risks military confrontation and global destruction.

Pax Americana Ad Interim

It may be useful first to take a quick look at how the American–Soviet competition developed and became so potentially virulent. For more than a century prior to World War II, Western colonialism, in one form or another, was the predominant motif of the world. The vast areas of Africa, Asia, and Latin America were largely under the sway of Western European powers and, beginning with the end of the 19th century, also the United States. The British Empire, whose fleets ruled the seven seas, was archetypical of the prevailing pattern of international organization.

From the viewpoint of long historical perspective, this was in many ways an anomalous situation, made possible essentially because of the development of nationalism and the industrial revolution in Europe at a time when ancient non-European societies had fallen into desuetude. This Western domination stimulated nationalism in the colonial areas and created an awareness of the material advantages of the industrial revolution. As a result, even before World War II "the natives were getting restless." When European power was destroyed as a result of the war, the colonial world broke down. In its place there emerged a new world which soon came to be dominated numerically by scores of new nations erected out of the colonial ruins—impoverished, intensely nationalistic, urgently striving for development and, burning with resentment, and often hatred, against their erstwhile Western masters.

The new world was essentially a revolutionary world. Internal political and economic stability was compounded by the fact that the very geographical and demographic contours of many of the new nations were formed not as a result of historical evolution but resulted from power relationships of the colonial powers during their dominance.

Initially, the Western pattern of political and economic organization prevailed in the new nations, essentially because of the impact of Western culture among the new governing elites. No matter how unsuited it might be under the circumstances, a capitalist, free-enterprise orientation existed throughout the Third World. Even though, in the years after World War II, the Western nations, and especially the United States, provided essential economic and military assistance to the new states, a certain economic colonialism remained. The new nations continued to provide raw materials for the industrialized countries of the West, receiving in return manufactured goods. Prices for the latter were comparatively high, prices for the former low. Consequently, material benefits of independence were disappointing. This in turn, in an era of "rising expectations," produced more resentment and political instability.

In terms of what might be termed "macro-international politics," the postwar world was dominated by the United States and the Soviet Union. More precisely, in the first decades after the war, it was dominated by the United States. Alone of all the nations, the United States had come out of the war stronger than before. From a prewar position of comparative isolationism, it had become a global power—indeed, *the* global power. The United States, and it alone, controlled the seas and the skies and, as a result of fighting the war, had military outposts all over the world. The United States alone possessed the combined military and economic might capable of projecting global power, and it— and it alone—possessed the atomic bomb.

American predominance in the world right after the war was not military. It was also ideological and economic. The American ideas of democratic capitalism, four freedoms, and a global open door for free trade followed the flag, as it were. Enterprising American businessmen were quick to take advantage of their country's ubiquitous position to establish themselves in most corners of the world. Only the Soviet Union and areas under its control—Eastern Europe and North Korea—were immune. It was a kind of pax Americana *ad interim*.

This new worldwide position of the United States was not only mutually unchallenged, in any meaningful way; it was unchallengeable. Hardly more than debilitated Western Europe and occupied Japan was the Soviet Union in a position to pose a challenge. Its productive capacity in ruins as a result of the war, which killed 20 millions of its citizens, the USSR had virtually no navy or long-range bombers, and its land forces, although large, were already over-extended in Eastern Europe and for a while, in North Korea. Exhausted both materially and psychologically from the war, the Soviet Union could only focus on its gigantic problems of recovery.

The Cold War—Soviet Isolationism

Challenges to the new American position were in the making, however. The American-Soviet alliance which won the war broke down almost as soon as the shooting stopped, not over competition in the Third World but over Eastern Europe and Germany. Even though the Truman Doctrine of 1947 perceived a Soviet threat in more or less global terms, the Cold War was initially Europe-centered. Without going into the controversy over which side was more responsible, suffice to say that mutual misconceptions were involved. The considerable expansion of Soviet power into Eastern Europe and Germany as a result of the war, plus Western European weakness, gave rise to Western fears of further Soviet expansion. Many in the West were convinced that Soviet Communist ideology impelled the USSR to seek "world domination." For its part, the Soviet Union interpreted Western opposition to its position in Eastern Europe, American global power and the change in American attitudes which accompanied the Truman presidency as manifestations of capitalist hostility and efforts at encirclement.[4]

The Soviet weakness *vis-à-vis* the capitalist world after World War II was not new. It had, in fact, existed ever since the Bolshevik Revolution in 1917. Lenin, ever the realist, recognized it in 1921 when he proclaimed the New Economic Policy, or NEP. NEP called for a limited and temporary reversion to capitalism at home and, with regard to foreign policy, postponement of efforts to produce worldwide revolution. The "objective conditions for revolution," Lenin concluded, were not present. NEP ushered in a long period of inward-lookingness and focus on domestic Soviet problems. Under Stalin, who jettisoned the internal aspects of NEP, the inward-lookingness became a sort of isolationism, as the USSR concentrated all its efforts on building "socialism in one country." There was, he said, an "ebb tide of revolution" in the world, and the task of the USSR was to build its strength against the day when this would become a "flow tide." Forced by the Nazis to enter the international political arena, Stalin got his fingers badly burned, first by the Munich agreement, and then by his efforts to counter it through the Nazi–Soviet pact.

Whatever his hopes may have been during the brief period of the World War II alliance with the West, it is clear that Stalin, looking out at the world from the sometimes-paranoid windows of the Kremlin in 1945–1946, felt the necessity to turn inward again at least temporarily. For Stalin, Soviet economic and military recovery constituted the overriding priority, along with maintaining and strengthening the Soviet hegemony in Eastern Europe.

For him, the world was divided—as Zhdanov told the first meeting of the Cominform in 1947—into two hostile camps.[5] One camp comprised the USSR and its satellites in Eastern Europe. The other camp consisted of the rest of the world, dominated, as Stalin saw it, by capitalist powers. No matter that new nations were a-building, many of them looking for ways to divorce themselves from their former colonial masters. Either they were Socialist countries—i.e., run by Communist parties, which meant subservience to Moscow—or they were part of the hostile world with which the Soviet Union would have no truck. Stalin seemed to be continuing the earlier conviction that "objective conditions for revolution" did not obtain except where the Red Army was in control, as in Eastern Europe. And Stalin considered the USSR too week and too preoccupied to try to promote them.

In fact, the revolutionary potential in the Third World was there and about to burgeon. But the domestic exigencies were too great for Stalin to see it, or at least to concern himself with it. As a result, there was virtually no Soviet involvement at all in the Third World in the years immediately following World War II.

The United States completely misconceived this Soviet abstention from the Third World. Goaded by Soviet intransigence regarding Eastern Europe and Germany and spurred by a rising anti-Communism at home, the widespread American belief was that the Soviet Union was seeking to extend its tenacles everywhere. If Stalin ignored rising nationalism and indiginous revolutionary forces, so did Truman and his successors. When the Communists took over China, for example, Dean Rusk, then Assistant Secretary of State for Far Eastern Affairs, attributed it to Soviet action and termed China a Soviet outpost. The fact was, of course, that not only did the USSR not aid the Chinese Communists in their revolution but that Stalin counselled them against making it.[6] The Korean war only convinced American decision-makers of the correctness of their evaluations and gave further credence to the idea of a Soviet Union bent on "world domination."

The Cold War—A Soviet Offensive

It was not until 1952 that Stalin shifted gears. By this time the Soviet Union was well on its way to a quite remarkable economic recovery. It was still militarily weak compared with the United States, but military recovery, too, was in sight. The USSR now had the atomic bomb and was ready to develop thermonuclear weapons. Moreover, fissures in the *pax Americana* were appearing. Anti-Western nationalist movement, some communist-oriented, some not, were apparent throughout the Third World, visible even to the blinkered Kremlin.

To Stalin, this combination of renewed Soviet strength and anti-Western nationalism meant that the long "ebb tide of revolution" had shifted to a "flow tide." At the 19th Congress of the Soviet Communist party, Stalin called on the communists to take advantage of it.[7] Nationalism, he said, was now a dominant force in the world, and it was being ignored by the capitalist states, especially by the United States with its multinational and supranational anti-communists pacts and diplomatic devices. It was up to the communists, Stalin declared, to exploit this by picking up "the banner of nationalism where it had been dropped by the bourgeoisie." Whether a regime was communist or not was not important, Stalin implied. The important thing was that it stood independent of capitalism and outside the world capitalist market. Such regimes should be supported, because their success would hasten the collapse of capitalism generally. The Soviet Union would help the process not only by extending aid to the new states and encouraging nationalist movements but also by economic competition with the capitalist countries for Third-World resources and markets.

What Stalin called for at the 19th party Congress, in short, was a foreign policy offensive in which competition with capitalism— i.e., especially the United States—in the developing countries was a major ingredient. Interestingly enough, this dramatic and significant shift in Soviet foreign policy outlook was virtually ignored in the United States, and for two main reasons: first, American policy-makers had already assumed there was an all-out Soviet effort to achieve influence in the developing countries; second, the implementation of the new foreign policy called for by Stalin was some time in the making and was not put into effect until after his death. Nonetheless, it was a shift of the utmost significance, and it ushered in the superpower postwar competition in the Third World.

By 1955, the Soviet Union had launched a foreign-aid program and began making overtures to dozens of developing countries all over the world.[8] The ensuing erosion of the *pax Americana*, however, occurred not so much because these countries were attracted to Soviet Communism as because the possibility of Soviet support gave them an alternative to dependence wholly on the West. The first and perhaps classic example was Nasser's Egypt, which opted for collaboration with the USSR after the United States refused to provide aid for the Aswan Dam.

The new foreign policy stemming from Stalin's 19th Congress position signaled an intensification of the Cold War. The United States was already beginning a global struggle against "Communism," called for in the famous National Security Council document #68, and Secretary of State Dulles, ready, as he said, to go "to the brink of war," was designing a worldwide system of anti-Soviet military pacts.[9] In a period when both sides now had thermonuclear weapons and missiles of global reach, the danger of military confrontation—heretofore virtually nonexistent because of Soviet reluctance and/or inability to project its power—loomed for the first time.

The New Soviet Global Reach

Khrushchev, in 1956, laid the groundwork for defusing the danger of superpower confrontation, but at the same time he set in motion an even more active Soviet foreign policy offensive. The foreign policy outlined at the 20th party Congress—and further spelled out at the 21st Congress in 1959—redefined the Soviet concept of "peaceful coexistence" to mean that war was no longer inevitable. Increased Soviet and communist strength provided the means of preventing it, he said, and the destructive nature of thermonuclear weapons was such that even capitalist nations—hitherto regarded as inevitably committed to warmaking—might be more restrained. Indeed, according to Khrushchev, it was now imperative to prevent war in the interest of the Soviet Union and communism, i.e., to avoid global destruction; and for this, agreements and a certain amount of cooperation with capitalist countries were necessary. Khrushchev also downgraded the idea of violent revolution, contending that new

political patterns in both developed and under-developed countries made a "peaceful transition to socialism" more likely. The
Soviet Union would henceforth compete "by example".[10]

At the same time, however, Khrushchev proclaimed two exceptions to Soviet abstention from international voilence. First, wars
of "national liberation" were inevitable and the Soviet Union
would support them, although it would not instigate them. Second, the Soviet Union would come to the defense of established
Socialist regimes if the imperialists sought to put them asunder.

The new coexistence position had two prerequisites—that the
Soviet Union be treated as an equal power in all respects, i.e.,
especially by the United States—and that communism be treated
as an equal world system, as legitimate as capitalism.

Both the exceptions and the prerequisites constituted a challenge to the West. The United States and its allies had heretofore
not only been predominant in both military strength and in their
overall role in the international system but had frequently inter-
vened—more of less with impunity—in underdeveloped areas to
suppress national liberation movements.

The new Soviet position did not explicitly threaten global
intervention, but it did put the United States on notice that
henceforth the USSR considered it had as much right to be anywhere in the world as the USA. It was a declaration of a kind of
"Ruth syndrome"—i.e., whither thou goest, I too will go, or at
least claim the right to go. This is more or less what Khrushchev
tried to tell President Kennedy when they met in Vienna in 1961.
Kennedy felt Khrushchev was threatening him. Certainly, in a
way, he was.

The new position reflected several factors. First of all, although
the Soviet Union still lagged behind the United States significantly
in virtually all indicators of strength, its growing economic power
and its thermonuclear arsenal did serve as "equalizers" to a considerable extent. Second, the Soviet Union had never given up its
goal of promoting communism where possible. "National liberation movements," even if not communist, were seen as means to
that end, both because they weakened capitalism—the Stalin
argument at the 19th Congress—and because they were likely
to opt for socialist rather than capitalist patterns; in turn, this
opened vistas for new relations with the Soviet Union which
could, in Moscow's view, ameliorate the USSR's unequal global

strategic position. Additionally, the fire-breathing Chinese communists, reluctant to accept the new coexistence formula, had to be reassured that it did not mean abandoning the cause of revolution. Increasingly, also, as the Chinese began to compete with the Russians for influence in the world Communist movement, a Chinese presence in developing countries was an added spur to Soviet intervention of one sort or another. (Indeed, with regard to foreign aid to developing countries, the Soviet performance seemed to have competition with China more in mind than competition with the United States. Invariably, when Chinese aid increased, so did Soviet aid. This was not necessarily the case as far as American aid was concerned.)[11]

The new Soviet "global foreign policy" was not long in manifestating itself. Sometimes, it seemed, the United States was almost consciously giving its opportunities—as, for example, in regard to Egypt in 1956 and Southeast Asia (especially Laos) in 1959-60. Soviet assistance was quickly extended to the new governments in India, Syria, Indonesia, Iraq, Guinea, Ghana, and Mali and later Yemen and Algeria. Soon there would be others.

Although military assistance was a prominent part of Soviet assistance to these regimes and increasingly bulked larger,[12] it was hardly "intervention" in the ordinary sense of the word. Nevertheless, it was a manifestation of the assumption by the USSR of a global role.

A Contradiction?

The Soviet pledge of support for "wars of national liberation" did not by itself necessarily threaten military intervention. In fact, Khrushchev specifically qualified the new stance by asserting that the Soviet Union would not intervene militarily if "the imperialists," i.e., the United States—did not. And then he went further: the Soviet Union would not necessarily intervene militarily even if the imperialists did, because, he said, imperialist intervention usually was self-defeating.[13] Even with these qualifications, however, the new Soviet position involved a potential contradiction. The overriding objective of the doctrine of coexistence was to avoid thermonuclear war, which, practically speaking, meant avoiding military confrontation with the United States. But if the Soviet Union were to support a national liberation movement which the United States was opposing, might this not risk military confrontation? Indeed, this almost happened in 1961, when the USSR began assisting communist forces in Laos, where the United States armed forces were already involved. Even though Soviet forces were not present in Laos, President Kennedy went on national television to warn that the situation risked World War III.[14]

Laos was, of course, far away from the United States, and probably Kennedy didn't really mean it. But, if a country in a core American security interest were involved, the outcome could have been much different. The Cuban missile crisis, which took the world to the very brink of thermonuclear war, is a case in point. Here it was not Soviet support of a national liberation war but the Soviet pledge to defend an established socialist regime— also an integral part of the new coexistence posture—which was in question.[15]

Of course, as long as the Kremlin itself can decide what "support" means and what is and what is not a "socialist regime"— or a "nationalist liberation movement"—it can, theoretically, avoid getting into situations considered too dangerous. But "bluff" invariably plays an important role in international politics, and misperceptions are more usual than unusual in foreign policy determination. Additionally, if Soviet pledges meant anything, it was not too difficult to envisage a scenario where the Kremlin might think it is necessary to honor them, even at great risk. Except for the Cuban cause, the Soviet union, in fact, has carefully abstained from any kind of intervention in clear American core interests. And even in regard to Cuba, the USSR may have been pushed beyond prudence by fears of Chinese competition— a pressure more or less dissolved during the 1960s. Nevertheless, even before the Cuban missile crisis—and, possibly, with it in mind—Khrushchev had denigrated the Monroe Doctrine and pronounced it dead.[16]

How "prudent" the Soviet Union might be in offering its support to Socialist regimes or national liberation movements would likely be determined, at least in part, by its military strength vis-à-vis the United States. It is not altogether accurate to say that the USSR "backed down" in the Cuban missile crisis, since the solution involved a non-intervention pledge by the United States. Nonetheless, it was clear in that affair that the Soviet

Union was "out-navied" and, despite Khrushchev's bravado, "out-missiled." Whether it was because of a relaization of this, or other factors, the 1960s saw the start of the steady Soviet military build-up which persisted throughout the following decade. As a result of this, the more or less "token" Soviet military equality which existed at the time of Cuba came to be a real, across-the-boards equality, not only in nuclear weapons but also naval strength and other "conventional" weapons. Without going into the argument about who's ahead in what variety of weaponry, it was unquestionably the fact that during the 1970s the Soviet Union became able to project military power far from Soviet borders in a way which had been impossible in earlier years.

In terms of competition in developing countries, the situation was thus far different—and far more dangerous—than it was before. The West, and principally the United States, had set the pattern of intervention, covert and open, in distant developing areas—Iran, Egypt, Lebanon, the Congo, and Cuba—and, of course, Southeast Asia. Although the Soviet Union had already followed suit in some instances, now its capacity to do so was roughly equal to that of the United States.

The Promise of Detente

A great many factors led to the American–Soviet detente of the early 1970s. If the major one was mutual fear of each other's growing nuclear capabilities, another was also a mutual under-standing that military confrontation in the Third World involved the danger that these might be used. While the idea of defusing competition in the developing nations did not arise explicitly in the detente negotiations, it hovered conspicuously in the background and was implicitly treated in the formal agreements. Indeed, the morass in which the United States had involved itself in Vietnam was the catalyst for the beginnings of detente.

A major ingredient in the American failure in Vietnam was the continuing supply of armaments by the Soviet Union to North Vietnam. Nixon and Kissinger concluded—correctly—that the leverage this gave Moscow over Hanoi could be utilized to persuade the North Vietnamese to negotiate arrangements permitting a U.S. withdrawal without the appearance of total defeat. To demonstrate that the United States could not be "pushed around," the Nixon administration attempted one last massive try—the bombing of Hanoi and the mining of the Haiphong harbor. It is ironical that the detente negotiations—one hope of which was to defuse American–Soviet competition in developing nations—got underway at the very time that the United States was utilizing penultimate military force in one of them intimately allied with the USSR.[17]

An awareness of the new strength of the Soviet Union was obviously among the reasons which led the United States to opt the policy of detente. Nixon and Kissinger saw an ordering and restraining of American-Soviet competition essential if military conformation and nuclear war were to be avoided. For the Soviet Union detente was, in a sense, a "tactic" to implement the co-existence "strategy." That is to say, concentrating on a new relationship with the United States to defuse the Cold War was considered necessary if the security and economic benefits originally envisaged in the coexistence doctrine were to be realized, above all, of course, avoidance of military confrontation and nuclear war. Detente could thus eliminate the contradiction in the coexistence doctrine.[18]

American–Soviet detente, as defined in the Declaration of Principles signed by Nixon and Brezhnev in May 1972,[19] appeared to meet Moscow's coexistence requirements of recognition of the Soviet Union as a fully equal power and communism as a legitimate and equal system in international affairs. In the Declaration, the United States and the Soviet Union pledged to respect each other's core interests, "based on the principal of equality."

The Declaration went on with both sides promising to "do their utmost to avoid military confrontations." They further agreed "always [to] exercise restraint in their mutual relations and . . . be prepared to negotiate and settle differences by peaceful means . . . in a spirit of reciprocity, mutual accommodation, and mutual benefit." Both countries "recognize[d] that efforts to obtain unilateral advantage at the expense of the other, directly or indirectly, are inconsistent with these objectives." Returning to the same theme a year later, an "Agreement on Prevention of Nuclear War" pledged the United States and the USSR to "act in such a manner as to prevent the development of situations capable of causing a dangerous exacerbation of their relations, [and] as to avoid military confrontation. . . ."[20]

As far as American-Soviet competition in developing countries is concerned, there were ambiguities in the detente agreements capable of differing interpretations—not so much of the overall purposes and objectives as of their application to specific situations which might arise. There was no thought—on either side—that the competition would diminish. Indeed, Kremlin spokesmen made it clear that the Soviet Union was not relinquishing its policy of support of national liberation movements and that "ideological competition" would, if anything, increase.[21] Likewise, that there would continue to be an adversary relationship was constantly stressed by Nixon and Kissinger.[22] But did the pleges of caution and restraint and promises not to seek "unilateral advantage at the expense of the other" mean no intervention anywhere? And what constituted intervention? Only intervention with armed forces? Covert operations? Military assistance? While these questions were not faced up to in the detente negotiations, it seems safe to say that what was envisaged was essentially no interventions which directly threatened one side or the other and especially no interventions by one side into an area where the other was already involved, or had recognized security interests, plus restraint in areas where both might be involved. But even these concepts are imprecise. It is doubtful if they could ever be otherwise. The importance of detente lay not so much in categorizing specific types of actions as in establishing an overall relationship in which various actions would not be threatening.

In considering such matters, one must distinguish between three types of geographic areas. One embraces the clear core interests of both powers, that is, those areas considered so vital to national security that a perceived threat to them is certain to bring an immediate, and usually violent, reaction—e.g., Eastern Europe for the Soviet Union and Latin America and Western Europe for the United States. A second is a gray area, where the superpowers are involved and have important but less than clear core interests. The Middle East is a classic example. A third consists of areas not affecting the security of either power and where neither have manifested significant interests. Prior to the mid-1970s, at least, southern Africa seemed to be one such an area.[23]

The mutual recognition of core interests was explicit in the Declaration of Principles. Even though these areas were not spelled out, it was abundantly clear to both sides what they were

Concretely, this meant, *inter alia*, that the Soviet Union would not intervene in, or seek directly to influence, those developing countries within the American security sphere, i.e., Latin America. And, although the Cuban connection was maintained, and even in some ways enhanced, aside from Cuba the Soviet Union abstained almost ostentatiously from Latin American affairs throughout most of the 1970s.

The call for restraint in the gray areas was almost equally explicit, since both sides agreed on the importance of "preventing the development of situations capable of causing a dangerous exacerbation of their relations" and promised "to do everything in their power so that conflicts or situations will not arise which would serve to increase international tensions." The 1973 Middle-East war brought a quick test to the validity of these principles. Although perhaps both the United States and the Soviet Union could have done more to prevent that conflict from arising, both did, generally speaking, exercise restraint and worked separately to limit and end the war.[24] Admiral Worth Bagley, commander-in-chief of U.S. Naval forces in Europe, for example, observed at the time that "the Soviets weren't overly aggressive. It looked at though they were taking some care not to cause an incident. On the whole, thieir overt posture was restrained and considerate."[24a]

Although it was too early in the detente process to have implemented the Soviet idea for joint American–Soviet peacekeeping, it it was clear that detente, then in its heyday, in all likelihood prevented a superpower confrontation in the 1973 war. As President Nixon commented, "without detente we might have had a major conflict in the Mideast. With detente we avoided it."[24b]

It was in regard to the third area, where neither side had manifested important interests, that the most serious problems arose. Detente was already encountering its first setback, in the Jackson-Vanik amendment to the Trade Act,[25] when, in the summer of 1975, a crisis broke out in the Portuguese colony of Angola. The Angolan affair involved no direct superpower confrontation, but it did result in damage to detente.

The Lessons of Angola

The Angolan situation had several distinctive characteristics. Angola was a country in limbo in 1975, neither a colony nor an independent state. The Portuguese had decided to grant independence as of November, but, with a political upheaval in Portugal itself, had already ceased to exercise authority there. Both the Soviet Union and the United States were giving low-level assistance to competing national liberation groups, and Gulf Oil Company had a concession.[26] But neither country had ever manifested especial concern about Angola or indicated they considered it important for security reasons. With independence nearing, the United States and the Soviet Union stepped up aid to their respective groups. By 1974, the Chinese as well as the South Africans had entered the contest, supporting yet a third liberation group. With the spread of virtual anarchy in Angola resulting from cessation of Portuguese authority, the USSR greatly increased military assistance to its favored group, the Movement for the Popular Liberation of Angola (MPLA), which in turn brought a further increase in Central Intelligence Agency (CIA) aid to MPLA's opponents. Finally, in part because the MPLA forces were unable to utilize the sophisticated weaponry supplied by Moscow, the Soviet Union flew in Cubans. Although Kissinger pushed for continued American intervention, his efforts were blocked by Congress. In the end the communist-oriented MPLA triumphed.[27]

The Angola situation quickly brought out differences in the interpretation of the still fledgling detente. Asserting that "detente is indivisible," Secretary Kissinger denounced the Soviet–Cuban intervention as a violation of its permissible boundaries.[28] The USSR, on the other hand, insisted there was nothing in the detente relationship to bar its actions in Angola since it did not threaten American interests and pointed out, moreover, that Soviet spokesmen had always said detente did not mean the USSR would not continue to support national liberation movements.[29]

These respective positions did more to confuse than clarify the real issue. Aimed specifically at avoiding military confrontations, the detente guidelines clearly prohibited either side from intervening, in any way, in the core interests of the other. They clearly called for restraint in gray areas such as the Middle East. But they said nothing about actions in areas of nonsecurity interest like Angola. It might be said that both sides, in a sense, violated the detente pledge to avoid developments "capable of causing a dangerous exacerbation of their relations," but what evidence was there to indicate either side thought its intervention was a "dangerous exacerbation?" Additionally, as we have seen, Angola, neither independent nor under Portuguese control, was "up for grabs," with not only the United States and the Soviet Union intervening but also the Chinese and the South Africans. Since the latter were opposing the pro-Soviet faction, even a mutual American-Soviet abstention would have resulted in a *de facto* defeat for Moscow. Of course, Angola was in this sense a unique situation.

One could say that the problem in Angola was not too much detente but not enough. That is, central to the detente relationship was the idea of avoiding superpower confrontation—above all military confrontation—but, implicitly, perhaps, also political confrontation. The only way this could be achieved, if it could be achieved at all, would be by high-level consultations about the nature of the two nations' respective interests. The core interest areas, as noted above, were fairly clear. If the situation was less clear in the gray areas, it was not clear at all in the noninterest areas. Yet there were no efforts to discuss these matters. Nobody proposed it. The Soviet Union had no reason to consider that Angola might be considered an important American interest. Indications were that Moscow was genuinely surprised at the intensity of the American reaction to events in Angola.[30]

This failure to discuss a *modus vivendi* for American and Soviet global interests was in some ways the greatest failure of detente. Discussions of this nature might not have led to agreement, but they could not have helped but clarify matters and might well have avoided the attribution against detente which ensued from the Angola affair. Perhaps the detente process was still not sufficiently advanced.

After mutual interventions were under way, Kissinger sought to persuade the Kremlin that a withdrawal from the conflict of all non-African powers was desirable.[31] There is some indication that the USSR responded to these overtures, since, after President Ford had met with Soviet Ambassador Dobrynin, it halted its military airlift to Angola on December 9, 1975, continuing the suspension until December 24. If, as Kissinger felt, the resumption was triggered by congressional prohibition on further U.S. aid to Angola, at the same time it apparently indicated a Soviet interest in avoiding confrontation.[31a]

Actually, by that time, it was doubtless then too late for effective cooperation, if only because the South Africans and the Chinese were already involved. Had such discussions come earlier, the outcome might have been different. Even the 1973 Middle East war, where restraint was in fact exercised by both sides, would have posed less of a strain on mutual relations had there been prior consultations about the nature and extent of American and Soviet interests. The difficulty was that such consultations can occur only in a cooperative relationship, but that without them the results inhibit development of such a relationship. In some ways it was like detente and SALT agreements. Detente would seem to be necessary in order to have arms limitation agreements, but, at the same time, it is doubtful if there can be detente without arms limitation agreements.

Competition in the Horn of Africa

Competition in the Horn of Africa subjected American–Soviet relations to further strain. But there the situation was much different than in Angola. In the case of Somalia and Ethiopia, fully established governments asked for Soviet military assistance. Even though strategic implications were involved—more clearly than in Angola—strictly speaking it is difficult to interpret the Soviet interventions *per se* as violations of detente, and no such accusations were officially made. What made some Americans feel threatened by Soviet intervention in the Horn of Africa was not only the Soviet presence, with the Cubans, and the volume of Soviet military supplies,[32] but the perception of these factors as a part of Soviet hostile intentions toward Middle Eastern oil. What a functioning detente relationship could have done was to have minimized the strategic implications and, in turn, avoided, or at least mitigated, the resulting strain on American–Soviet relations.

The military coup of 1969 in Somalia occurred before the American–Soviet detente relationship was formalized, but the Russians seem to have had little if anything to do with it. Prior to this time, the United States, the USSR and China all had given assistance to Somalia, with Moscow the biggest supplier of military aid.[33] Following the coup, Siad Barre proclaimed Somalia a socialist state. The Soviet Union, having greatly stepped up its military support, then proceeded to construct extensive military and naval facilities. A certain American and Chinese involvement continued, however, until 1975, when the Soviets again upped their aid package and supplemented it with Russian and Cuban military advisers to help train the Somalian forces.

Even if the strategic implications of Soviet bases on the Indian Ocean could have raised questions about detente in regard to Somalia, it is less clear that the bases were the major Soviet objectives. By 1977, Moscow, in effect, abandoned them by switching its support to Ethiopia, which was engaged in military conflict with Somalia. The Russians, along with the Cubans, were then expelled from the country.[34]

Soviet competition with the United States in Ethiopia presents a more complicated and more ambivalent set of circumstances than that in Somalia. Until Emperor Haile Selassie was overthrown in 1974, Ethiopia was, more or less exclusively, an American "client," with almost no Soviet presence. While hardly a vital U.S. strategic interest in the sense of, say, the Caribbean, it was nonetheless clear that the United States considered it of strategic importance.[35] This continued to be the case even after the Dergue came to power, although the increasingly radical socialist·leaning of the new regime, with indications it was flirting with Moscow, was causing reevaluation in Washington. When Mengistu, the new Ethiopian strong man, took over in February 1977, Ethiopian relations with the Soviet Union became much closer, and small military supplies began to trickle in. The actual American replacement by the Russians did not come until after President Carter, as a part of his "human rights" emphasis, cut off military aid to Addis Abbaba. Mengistu then expelled the Americans and promptly went to Moscow seeking aid. It was only toward the end of 1977, however, that the massive influx of Soviet military assistance into Ethiopia began.[36]

U.S.–Soviet competition in Ethiopia resembles in some ways what occurred in Egypt after the 1973 war. There, the Russians were expelled, in part because of Moscow's reluctance to supply the Egyptians with the arms Cairo thought it needed, and it was the Americans who rushed in to fill the gap.

Although the Soviet Union came into Ethiopia at the invitation of the government and only after the Americans had been ousted, nevertheless the shift from an American to a Soviet military presence did constitute a change in the strategic balance in the Horn of Africa.[37] (It remained to be seen, of course, whether the Soviet-Ethiopian alliance would prove to be more lasting than that between the USSR and Somalia.) The Ethiopian affair in particular illustrates one of the knotty aspects of the whole problem. With the Americans no longer present, and Moscow, beseeched by the Ethiopian government to supply it with military aid, it would be ridiculous to have expected the Kremlin to say, in effect, "No, we can't because it would involve obtaining 'a unilateral advantage at the expense' of the United States." To the extent that American objections to the Soviet presence in Ethiopia were based on considerations of detente, it was an indication of how unrealistic these considerations were.

The competition in the Horn of Africa seems to demonstrate that detente is more important in creating an overall relationship defused of military threat than it is in proscribing this or that national action. It is also clear from developments in the Horn of Africa that detente is no substitute for an otherwise intelligent and realistic foreign policy.

Afghanistan

The question of detente enters into the question of Soviet intervention in Afghanistan only peripherally. The intervention occurred in December 1979. Not only had Afghanistan been oriented almost altogether toward the USSR since at least the spring of 1978, but, given its geography, it is an obvious security interest of the Soviet Union. Just as obviously, it is not a security interest of the United States and was never so claimed until after the Soviet interventinon. Whether or not the Soviet intervention was legitimately requested by the government of Afghanistan, it changed no strategic balance in the area. It is understandable that many governments found the intervention by actual Soviet armed forces, rather than proxies, disquieting. It is less understandable that some saw it as a threat to Iranian oil. Had the Soviet Union wished to invest Iran, it had a direct route of easy access through Azerbaijan and across the Soviet-Iranian border as well as via the Caspian sea. Only one totally unfamiliar with the virtually impassable terrain between Kabul and the Iranian oil fields could suggest that a concentration of troops around the former threatened the latter.

245

How much validity there was to Soviet charges of American and Chinese collusion with anti-Afghan guerrillas prior to the Soviet intervention is impossible to determine. What is clear is that American–Soviet relations were already in such a state of disrepair that considerations of detente, if they existed at all, could only have been minimal at that point, to either side.[38] Nevertheless, it is also clear that if there had been a flourishing detente relationship, events in Afghanistan would have likely taken a different turn and one more salutary for international stability.

A New Ballgame for International Politics

The importance of the Afghanistan events of detente, of course, is that the Soviet intervention brought on American reaction which not only destroyed what there was left of the detente relationship of the 1970s but in all likelihood destroyed its framework as well. Regardless of what happened after the Soviet intervention, it would be extremely difficult—perhaps impossible—to return to the state of relations which existed earlier in the 1970s. Humpty Dumpty, once fallen, is very hard to put back together again.

What exists in the wake of Afghanistan—the Soviet intervention and the American reaction—is a wholly new ballgame in international politics. Prior to the 1970s, the United States could act with more or less impunity anywhere in the world because of its unquestioned military superiority, while the Soviet Union, because of its comparative weakness, had no such option. During the 1970s, the Soviet Union, having approached military equality with the United States, had vastly more power to project its influence globally. It did so to a certain extent, but in this period both the USSR and the USA were inhibited, at least in part, by the detente relationship. The world entered the 1980s with American–Soviet military equality but without American–Soviet detente and, it appeared—given the American failure to satisfy SALT II—without institutional limitations on thermonuclear arsenals or other types of weapons.[39]

With both the United States and the Soviet Union feeling that detente had failed—which it had, although not necessarily for the reason adduced in Washington and Moscow—the prospect was for renewed foreign policy offensives on both sides, greater emphasis placed on securing strategic advantages and the likelihood that the developing countries would become an arena for a competition more virulent and more dangerous than ever. Under these circumstances, the ultimate hope that there might be superpower cooperation to assist development in the Third World seemed further away than ever. Such a prognosis constituted a grim prospect for the developing countries, for the United States and for the Soviet Union and, indeed, for the whole world.

The American-Soviet detente of the 1970s turned out to be a faulty instrument for curbing competition and intervention in the developing countries. But was it the fault of the detente mechanism or the failure of national leaders to utilize it properly? Is another, and more effective, type of detente relationship possible? Is there an alternative to *some* kind of detente, if military confrontation and its likely result—thermonuclear war—are to be avoided? In his address to the Pacem in Terris Convocation in 1973, Henry Kissinger observed that "opportunities cannot be hoarded; once past they are usually irretrievable."[40] The world will now have to wait and see if he was correct.

FOOTNOTES

1. Testimony before Committee on Senate Foreign Relations, September 19, 1974, reported in *Department of State Bulletin*, October 14, 1974, p. 154.

2. The Soviet "gains" and "losses"—with the latter considerably outweighing the former—are well discussed in *The Defense Monitor* (Washington, Center for Defense Information), 9(1) (January 1980).

3. O. M. Smolansky, "The United States and the Soviet Union in the Middle East," Grayson Kirk and Nils H. Wessell, *The Soviet Threat: Myths and Realities* (New York: The Academy of Political Science, 1978), p. 102.

4. Cf. Fred Warner Neal, *U.S. Foreign Policy and the Soviet Union* (Santa Barbara: Center fror the Study of Democratic Institutions, 1961), esp. pp. 8-18.

5. Andrei Zhdanov, *The International Situation* (Moscow: Foreign Languages Publishing House, 1947).

6. Neal, *U. S. Foreign Policy and the Soviet Union, op. cit.*, p. 20; and ed. Elaine H. Burnell, *Asian Dilemma: The United States, Japan and China* (Santa Barbara: Center for the Study of Democratic Institutions, 1969), p. 51.

7. Stalin's main thesis was actually published on the eve of the 19th Congress and supplemented by his concluding remarks to that conclave. See

Malenkov's report, ed. Leo Gruliow, *Current Soviet Policies I* (New York: Praeger), pp. 6-8 and 235-236.

8. Soviet economic credits and grants to non-communist developing countries after 1955 are detailed in a CIA study, *Communist Aid to Less Developed Countries of the Free World, 1977*, Research Paper ER 78-10478U, November 1978.

9. Cf. Lawrence S. Kaplan, *Recent American Foreign Policy: Conflicting Interpretations* (Homewood, Illinois: The Dorsey Press, 1968), pp. 166-186.

10. See *Current Soviet Policies III, op. cit.*, pp. 57, 202. For a discussion, see Neal, "Coexistence: Practical Problems and Politics," *Coexistence*, 3(1): 11, and *U.S. Foreign Policy and the Soviet Union*, pp. 28-30.

11. Joseph Pelzman and Anne T. Sloan of the University of South Carolina demonstrated this fact in a paper presented to the 1980 meeting of the International Studies Association. See also Robert Legvold, *Soviet Policy in West Africa* (Harvard: 1970), p. 13.

12. Soviet military aid to non-communist developing countries in the period 1955-74 amounted to $12,010,000,000, according to a report of the Library of Congress Congressional Research Surface, *The Soviet Union and the Third World: A watershed in Great Power Policy?* (Washington: U.S. Government Printing Office), p. 69.

13. *Pravda*, January 25, 1961. See discussion in *Coexistence, op, cit.*, p. 12.

14. *The New York Times*, March 24, 1961.

15. See Communist party Program at 22 Congress, *Current Soviet Policies IV, op. cit.*, p. 14; and Khrushchev, "On Peaceful Co-Existence," *Foreign Affairs* (October 1959): 8.

16. Khrushchev's statement, made at a Moscow press conference, was reported in *The New York Times*, June 13, 1960.

17. Cf. *A Survey of Detente, op. cit.*, pp. 7, 16.

18. See discussion in *A Survey of Detente*, pp. 5-8.

19. "Basic Principles of Relations between the United States of America and the Union of Soviet Socialist Republics, 29 May 1972," *Department of State Bulletin*, 66(1772) (June 26, 1972): 898-899.

20. "Agreement Between the United States of America and the Union of Soviet Socialist Republics on the Prevention of Nuclear War, 22 June 1973," *Department of State Bulletin* (July 23, 1973): 160-161, 69 (1778).

21. *Pravda*, January 10, 1976. See also Brezhnev's Report to the 25th Congress of the Soviet Communist Party, *Pravda*, February 24, 1976.

22. Cf. *A Survey of Detente, op cit.*, pp. 10-11. See also Kissinger statement to Senate Foreign Relations Committee, *Department of State Bulletin* (October 14, 1974), pp. 505-519.

23. The concept of differing areas is discussed in Neal, "A New Foreign Policy Based on Core Interests," *Center Magazine*, May 1972.

24. One of the most complete and authoritative accounts is that by Galia Golan, *Yom Kippur and After: The Soviet Union and the Middle East Crisis* (Cambridge University Press, 1975). See esp. pp. 108-126.

24a. Quoted in *U.S. News and World Report*, December 24, 1973, pp. 27-28.

24b. The Insight Team of the *London Sunday Times, The Yom Kippur War* (New York: Doubleday, 1974), p. 419.

25. *A Survey of Detente*, pp. 11-13.

26. For a discussion of the Soviet Union and Angola, see Legvold, *op. cit.*; Colin Legum, "The Soviet Union, China and the West in Southern Africa," *Foreign Affairs* (July 1976): 748-751; Richard Bissell, "Southern Africa: Testing Detente, *The Soviet Threat: Myths and Realities, op. cit.*, pp. 89-94.

27. Bissell, *op. cit.*, p. 92. See also Christopher Stevens, "The Soviet Union and Angola," *African Affairs*, 75(299) (April 1976): 136-138.

28. "The Permanent Challenge of Peace: U.S. Policy Toward the Soviet Union," *Department of State Bulletin* (February 23, 1976): 210-211. See also *A Survey of Detente*, pp. 16-17.

29. Cf. *Pravda*, January 10, 1976. See also Report to 25th Congress, *op. cit.*

30. *A Survey of Detente, op. cit.*, p. 16.

31. Bissell, "Southern Africa: Testing Detente," *op. cit.*, p. 91. Kissinger also later alluded to such overtures. Cf. "The Permanent Challenge of Peace: U.S. Policy Toward the Soviet Union," *op. cit.*, p. 210.

32. Early in the 1970s, Somalia became the largest Soviet arms client in Africa. The developments in Somalia are discussed in Bowyer Bell, "Strategic Implications of the Soviet Presence in Somalia," *Orbis* (Summer 1975), and Gerard Chaliand, "The Horn of Africa's Dilemma," *Foreign Policy* (Spring 1978).

33 *Ibid.*

34. See account by Richard Bissell, "Soviet Policies in Africa," *Current History* (October 1979).

35. Chaliand refers to the Kagnew air base as having been "the most important U.S. communications station in Africa and the Indian Ocean." "The Horn of Africa's Dilemma," *op. cit.*, p. 117.

36. *Strategic Survey 1977* (London: International Institute for Strategic Studies, 1978), pp. 18-21; and Marina and David Ottaway, *Ethiopia, Empire in Revolution* (New York: Africana Publishing Company, 1978), pp. 166-168. The Soviet arms supply to Ethiopia is chronicled in *Time* (February 20, 1978)

37. Assuming, of course, the Russians do not get bogged down in Ethiopia's incredibly complicated domestic and foreign policy problems. Cf. *The Defense Monitor, op. cit.*, p. 10.

38 Moscow concluded the administration had adopted an antidetente policy once it decided to place new missiles in Western Europe and prospects for SALT ratification vanished. For a discussion of an earlier dismal Soviet view of Carter's foreign policy, see Neal, "Detente and Jimmy Carter," *World Issues* (April/May 1978): 3-10.

39. SALT II appears to have been a prerequisite for agreements limiting conventional weapons, banning all tests and reducing nuclear arsenals.

40. Ed. Fred Warner Neal and Mary Kersey Harvey, *The Nixon-Kissinger Foreign Policy: Opportunities and Contradictions* (The Center for the Study of Democratic Institutions, 1974), p. 10.

INDEX

Latin American Economic System
  (SELA), 120, 131
Lebanon, 237
Libya, 5, 25-26, 28, 126-133
LeDuan, 91
Lin Piao, 96
Malaysia, 6
Mali, 29, 133, 167, 179, 235
Mao Tse-tung, 68 ff, 95
Martinique, 132
Mendes-Frence, Pierre, 76-78, 80
Mexico, 32, 124, 132, 137, 211
Mikoyan, Anastas, 81, 200
Mirskiy, G. I., 167, 180 ff
Molotov, 70, 75-80
Morocco, 23-24, 27, 133
Mozambique, 5, 27, 34, 126-133
N.A.M.U.C.A.R., 120, 131
National Bourgeoisie, 202, 232
Nationalization, 205, 218
N.A.T.O., 66
Navarre Plan, 69
New Economic Policy (NEP), 214,
  230
New International Economic Order
  (N.I.E.O.), 227
Nicaragua, 7, 120, 125-131, 139
Nigeria, 28
Nixon, Richard M., 92, 100,
  237-240
Nkrumah, Kwame, 169 ff
North Vietnam, 63 ff, 80-82, 84,
  90, 237
Oman, Pop. Front for Liberation
  (PFLO), 154 ff
OPEC, 17, 147 ff
  and CMEA (COMECON), 42, 149
Organization of African States
  (OAV), 137
Pahlavi. Mohammed Rez-(Shah),
  146, 156
Pakistan, 27, 137, 153, 159
Palestine Liberation Org. (PLO),
  127-131, 159

Panama, 121-125, 131-135
Paraguay, 132, 137
Peoples Democratic Republic of
  Yemen (PDRY) (South
  Yemen), 6, 145, 152 ff
  Pres. Abdul Fattah Ismail, 155,
  159, 179
Peoples Republic of China (PRC),
  64 ff, 137
  Chairman Hua Guofeng, 158,
  235, 243
Peru, 25
  USSR Military Presence, 119,
  125, 243
Pham Van Dong, 92
Phillipines, 6, 152
Poland, 42 ff
Portugal, 241
Puerto Rico, 120
Qatar, 149
Revolutionary Movement, 173 ff,
  183, 202, 215, 228
Rhodesia (Zimbabwe), 128
Romania, 34-37, 149
Rusk, Dean, 231
SALT II, 139, 243
Sandinista Guerrilla, 122-133, 138
Sapozhnikov, B. G., 183
Saudi Arabia, 146 ff
Selassie, Haile, 244
Shao-Chi, Liu, 87
Singapore, 6
Socialism, 166 ff, 202-216, 234
Socio-economic development, 170,
  177-180, 207-215
Somalia, 4, 5, 26-28, 133, 137,
  145, 151, 156, 188, 242
Somoza, Anastasio, 120, 139
South Africa, 243
South Vietnam (NLF), 85 ff
South Yemen, 5, 25, 27, 126-133
Spain, 129, 152
St. Lucia, 132
Sudan, 6, 156, 179